GREATEST MOMENTS IN TCU FOOTBALL

Edited by

DAN JENKINS & FRANCIS J. FITZGERALD

Includes Selected Stories from the Sports Pages of the

Fort Worth Star-Telegram

Published by

Louisville, Ky.

ACKNOWLEDGMENTS

Research Assistance: Glen Stone, Kent Johnson, Trey Carmichael, Debra Grubb, Kristin Johnson and the TCU Sports Information Office; Larry Lauer; Kevin Dale, Sports Editor of *The Fort Worth Star-Telegram*; Kent Stephens, The College Football Hall of Fame; Kathy Belcher and Marcia Melton, *The Fort Worth Star-Telegram*; Jerry Stafford, University of Texas at Arlington Special Collections Library; Bo Carter, The Southwest Conference; Charlie Fiss, The Cotton Bowl Classic; the Sugar Bowl and the Federal Express Orange Bowl.

ISBN 1-887761-04-7

Cover Design by Shayne Bowman, Visual Solutions, Detroit.
Book Design by David Kordalski
Typeface: Parkinson, Kis-Janson

PUBLISHED BY:
AdCraft Sports Marketing
Kaden Tower, 10th Floor
6100 Dutchmans Lane
Louisville, KY 40205
(502) 473-1124

This book is dedicated to

AMON G. CARTER

*publisher of The Fort Worth Star-Telegram
and long-time friend of Texas Christian University.*

CONTENTS

Contents

IN JANUARY 1953, when I arrived at TCU for the first time, I realized I was at an institution rich in football tradition. This was the school Sammy Baugh and Davey O'Brien made famous. TCU had already played in the Orange Bowl, the Sugar Bowl twice and the Cotton Bowl three times.

TCU has a tradition that is second to none.

Horned Frog football got its start in 1896, when the school was still called AddRan College and was located in Waco, Texas. But the sport didn't take off until Matty Bell arrived in 1923 and convinced us to join the fledgling Southwest Conference. In the late 1920's, Francis Schmidt took over the TCU coaching reins and won more games in a five-year period than any other coach in Southwest Conference history.

Dutch Meyer, who invented the spread formation and was the first proponent of the forward pass in the Southwest Conference, would succeed Schmidt in 1934, when he left to take a lucrative offer from Ohio State. Dutch had those great TCU national championship teams of 1935 and 1938 and the many powerhouse SWC championship teams of the 1930's, 40's and early 50's.

Abe Martin followed Dutch in 1953 and he led us to three Cotton Bowls in the 1950's. In the 1980's, Jim Wacker took the helm and helped us stabilize the Horned Frog football program following a two-decade decline in the 1960's and 70's. And, now, Pat Sullivan has brought us back to the level where TCU is again competing for conference titles, national rankings and a taste of the glory we once enjoyed so very much.

There have been many heroes who have worn those purple TCU jerseys — the all-Americans, the All-SWC players and the one who won the Heisman, the Maxwell and the Walter Camp trophies.

Maybe the greatest quarterbacks to ever play the game of college football — Sammy Baugh and Davey O'Brien — were TCU Horned Frogs. So was the greatest tackle ever — Bob Lilly.

Switching to pure artistry, Jim Swink was the most elusive runner in our history.

The greatest TCU game in my football memory bank? That's an easy one. I will never forget the Son-

Frank Windegger with Abe Martin.

ny Gibbs pass to Buddy Iles for a touchdown to beat undefeated, No.-1 ranked Texas in 1961. However, I would have loved to have seen the 1935 shootout between TCU and Southern Methodist.

It has been a pleasure, indeed, to have lived a part of the rich and glorious legacy of TCU football. I hope it lasts forever.

FRANK WINDEGGER
Director of Athletics
Texas Christian University
June 20, 1996

Sam Baugh launches a pass under a heavy rush in TCU's 28-0 victory over Baylor in 1936.

BY DAN JENKINS

A friend once said that if you were to cut me open, the first thing you'd find is a piece of Davey O'Brien's helmet somewhere near my heart.

My friend was being hilarious, of course. Then one day a while back a team of surgeons did slice open my chest to fix something or other, and they didn't just stumble upon a piece of Davey O'Brien's helmet, they found it resting comfortably in there next to a shred of Sam Baugh's jersey and a cleat from Jim Swink's shoe.

An amazing thing. Amazing, too, that those objects were so well pre-

Davey O'Brien, an all-America quarterback in 1938.

served, considering that they'd been co-existing for so many years with all that barbecue, Tex-Mex food, country sausage, cream gravy, biscuits, cigarette smoke, and the occasional adult beverage of my choice.

How the artifacts invaded my body is somewhat mysterious, I agree, but it's probably no more of a mystery than how Papa Hemingway's leopard managed to get himself up there on Kilimanjaro.

Sorry. Little literary reference there. Just to prove I once got myself a semi-education at the campus on University Drive, or rather in a booth of the soda fountain in the old drugstore on the corner.

Anyhow, what the discovery of those cherished gridiron artifacts did was reveal that I occasionally bleed purple and white, which was hardly a news bulletin to my wife or kids or close pals.

Personally, I blame it on my youth.

You can't let a kid grow up within bicycle distance of TCU Stadium, and let him spend his formative years watching Sam Baugh and Davey O'Brien throw touchdown passes and win national championships —

not only for the school but for the old home town —
and not expect that kid to be bent, twisted, warped.

But in the best possible sense, right?

Sports heroes are heap good medicine for kids. And
today there are sports heroes of all kinds leaping about
and entertaining kids all across America — and doing it
in so many cities that have become major league in one
sport or another they are too numerous to count, I might
add — but this is all for the good. The heroes, I mean.

Better a sports hero than a bag of dope, as they say.
I would even take it a step further and say better a
sports hero than an electric guitar and an amp, but
that would just underline the fact that I am of the
geezer/codger persuasion and my boyhood heroes
wore leather helmets instead of armor plate or
bloomers.

Of course, the older one gets, the harder it is to
remember yesterday. I'll vouch for that, in as much as
I can still see Baugh and O'Brien flipping passes quite
clearly, but I can't recall the 1970's at all.

That's just one example. I have to confess that I
can't see very much of the 1980's either — or even
care to — but nothing is clearer than Jim Swink mean-
dering all over the field on one of his dazzling touchdown runs. It brings the 1950's back to me more vivid-
ly than thoughts of my overheating Buick.

By then, I was being paid by a newspaper to see all
of TCU's games. A glorious task throughout those
blissful 1950's, covering nifty teams that usually went
to bowl games and finished in everybody's Top 10.

It was a pure treat for a newspaper guy to deal with such
legendary coaches, such unique individuals, as Dutch Meyer and Abe Martin.

Gruff, growling Dutch, a master bridge player, by
the way. Strategist supreme, dreaming up the nine-
man defensive line, inventing the exciting Spread formation, which others would later name the Shotgun
and claim as their own. Chewing his tobacco, moti-
vating by fire and brimstone, having no respect for
anyone who didn't stand up to him.

I recall asking Dutch a question one day in the early 1950's. It was after the coaches' offices had been
moved to better quarters, down to the stadium from
the tiny old rooms with concrete floors in the building on the main campus known as Little Gym.

"This is nice, Coach," I said, looking around at the

new furnishings in the larger offices. "How do you
like it?"

"Nowhere to spit," Dutch muttered.

I enjoyed luring Dutch into conversations about
his great teams of the 30's. Sam and Davey and them.

It must have been fun to have been a grownup fan
back then, I'd always felt. Ride the special trains to the
out-of-town games, Stetson squared away, flask handy,
dinner in the diner. What a giddy time for the fans
who could afford to travel with the Frogs in '35 and
'38, the national championship seasons.

There was this day in Dutch's office when I was
getting him to dwell on '38 in particular. Suddenly,
he thought of something that angered him. It had to
do with a group of TCU's most affluent fans.

"It was sometime in January after we'd come back
from the Sugar Bowl," Dutch remembered. "A bunch
of those rich fellows invited me to lunch. They took
me downtown to the Fort Worth Club. We had a nice
meal, then they got down to the real reason I was there.
They said, 'Dutch, we had a helluva good time this
season. It was great for the school, great for the city.
We want to keep on doing it. So how much money is

Ki Aldrich, a 3-time All-SWC center in 1936-38 and
all-America in 1938.

Jim Swink — the greatest halfback in TCU's history.

Dutch Meyer, Davey O'Brien and Amon Carter wave before departing to attend the Heisman Dinner in 1938.

it gonna take?"

Dutch recalled that one or two of the gentlemen even pulled out their checkbooks and their fountain pens, right there at the table.

"I've never been so insulted," Dutch recalled. "I stood up and told 'em off good and proper, and walked out of the room. And that was the end of *that*."

As Dutch sat there looking satisfied with himself after relating the story, I couldn't fight off a grin.

"Damn, Coach," I said. "Do you realize if you had-n't stormed out of that lunch, we could be Notre Dame now?"

Dutch stared at me for a long, cold moment, then rewarded me with a smile he reserved for newspaper cynics. But he didn't have my words engraved on any campus marble.

Honest Abe Martin was a whole other character. Folksy, sweet natured, trusting, master recruiter, gnaw-ing on his cigar, wearing his lucky brown suit or his lucky brown hat on the sidelines, but streamlining TCU's offense with the Multiple-T while underplay-ing his guile and savvy.

Abe had a way of making print, no matter what he said.

During the fun-filled season of '55, when Jim Swink was making every opponent's defense look stupid and clumsy, and making everybody's all-America team, I asked Abe at one point if he could describe Swink's ball-carrying style. None of us sportswriters had been able to do it satisfactorily.

Abe leaned back in the swivel chair at his desk, toyed with his cigar, and said, "Aw, he's just a little old rub-ber-legged outfit nobody can catch."

Abe's linemen were frequently "big old green peas," but for three seasons, from '58 through '60, he had an all-American tackle named Bob Lilly, who would "stand in there for you like a picket fence."

Honest Abe, as some knew him, took a dim view of the game's new terminology, much of it introduced by Bear Bryant.

"*Pursuit*," Abe would remark in a disparaging tone. "Everybody's talkin about *pursuit* now. Hell, that ain't nothin' but chase 'em and catch 'em."

Abe had a term of his own for the goal-line. He called it "the alumni stripe." And what a successful coach need-ed to do to keep his job, according to Abe, was always have a team that could "push that dern football across the alumni stripe with a degree of regularity."

A story concerning Abe on the sideline during a TCU-Rice game in the late 1950's has long since passed into legend.

It seems the Owls were hurting the Frogs badly with a wide pitch, a sweep around the end. Abe wanted it stopped. He motioned to a player on the bench. The kid jogged up to Abe, purple helmet in hand, wide-eyed, eager to get into action.

Abe said, "Billy, I want you to look at what they're doing to Tommy on that sweep. They're wearing Tommy out. Now Billy, I want you to go out there and stop that sweep for me."

The kid fastened his chin strap, hopped up and down.

"I'll try, Coach," he said excitedly.

Abe gently patted the kid on the shoulder.

"Sit down, Billy," Abe said calmly. "Tommy's *tryin.*"

★ ★ ★

Yeah, it's true. I'm under doctors' orders not to think about the Southwest Conference breaking up. That business about Texas, Texas A&M, Baylor and Texas Tech going over to the Big Eight and forming the Big 12 — purely for TV money.

Which in turn left the Frogs, Mustangs and Owls looking for a new home. Right, TCU, SMU and Rice. Three schools that contributed more lore to the grand old Southwest Conference in a single decade than Texas Tech and Baylor did in a lifetime.

As a matter of fact, the combined football history of Texas Tech and Baylor wouldn't put a grass stain on the elbow of Davey O'Brien's jersey!

Sorry to shout just then, but I wanted to make sure the jerks who orchestrated the Big 12 could hear me.

Happily, as we know, the Frogs, Mustangs and Owls have become part of the Western Athletic Conference, the WAC, where new friendships will be formed, new rivalries developed, new regions explored. And in the long run, it may all be for the best.

Meanwhile, only those who played the game of football in the 80-year old Southwest Conference have a right to take its demise harder than those of us who grew up with it and watched it for so many thrilling years.

"The Big 12 was an idea whose time had come."

Abe Martin and his star quarterback, Sonny Gibbs, on the sidelines in 1961.

That was the explanation we heard.

Well, wrong. *Greed* was an idea whose time had come.

It was that simple. And I think the thing that annoys us geezers and codgers the most is the thought that the three-piece suits primarily responsible for killing the Southwest Conference were bottom-line nerds who never saw Sam Baugh, Davey O'Brien or Jim Swink play football, much less a Doak Walker, Kyle Rote and Bobby Wilson at SMU; a Jack Crain, Bobby Layne and James Street at Texas; a John Kimbrough, Dick Todd and John David Crow at Texas A&M; a Billy Patterson and Larry Isbell at Baylor – OK, I'll throw Baylor a bone – a Clyde Scott and Lance Alworth at Arkansas; or a Bill Wallace, Froggie Williams and Dicky Moegle at Rice. Or many, many others, including all the stalwarts who either blocked for them or tried to tackle them.

I plead guilty to insisting it was a better world then. Which leads me to point out that one of the benefits of living in the past is the luxury of being able to clear rooms of vast swarms of people.

For instance, you can be a part of a conversation about the problems in the Middle East and get to watch people drift away as you say, "That's all well and good, but what about the fact that TCU won more football games in the 1930's than any other major college team in the country? I have the exact totals right here. The Frogs had 84 victories, Alabama and Tennessee come next with 79. Notre Dame's not even in the first 10, by the way."

Being part of a conversation about the turmoil in the Balkans, I've found, affords you an excellent opportunity to blurt out, "That might be true, but I think it's far more important that in the first 37 years TCU was in the Southwest Conference, from 1923 through 1960, the Frogs won more games than any other school, including Texas, and at the same time produced almost twice as many all-Americans as anybody else."

In most conversations about reducing the federal deficit, I like to butt in and say, "Frankly, I'm not sure what this has to do with TCU being the first Southwest Conference team to play in the Sugar Bowl, Cotton Bowl, Orange Bowl and Bluebonnet Bowl."

Actually, one of my favorite topics is the national championship thing. Quick history. You may not know it, but ratings and polls to determine the nation's No. 1 team did not begin until 1924. Before that, the mythical national champion was whatever team from the East or Midwest that might be chosen by one lonely – and usually prejudiced – gentleman, a coach or historian, who would write an article about it in some national publication such as *The Spalding Guide* or *Harper's Weekly*.

But along came '24 and a man named Frank G. Dickinson, a professor of economics at the University of Illinois. It was Dickinson in that year who originated the first mathematical system, or formula, for rating teams. Basically, Dickinson's system measured a team's number of victories against the strength of its opposition.

This wasn't anything to overtax the brain, but nobody had thought of it before, so naturally it gained immediate popularity in newspapers across the land. Perhaps, this should have been

A trio of Carnegie Tech defenders tries to bring down TCU's Johnny Hall in the 1939 Sugar Bowl.

TCU's defense converges to stop a threatening LSU attack deep in Frogs' territory in the 1936 Sugar Bowl.

expected during that so-called Golden Age of Sport, what with all those Red Granges and Four Horsemen romping about.

In any case, Dickinson started something. Other systems were designed in the late 1920's by other authorities in other parts of the country, but only one of them caught on big and rivaled Dickinson. This was the Paul O. Williamson System, out of New Orleans. It quickly gained nation-wide respect and a large syndicated circulation. The Fort Worth Star-Telegram, I might mention, was a subscriber to Williamson's weekly ratings and final rankings in the 1930's.

So that was it. Dickinson and Williamson. That was the whole ball game where No. 1 was concerned before the wire-service polls began, before the Associated Press started its writers' poll in 1936 and the United Press followed up with the coaches' poll in 1950.

You may ask what all this means, what I've been leading up to, what's the deal here with the history lesson. I'm more than happy to tell you.

In all of these football seasons since the ratings system began, more than 70 years as of 1996, it just so happens that TCU is one of only 38 schools that have

won a national championship. Uh-huh. That few.

Better still, the Frogs are one of only 24 schools that have won two or more national championships. Pretty elite, huh?

The thing I feel compelled to do now is celebrate our two national championship seasons in a special kind of way. Those seasons of '35 and '38 obviously represent the most glorious time in TCU's gridiron history. They deserve the permanence of hardcover.

But as I take you on this stroll down memory lane, it occurs to me that I ought to do it with as much reverence as possible. Therefore, if it will help, think of me for a few moments as a wire service writer on heavy medication.

TCU's National Championship of 1935

TCU 41, Howard Payne 0

FORT WORTH, SEPT. 21 — The Howard Payne Yellow Jackets from Brownswood, Texas, came to town as defending champions of the Texas Conference, undefeated the previous season, but they were no match for the white-jerseyed Frogs. Before a crowd of 10,000 in warm, sunny weather, quarterback Sam Baugh scored in the first quarter by running 15 yards after taking a lateral from fullback Tillie Manton. Moments later, substitute quarterback Vic Montgomery intercepted a Yellow Jacket pass and ran 30 yards for a touchdown. It was 14-0 at the half.

Early in the third period, Baugh tossed a 12-yard touchdown pass to halfback Dutch Kline. A short time later, end Walter Roach intercepted a pass and sailed 40 yards for a score. The fourth quarter was turned over entirely to reserves. Alan House, a third-string quarterback, passed 25 yards to halfback Scott McCall for a touchdown. TCU's final score came when substitute fullback Glen (Donkey) Roberts intercepted yet another Yellow Jacket pass and took it back 35 yards for a touchdown.

TCU 28, North Texas State 11

FORT WORTH, SEPT. 28 — The Frogs wore their new dark purple jerseys at home for the one and only time during the season, and a fierce south wind helped hold down the score. With the wind helping, North Texas scored first. Tailback Johnny Stovall, North Texas' star, romped over on a 10-yard run, and the Eagles from Denton led, 7-0. TCU quickly took command in the second quarter, however. With the wind now behind the Frogs, Dutch Kline skipped across the goal from 7 yards out to cap an 80-yard drive. Later, Sam Baugh circled end from 5 yards away to top off another long drive, and it was 14-7 at halftime.

TCU had the wind again in the third quarter. That's when Kline plunged for two more touchdowns after Baugh mixed runs and passes on two more sustained drives. Kline, a senior from Gregory, Texas, thus accounted for three touchdowns in the game.

Safely leading 28-7 and fighting the strong wind in the fourth quarter, Baugh twice stepped out of his own end zone, surrendering two safeties to North Texas in order for the Frogs to pull out of deep holes.

TCU 13, Arkansas 7

FAYETTEVILLE, ARK., OCT. 5 — All of the scoring happened in the first quarter as the white-jerseyed Frogs won in the Ozarks, which is never easy. A freak play led to TCU's first touchdown. Tackle Wilson Groseclose blocked an Arkansas punt. End L.D. (Little Dutch) Meyer, a nephew of TCU's head coach, caught the ball in mid-air and ran 20 yards, then pitched a lateral to Sam Baugh. Baugh rambled on for 25 more yards, all the way to the Razorbacks' 4-yard line. Halfback Jimmy Lawrence bulled into the end zone from there. The extra point was missed, but TCU had the lead, 6-0. Moments later, however, the red-shirted Hogs recovered a fumble at TCU's 23-yard line, and Arkansas' gifted quarterback, Jack Robbins, threw a touchdown pass. The conversion was good, and now Arkansas led, 7-6.

But not for long. Jimmy Lawrence jarred and side-stepped his way to a 40-yard kickoff return, going all the way to Arkansas' 24-yard line. And just as quickly, Sam Baugh lofted a spiral into a far corner of the end zone where end Willie Walls, who alternated throughout the season with L.D. Meyer, made a sensa-

tional catch for a touchdown between two Arkansas defenders. The Frogs continually threatened to score again over the last three quarters while Arkansas never crossed midfield again. TCU would liked to have had more points on the board, but getting out of Arkansas with any kind of win was always a cause to celebrate.

Sam Baugh, an all-America quarterback in 1935 and 1936.

TCU 13, Tulsa 0

TULSA, OKLA., OCT. 12 — Gloomy Gus Henderson's Tulsa teams had been powerhouses in their region for 10 years, averaging eight victories a season, and the purple-clad Frogs knew they were in for a rough afternoon. The game was scoreless after three quarters, during which time several Frogs were sidelined with injuries, including the all-America center, Darrell Lester. Sam Baugh's repeated drives had produced no points, primarily because Coach Dutch Meyer had refused to settle for field goals, as he had against Arkansas. But the fourth quarter found Baugh in the middle of a 60-yard drive in which he flipped crucial passes to end Walter Roach and the speedy halfback, Rex Clark, who often shared time with Dutch Kline. Baugh eventually plowed over from the 1. Later on, TCU got an insurance TD when Glen (Donkey) Roberts galloped 30 yards with an interception.

TCU 19, Texas A&M 14

FORT WORTH, OCT. 19 — As the saying goes, it wasn't as close as the score indicates. By winning over the Aggies for the eighth straight year — the longest stretch in which TCU would dominate any Southwest Conference team — the Frogs bombarded A&M in the first two quarters before a near-packed stadium of 25,000, building a 19-0 halftime lead.

In the first quarter, Jimmy Lawrence tore loose on a 62-yard jaunt to set up the first touchdown. Dutch Kline carried over on the next play from 4 yards out. It was in the second quarter that Sam Baugh fired touchdown passes of 35 and 39 yards to the fleet Rex Clark, who simply outran his defenders.

The Aggies scored late in the third quarter against TCU's reserves, and scored again against a lineup mostly consisting of third-stringers just before the final gun sounded.

TCU 27, Centenary 7

SHREVEPORT, LA., OCT. 26 — For the third year in a row the TCU-Centenary game was an attraction of the Louisiana State Fair, and it was no secret that the maroon-clad Gentlemen had risen as a national power. They were undefeated in '32 and '33, had fashioned a 10-2 record in '34, and on this day took the field with a 4-1 record against the Frogs.

All of which had something to do with Dutch Meyer devising a few new plays for the occasion. The Frogs scored first in the second quarter on a 12-yard pass from Sam Baugh to end L.D. Meyer after a sustained drive of 65 yards. An interception set up the Frogs' second touchdown, which came on a fancy new play. Jimmy Lawrence took a wide lateral from Baugh and threw a 5-yard pass to Bob Harrell, a substitute end. Centenary fought back and scored a touchdown that made it 14-7 at the half.

It was in the second half that the Frogs unleashed a varied attack that all but ran the Gentlemen off the field. Baugh drove the Frogs 70 yards and flipped another touchdown pass to L.D. Meyer, this one for 8 yards. And in the fourth quarter, the half-

Dutch and TCU assistant Mike Brumbelow.

back pass worked again as Jimmy Lawrence hurled a 30-yard scoring aerial to second-string halfback Scott McCall.

In the following Tuesday's newspapers, TCU was suddenly rated No. 7 in the nation by the Williamson System's weekly rankings.

TCU 28, Baylor 0

WACO, NOV. 2 — Carroll Field was a complete sellout, standing room only, for a battle of undefeated teams. TCU and Baylor were both 6-0. The game was further advertised as a duel between field generals, Sam Baugh of the Frogs and Lloyd Russell of the Bears.

The Frogs in their white jerseys exploded in the second quarter against the green-shirted Bears. Baugh sparked a 55-yard drive that carried to the Baylor 12, from where Jimmy Lawrence spiraled a halfback pass into the arms of end Willie Walls for a touchdown. On their next possession, Baugh shot a 35-yard scoring strike to Rex Clark, who was racing clear down the sideline. The Frogs led at the half, 14-0.

The teams battled evenly in the third quarter, but Baugh engineered a long drive in the fourth that ended with his 9-yard touchdown pass to Charlie Needham, a reserve end. Near the end of the game, Baugh intercepted a Lloyd Russell pass at Baylor's 34 and promptly hit Needham again for the last touchdown. It was Baugh's third scoring pass of the game against a very good Baylor team that would wind up the season with an 8-3 record.

TCU 14, Loyola of the South 0

NEW ORLEANS, NOV. 8 — This was a Friday night game played in rain, mud and fog under the dim lighting of the Wolves' tiny stadium.

The Frogs scored in the first quarter at the end of a 50-yard march when Jimmy Lawrence dived over from the 2-yard line.

In the second quarter, Sam Baugh piloted another drive of 60 yards. The touchdown came on one of Dutch Meyer's trick plays. From the 6-yard line, Baugh slipped an underhanded pass — a shovel pass, it would become known — into the hands of Lawrence, and he zipped across the goal untouched, practically unnoticed. With a two-touchdown lead and the elements worsening, TCU fell back on its defense throughout the second half. Loyola never threatened to score.

TCU's season record was now 8-0 and in Williamson's weekly rankings the Frogs climbed to fifth place in the nation behind Minnesota, Princeton, Notre Dame and LSU. Meanwhile, SMU, the Southwest Conference's other undefeated and united team, was rated sixth, and the Frog-Mustang game, three weeks away, was starting to look huge.

TCU 28, Texas 0

AUSTIN, Nov. 16 — It was dark purple against dark orange on a cold, dreary day in Memorial Stadium, and the Frogs were prepared for a tough contest against the Longhorns, who had a 4-3 record and two of the most sought-after backs in the country, quarterback Ney (Red) Sheridan and fullback Hugh Wolfe. But Sam Baugh made it no contest.

Baugh found end Willie Walls with a 22-yard touchdown pass in the first quarter. He hit Jimmy Lawrence with a 20-yard scoring pass in the second quarter. Baugh then iced away the game early in the third period. He drove the Frogs 70 yards and concluded the drive with a 13-yard toss to end L.D. Meyer. Later in the third, end Walter Roach scooped up a punt blocked by guard Tracy Kellow and tackle Drew Ellis and raced 30 yards for the last score.

On the strength of their overwhelming win over Texas, the Frogs jumped to No. 3 in Williamson's national rankings.

TCU 27, Rice 6

FORT WORTH, Nov. 23 — It was the first of two successive Big Game weekends for the Frogs. The stadium sold out at 30,000. TCU had a 9-0 record. Rice, the defending conference champion, in town with a 8-1 record, led by its famed "Touchdown Twins," Bill Wallace and Johnny McCauley, who had made all-America in '34. In fact, the Owls, in bright blue jerseys and gold satin pants, had been Williamson's pre-season pick for the national title.

Walter Roach, a 3-time All-SWC end in 1934-36.

TCU's big team may have peaked this day. Dutch Kline returned the opening kickoff 75 yards to Rice's 11-yard line. Jimmy Lawrence cut through tackle to score standing up on the first play from scrimmage. In the second quarter, Sam Baugh all but buried the Owls. He hit Lawrence with a 22-yard touchdown strike to end a 65-yard march. He hurled a 21-yard touchdown pass to L.D. Meyer to cap an 80-yard drive. Rice scored in the third quarter to make it 21-6, but early in the fourth, Baugh ended the scoring with another pass to Meyer, this one for 21 yards. Baugh had now thrown three touchdown passes against Baylor, Texas and Rice.

Success brought a burden. Williamson boosted TCU to No. 1 in the U.S. and placed SMU No. 2, just in time for the biggest game in SWC history.

SMU 20, TCU 14

FORT WORTH, Nov. 30 — The Game of the Century had everything. Each team with a 10-0 record. Battle for the Rose Bowl bid. National championship at stake. Six all-Americans on the field. Stadium expanded with temporary bleachers to hold 35,000, but still brimming over with fans, celebrities from stage and screen, and famous sportswriters and broadcasters from across the country. The city had never known anything like it. Neither, for that matter, had the state.

SMU almost blew the Frogs away in the early going. The Ponies drove 72 yards to a touchdown in the first quarter. The big play was a trick. Fullback Bob Finley lateraled to halfback Shelly Burt who fired a 30-yard pass to quarterback Johnny Sprague. Finley then plunged over from the 1. Early in the second quarter, SMU drove 80 yards to score again. The crucial play this time was a 33-yard pass from Finley to end Maco Stewart, who made a diving catch at TCU's 9-yard line. From there, all-America halfback Bobby Wilson, the "Corsicana Comet," swept around end for the touchdown.

In the meantime, two long drives produced no points for the Frogs, but they finally scored before halftime after recovering a fumble in SMU's end of the field. Jimmy Lawrence plowed over from 4 yards away, and it was 14-7 in favor of the Mustangs at intermission.

TCU cranked up the 60-yard drive in the third quarter that tied the game. Baugh hit Lawrence for 18 yards, Willie Walls for 22 yards, then Lawrence with a 7-yard bullet

The 1935 TCU starting eleven who defeated LSU in the 1936 Sugar Bowl and led the Frogs to a national championship.

for the touchdown on the first play of the fourth quarter. The game was now tied, 14-14, the Frogs were outgaining SMU comfortably, and momentum seemed to be on their side, although Lawrence injured his ankle on the touchdown play and was lost for the rest of the game.

But SMU had another surprise. After pushing to the Frogs' 37-yard line, the Mustangs faced fourth down and long yardage. That's where Bob Finley, from punt formation, stunned the Frogs with that long desperate heave to Bobby Wilson, who leaped high, twisted in the air, made a circus catch, and fell over the goal for the biggest touchdown of the 1935 season.

SMU fans danced in the streets and TCU hearts were broken, but everyone agreed they had seen one of the greatest games ever played.

TCU 10, Santa Clara 6

SAN FRANCISCO, DEC. 7 — TCU's first trip ever to the West Coast for a game against the highly-regarded Santa Clara Broncos, a four-day journey by train, would have been a happier occasion if the Frogs hadn't still been trying to recover from the crushing loss to SMU, which had moved up to No. 1 in the nation while the Frogs dropped to fifth.

The special train, sponsored by The Star-Telegram, was loaded with fans, team and band as it made stops for the Frogs to hold workouts in Amarillo, Flagstaff and Salt Lake City.

Uniquely, the team took time to be serenaded by the Mormon Tabernacle Choir during the stopover in Utah.

As for the game, the Frogs were without Jimmy Lawrence, but they got a big break in the early moments before a crowd of 30,000

in Kezar Stadium. A quick kick by Sam Baugh was fumbled on the Santa Clara 5-yard line by Bronco tailback Nello Falaschi, who would make all-America a year later, and tackle Drew Ellis recovered. An instant later, Baugh pegged a touchdown pass to Harold McClure, who was subbing for Lawrence. It was in the second quarter that the Broncos turned a Frog fumble into a bizarre 77-yard touchdown play, but the conversion was missed and TCU held a 7-6 lead at the half.

In the third quarter, Coach Dutch Meyer hinted that he had learned his lesson about passing up field goals, two of which might have made a big difference against SMU. When a drive stalled, Dutch ordered the 33-yard field goal from fullback Tillie Manton. The purple defense did the rest.

As TCU finished the regular season 11-1, SMU breezed past Texas A&M, 24-0, and the Mustangs' 12-0 record earned them the national championship of the Dickinson System. Curiously, the Williamson System did something else. On the basis of LSU demolishing a strong Tulane team 41-0 in its last game and ending up with a 9-1 record, Williamson put the Tigers No. 1 with SMU second and TCU third. Then Williamson announced that its final rankings would not be made until after the post-season games, the reason being that too many candidates were involved. No. 2 SMU was going to the Rose Bowl to meet No. 5 Stanford, and No. 1 LSU was taking on No. 3 TCU in the Sugar Bowl.

The season wasn't quite over.

TCU 3, LSU 2 (Sugar Bowl)

NEW ORLEANS, JAN. 1 — Drizzling rain, mud and a cold wind did not keep 40,000 fans from filling Tulane Stadium for the Sugar Bowl Classic, nor did it keep the Frogs and the LSU Tigers

Although just 5-foot-7, Davey O'Brien led TCU to a national championship in 1938.

from playing an exciting, hard-hitting, suspense-filled game that would be decided by a baseball score.

Sam Baugh had a hand in all the scoring, as it turned out. Early in the second quarter, the wet ball slipped off his hand as he attempted a pass from his own end zone. The ball fell to the ground for an automatic safety.

LSU led, 2-0.

But later on in the same quarter, after Baugh had punched the Christians downs to the LSU 19-yard line, he held the ball and Tillie Manton booted the 26-yard field goal that ultimately made the difference.

Backing the line on defense, Manton was one of TCU's defensive stars as well, along with Walter Roach, an end, and the guards, Tracy Kellow and Cotton Harrison. Three times the Frogs staged goal-line stands, sending the Tigers away with no points.

While SMU was losing to an inferior Stanford team in Pasadena, 7-0, the purple-clad Frogs had all they could handle with the star-studded Tigers, who wore white with slashes of purple and gold, and are still regarded as one of LSU's greatest teams. All-America Gaynell Tinsley was at one end, and the backfield was led by triple-threat Abe Mickal and the bull-dozing Bill Crass.

To keep the Tigers in the hole, Baugh punted 14 times during the afternoon, often with a water-logged ball, and his kicks averaged an astonishing 45 yards. Numerous times, Baugh coffin-cornered his punts inside the LSU 5-yard line. Baugh also ripped off the longest gain of the day from scrimmage, a 43-yard jaunt that left the Frogs down close and threatening to score again at the very end of the game.

It was mid-January before the final Williamson Rankings were released, declaring TCU the nation's No. 1 team. Inasmuch as SMU had already been given the No. 1 award by the Dickinson System, this marked the only time in the history of the Southwest Conference that two of its member schools could boast of a national championship in the same season.

Dallas laughed first, Fort Worth laughed last.

TCU's National Championship of 1938

TCU 13, Centenary 0

FORT WORTH, SEPT. 24 — The Centenary Gentlemen came to town with one of their best teams. Led again by a do-everything halfback, Weenie Bynum, these were more or less the same gents who had upset the Frogs, 10-9, the year before. A big question was how much had TCU improved?

Davey O'Brien answered that question quickly after the big white team took the field before a shirt-sleeve crowd of 15,000. In the first quarter Davey connected with end Don Looney on a towering 65-yard touchdown pass. In the second quarter O'Brien hit halfback Johnny Hall with a 43-yard spiral that carried to Centenary's 3-yard line. Sophomore fullback Connie Sparks took it over from there. Thereafter, the Frogs fell back on their defense,

which was anchored by center Ki Aldrich and tackle I.B. Hale. Centenary never came close to a score. It was cheerful news to Coach Dutch Meyer that O'Brien's ability to hit the long pass had greatly improved over his junior year.

TCU 21, Arkansas 14

FORT WORTH, OCT. 1 — On a blistering afternoon, TCU proved it also had a running attack. With the big, powerful Connie Sparks gaining over 100 yards, the Frogs rolled up 296 yards on the ground, and won over the Porkers far more easily than the score insinuated.

Not that the passing game was ignored. On TCU's first possession, Davey O'Brien fired a 50-yard touchdown strike to halfback Earl Clark, a vicious blocker who played violin for a hobby and would become Davey's favorite passing target. Moments later, O'Brien hurled a 30-yard pass to Clark that went to the Hogs' 2, from where Connie Sparks plunged across. Arkansas' Kay Eakin, who in '39 would follow O'Brien as the nation's leading passer, guided the Hogs to a touchdown that made it 14-7, but Davey answered by darting 20 yards up the middle, then shooting a beautiful lateral out to Sparks, who rumbled 31 more yards for the touchdown that made it 21-7 at halftime. Frog subs played the entire second half and gave up a meaningless score at the end.

Overwhelmed by TCU's strength, Arkansas coach Fred Thomsen predicted that no other team would score twice on the Frogs in '38.

Johnny Hall, a speed demon on wide sweeps.

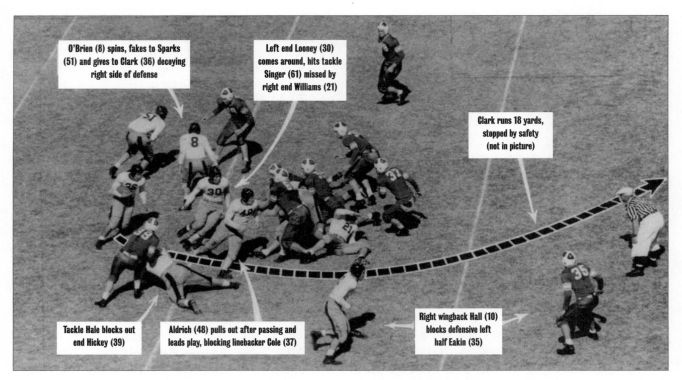

O'Brien & Co. execute the perfect play against Arkansas in 1938.

TCU 28, Temple 6

PHILADELPHIA, OCT. 7 — The Frogs faced Coach Pop Warner's Temple Owls on a chilly Friday night after a three-day train trip, but none of that mattered to Davey O'Brien — he chose the occasion to stage one of his greatest passing exhibitions, and all in the second quarter.

O'Brien hit the striding Earl Clark for 49 yards for the first touchdown. He dropped a 28-yard spiral into Johnny Hall's arms for the second touchdown. Just as rapidly, he sailed a 56-yard bomb into Hall's hands for the third touchdown. It was 21-0 just like that, and no TCU regular played a single down in the last two quarters.

Afterward, the legendary Pop Warner said, "That little Davey O'Brien is the greatest passer I've ever seen, and I've been looking a long time."

TCU 34, Texas A&M 6

COLLEGE STATION, OCT. 15 — Davey O'Brien was apparently just getting warmed up against Temple. He tossed three touchdown passes and ran for another against the Aggies in a game that was considered a dead-even contest before it began. All this in front of a record Kyle Field throng of 32,000. Moreover, it was A&M's worst defeat by a Southwest Conference opponent since the league was formed in 1915.

O'Brien's first touchdown pass went to Johnny Hall from 12 yards out. The second score came on a play that covered 55 dazzling yards. O'Brien hit Hall over the middle, whereupon the halfback tossed a long lateral out to Fred Shook, a second-string guard, who dashed the rest of the way untouched. TCU led 13-0 at the half.

The Aggies briefly cut the score to 13-6 in the third quarter, but O'Brien stormed right back to score on a 6-yard burst through tackle after an 80-yard march that featured a variety of reverses and shovel passes. Davey then popped a 20-yard touchdown pass into the wide-open arms of Charlie Williams, a reserve end. TCU's subs played the whole last quarter.

Coach Homer Norton of the Aggies exclaimed, "TCU has the best all-around football team I've ever seen."

The victory hurtled TCU into the No. 7 spot in the weekly AP poll, which had been led from the beginning by the Pitt Panthers.

TCU 21, Marquette 0

MILWAUKEE, OCT. 22 — Another three-day journey by train failed to bother the Frogs or Davey O'Brien. They needed only a few moments of the first quarter to destroy the host team.

O'Brien pitched 25-yard touchdown passes to Johnny Hall and Earl Clark, in that order. In fact, O'Brien completed the first seven passes he threw. While he was at it, he squirted around end for 5 yards and a touchdown of his own.

All this in the game's first 12 minutes, mind you.

TCU's second and third stringers were on the field the rest of the afternoon. The score could have been anything the Frogs chose to make it, for they piled up 410 yards of total offense to just 71 for the Golden Avalanche.

The easy win on the road elevated TCU to fourth place in both the AP and Williamson rankings.

TCU 39, Baylor 7

FORT WORTH, OCT. 29 — There had not been a more anticipated event in the city, or a tougher ticket, since the SMU game of '35. TCU's stadium overflowed with a crowd of more than 30,000. What they had come to see was a clash of undefeated teams plus a duel of two glamorous quarterbacks — the Frogs' Davey "Slingshot" O'Brien and Baylor's "Bullet Bill" Patterson.

It's likely the Frogs hit their '38 peak against the Bears.

O'Brien threw touchdown passes of 27 and 38 yards to Earl Clark, whose broken-field running and pass-receiving made him a co-star with O'Brien on this crucial afternoon. It was 14-0 by halftime.

Early in the third quarter, Davey fired a 35-yard touchdown pass to Pat Clifford, a speedy second-string halfback. Connie Sparks plunged for three touchdowns after O'Brien's air game set them up.

In all, the Frogs ate up 520 yards in total offense against Baylor's best team in years. In the aftermath, Baylor coach Morley Jennings said, "If there's a better team in the country, I don't know where it is."

The size of the score no doubt had much to do with TCU moving up to No. 2 in the rankings, close behind Pitt and its celebrated "Dream Backfield."

TCU 21, Tulsa 0

TULSA, NOV. 5 — The Frogs had a stockpile of injured players when they met Tulsa on a brutally windy day. Connie Sparks and Johnny Hall sat out the game. They were replaced by Ward Wilkinson and Pat Clifford, respectively. Other key men — Earl Clark, tackle Allie White, guard Forrest Kline — missed the second half. TCU was facing a fine golden-suited Tulsa team piloted by quarterback Tommy Thompson, a future star in the National Football League.

Not that any of this kept Davey O'Brien from doing his normal thing. With the wind at his back in the first quarter, he passed 26 yards to Pat Clifford for the first touchdown. Then his passes to his ends, Don Looney and Durward Horner, set up touchdown plunges by Ward Wilkinson.

The score was 21-0 in 15 minutes, after which Ki Aldrich led a Frog defense that totally shut down Tulsa's fancy offense.

It was on this same Saturday that Carnegie Tech rudely upset No. 1 Pittsburgh, 20-10, and the result was not lost on Fort Worth. The banner headline of Sunday's Star-Telegram sports section read:

Tartans Topple Pitt! Frogs Beat Tulsa 21-0

And sure enough, the Frogs bolted to No 1 in the polls.

Connie Sparks, an All-SWC fullback in 1938, was also a great punter for the Frogs.

TCU 28, Texas 6

FORT WORTH, NOV. 12 — The Frogs were without four starters this time — Earl Clark, Johnny Hall, I.B. Hale and Forrest Kline — but it hardly mattered. Davey O'Brien was perfectly healthy.

O'Brien struck with his usual quickness. He nailed Pat Clifford with a 35-yard touchdown pass in the first quarter. Connie Sparks rammed across for two scores after O'Brien's passes moved the Frogs down close in the second quarter. Lacy McClanahan, a third-team fullback, plunged for the last score in the third quarter. Subs played the final 15 minutes as TCU made it four victories in a row over the University of Texas.

After the Frogs had easily protected their No. 1 ranking, Texas Coach Dana X. Bible said, "This TCU team doesn't have a single weakness."

TCU 29, Rice 7

HOUSTON, NOV. 19 — The Rice Owls were the defending conference champions and were flying high with a new set of "Touchdown Twins," big Ernie Lain and shifty Ollie Cordill. But so what? Davey O'Brien had saved his greatest single day for the Owls.

Along with throwing three touchdown passes, O'Brien scampered for 109 yards from scrimmage, averaging a whopping 9.9 yards per carry. Before the white-shirted Owls in their gold satin

Halfback Earl Clark — a great broken field runner and Davey O'Brien's favorite target.

pants and shiny gold helmets could blink, O'Brien pitched touchdown passes of 30 and 40 yards to Don Looney and Earl Clark. In the second quarter, he hit Durward Horner with a 15-yard scoring pass, then ran one in himself from 8 yards away. The score was a staggering 27-7 by halftime. TCU's reserves did everything they could to hold down the score in the second half, but Rice still gave up a safety.

O'Brien's performance could not have come at a better time where all-America selectors and Heisman Trophy voters were concerned. This may well have been the afternoon Davey wrapped up both. At the same time, however, the Frogs learned a hard lesson about the popularity of Notre Dame. With an unbeaten team themselves, and despite TCU's impressive victory over Rice, the Irish inched ahead of the Frogs in the polls.

TCU 20, SMU 7

DALLAS, NOV. 26 — For all of their success, the Frogs still had a tough chore left. The Mustangs were 6-2, unbeaten in conference play, and tradition was a large obstacle. SMU had a habit of breaking TCU hearts in big games.

Not this time. Before a standing-room-only crowd of 27,000 in Ownby Stadium, Davey O'Brien — a Dallas boy, incidentally — sparked the Christians to a quick touchdown. Doing most of the ball-toting himself against a strong wind, Davey drove the Frogs 70 yards, and Connie Sparks pushed it over for the score. A short time later, O'Brien found Johnny Hall wide open on a deep pattern and hit him with a 37-yard spiral for another touchdown.

A blocked punt in the second quarter gave the Mustangs a touchdown to make things uncomfortable at 13-7, but O'Brien settled the issue in the third quarter when he directed a 75-yard scoring drive. Sparks again took it over on a plunge. Though only a soph, big Connie from Panhandle, Texas, would land himself a spot on the all-conference team along with O'Brien, Aldrich, Hale, Looney, White and Kline.

As if they had saved themselves for just such an occasion — to lock up a perfect season — O'Brien, Aldrich, Hale and four other Frogs played a full 60 minutes against the Mustangs. O'Brien and Aldrich were unanimous all-America selections. Hale made some teams. O'Brien was everybody's Player of the Year, winning the Heisman, Maxwell and Camp awards.

The Frogs still trailed Notre Dame in the polls, but only for another week. On Dec. 3 in Los Angeles the Irish were soundly trounced by Southern California, 13-0, and the Trojans may well have heard people cheering for them as far away as Fort Worth.

As a consequence, the Horned Frogs led the final AP poll by a wide margin, went to the top of Williamson's final rankings as well, received the Helms Athletic Foundation's award for No. 1 and went to the Sugar Bowl as college football's indisputable national champions.

TCU 15, Carnegie Tech 7 (Sugar Bowl)

NEW ORLEANS, JAN. 2 — Although TCU was disappointed to be denied the Rose Bowl bid it fully expected — the Duke Blue Devils somehow came up with better lobbyists — the Frogs were eventually delighted to be matched in the Sugar Bowl against Carnegie Tech, a big, powerful team with a 7-1 record, No. 4 in the country, the new "Beast of the East," winner over notorious Pitt. To top it off, the Tartans were a squad with a heralded backfield tandem of George Muha and Merlyn Condit. Beloved by the Eastern press, Carnegie Tech would give the Frogs a chance to prove they deserved the No. 1 title.

Indeed, the Frogs almost got more than they wanted from the Eastern bruisers — the two teams played an absolute thriller.

In his customary fashion, Davey O'Brien gave TCU a 7-0 lead in the second quarter. He ignited a 60-yard drive and Connie Sparks cracked over from the 1-yard line. Another Purple march carried deep into Tech territory but ended with a dropped pass on fourth down at the Tartans' 2.

The Frogs remained in control of things until there was only a moment left in the first half. Suddenly, Carnegie Tech scored on a 47-yard pass from Pete Moroz to George Muha. And when Tech converted, TCU was behind for the first time all season, 7-6.

A Star-Telegram feature writer roving the stadium claimed to have noted strong men in Stetsons weeping at halftime.

Fortunately, Davey O'Brien didn't let his fans weep for long. On TCU's first possession of the third quarter, Davey called a play he'd been saving up. He flicked a pass over the middle to end Durward Horner, who was free and in full stride, and the end raced untouched for a touchdown, the play covering 45 yards.

It was O'Brien's 20th touchdown pass of the season, a Southwest Conference record that would stand for 30 years, or well into the era of one-way players and specialists.

O'Brien then led the Frogs on a grinding, time-consuming drive of 60 yards that reached the Carnegie Tech 1-yard line, fourth down. Which is where Coach Dutch Meyer did the smart thing and called for Davey to placekick the field goals that put the contest out of reach.

For the rest of his days, when asked about it, Dutch would say, "That SMU game in '35 was a great one, but from the standpoint of hard-hitting, plenty of emotion, good execution by both teams, and all the drama you could ask for, I believe our game with Carnegie Tech was the greatest football game I ever saw."

★ ★ ★

As it happens, I saw the Rice and SMU games in '35 and just about every home game from then on through my teenage years. I was only 7 years old when I watched Slingin' Sam throwing bullets, though I

recall it better than two hours ago. And then, of course, I was a vastly mature 10 years old when Davey O'Brien was lofting spirals.

My family's seats in those impressionable pre-teen years were on the west side of the stadium, the press box side, down around the 25-yard line at the north end.

Consider for a moment the fact that the first two college games I ever saw were the epic battles in '35 with Rice and SMU. Pardon me, then, for thinking that every TCU game was obviously a sellout. Football must be more important, I thought, than all of the Germans and Italians who were hollering and marching in the newsreels. There must have been four or five million people in the stadium on those Saturdays.

Naturally, I was taken somewhat by surprise in '36 when I went to the home opener against Arkansas and the stadium wasn't totally full. Must be an epidemic of measles in town, I decided.

About that '35 spectacle with SMU, the Rose Bowl game. I well recall my dad saying before the opening kickoff that the Frogs were going to win for sure, because our guys in the white jerseys and gold-looking canvas pants and black helmets were the greatest football team God had ever put on Earth, and after they won this game everybody in Fort Worth was

The 1938 starting line who paved the way to a national championship for the Frogs.

going out to Hollywood to hang around with Ginger Rogers and Clark Gable and other movie stars.

Then after the game was over we sat in the stands for a long time. I mostly watched gown people crying and cussing and my dad drinking something out of a flask that he said was cough medicine.

Three years later, I recall the buildup to the TCU-Baylor game in '38 as stirring almost as much excitement as that SMU game, although the Bears came to town in mid-season rather than at the end.

This time, it was a football-silly uncle who took me to the festivities. First, we went to the downtown parade on Saturday morning. That's where lovely coeds in Greta Garbo hats waved from convertibles and where both school bands marched and cowboys rode horses.

If there had been a contest between the bands, the Frogs would have won easily with what was known in those days as "the Texas Christian University Swing Band," a small group of Benny Goodmans and Tommy Dorseys in white suits and policemen's caps that made you tap your foot when they swung into the TCU fight song Dixieland style.

The football-silly uncle prepared me for the quarterback duel between Davey O'Brien and

Baylor's Billy Patterson as if it were a heavyweight fight. And I distinctly remember being startled by the Bears' uniforms. They wore bright yellow pants with green stripes up the back, and bright yellow helmets with green stripes from ear to ear and front to back, and their jerseys were dark green with yellow rings around the sleeves, yellow shoulders, and yellow numbers. Frankly, I thought they looked more like something out of ready-to-wear than football players.

I marveled throughout that swell afternoon as Davey O'Brien and the Frogs mauled the Bears without much mercy, 39-7. Informed by the football-silly uncle that TCU might very well be on the way to the national championship, I could have sworn I was living in the sports capital of the universe — and felt kind of sorry for anyone who didn't.

O'Brien was a wonder to behold. Operating out of the single and double wing, hitting his receivers 50 yards downfield with perfect spirals, bouncing around, hiding the ball on his hip, darting for yardage this way and that, now and then shooting a long, magical lateral out to an associate in a white jersey, who would prance on down the sideline for a touchdown.

What do you mean you don't remember? It was only yesterday.

Darrell Lester was inducted into the College Football Hall of Fame in 1988.

CHAPTER I

AddRan's first team in 1896 posted a record of 1 win, 1 loss and 1 tie.

FIRST GAME, FIRST VICTORY

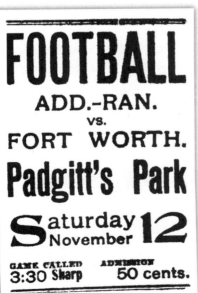

FOOTBALL
ADD.-RAN.
VS.
FORT WORTH.
Padgitt's Park
Saturday **12**
November

GAME CALLED   ADMISSION
3:30 Sharp   50 cents.

Special to The AddRan Collegian

WACO, DEC. 7, 1896 — The AddRan boys were too strong for Toby's team.

TCU	8	0	8
Toby	0	6	6

The first football game in Add-Ran history was played on the university campus, resulting in an 8-6 score. Our boys fought the game without calling on the substitutes.

In the first half, AddRan halfback Claude McClellan made the first touchdown. Burger of AddRan later ran 50 yards for the second. In the second half, Sparks marked a touchdown for Toby and Lampkin kicked the extra point. Parrott of Toby's team was disabled in the second half.

We regard this as good practice for the battle with the Houston Heavyweights team. Toby Business College is strengthening its team with the hopes of playing New Year's Day. We will be glad to accept their challenge.

CHAPTER 2

The 1909 TCU squad won 5 games, lost 2 and tied 1.

CHRISTIANS VICTORIOUS

Special to The Waco Daily Times-Herald

WACO, Oct. 16, 1909 — Carroll Athletic Field yesterday was the site of the first of the season's gridiron contests between the local old-time rivals, TCU and Baylor. The Christians gave the Baylorites a neat coating of whitewash and netted to their own credit a field goal and a touchdown.

TCU	3	0	6	0	9
Baylor	0	0	0	0	0

Nearly a thousand people were present and college spirit ran high. The grandstand was one mass of col-or, and the singing and rooting of the enthusiastic collegians, together with the music of the band was inspiring in the extreme. The weather was rather warm for a pigskin contest and the players suffered accordingly. A stiff breeze from the south made the handling of punts a difficult matter.

The teams were very evenly matched in weight — TCU already had one victory and tied with the heavy Texas A&M team, and Baylor had two victories to her credit — and for most of the game the outcome was in doubt. On the whole, however, the result can hardly be considered a forecast of the other two games between the same teams which are to follow. TCU

FIELDS

GRISSOM   ROBINSON

RATTAN

TCU and Baylor met on 3 occasions during the 1909 season.
TCU won 2 of these contests.

*Milton Daniel captained the
1911 Horned Frogs.*

undoubtedly played the best ball, but the green and gold gladiators put up a hard fight.

TCU had the best of the argument except at one time during the first half, when Baylor made repeated plunges for good gains through the line. Baylor outclassed her opponent in passing, but few spectacular plays were executed. Baylor, however, met her fate due to onside kicks more than any other cause. In punting, T.P. Robinson outdistanced his rival.

Marshall Baldwin's stunt in receiving Grissom's onside kick and running 65 yards for a touchdown was the feature of the game. Manley Thomas' return for 40 yards on a kickoff was a stellar play as was C.T. Rattan's run around left end for 30 yards. Hefley scintillated the crowds by receiving two forward passes for 20 yards each, while John Fouts did brilliant work in tackling. Bill Massie's place kick from the 20-yard line provided the first score for TCU.

Game in Detail

Baylor won the toss and chose the south goal.

Both teams, however, were unable to move the ball consistently in the opening drives.

Following several exchanges of punts, Thomas fielded Robinson's punt at the TCU 33 and returned it 8 yards to the 41.

On a crossbuck, Charles Fields rammed off tackle for 6 yards. Rattan followed with a 3-yard carry. Then Fields and L.C. Wright added 2 yards each.

From the Baylor 46, Thomas connected with Baldwin on a pass for 15 yards. G.P. Braus plunged into the Baylor middle for 4 yards and Paul Tyson added 2. Massie's 25-yard field goal, however, missed the mark thus halting the Christians' drive.

Later in the period, Robinson booted a 30-yard onsides kick that Thomas scooped up and returned 5 yards to the TCU 25.

Fields and Baldwin quickly punched for 5 and 4 yards. Fields and Baldwin added 5 and 3 yards. Wright then battered for 2 yards. On third down Thomas attempted a punt but it was blocked and recovered by a TCU teammate.

Hoping to seize the momentum, Rattan faked a punt and swept left end for 30 yards. Milton Daniel then hit on a crossbuck for 4 yards to move the ball to the Baylor 22. Wright added 2 yards on the next

FIELDS

TYSON

BRAUS

BALDWIN

The initial TCU-Baylor match in 1909 attracted a crowd of 5,000 to Carroll Field.

carry. On the final play of the period, Massie's 20-yard field goal soared true to give TCU a 3-0 lead.

The second quarter proved to be a punting duel for both squads. Baylor, however, briefly managed to control the ball with a passing and running exhibition led by Robinson, Hefley, Grissom and Grady Isbill.

But the period ended with the ball on the Baylor 45 and TCU leading, 3-0.

The TCU-Baylor chess match continued well into the third period when Baldwin picked up a 2-yard onsides kick by Baylor's Grissom and ran 65 yards for a TCU touchdown — which gave the Christians a 9-0 lead.

In the fourth quarter, Thomas of TCU gave the sideline spectators a thrill with his 40-yard kick return. The Christians then used the time remaining to their advantage by grinding for tough yardage.

*Cy Leland, nicknamed the "Lubbock Jackrabbit" and an All-SWC halfback in
1929, would later broadcast TCU games on radio with
Kern Tips in the 1930's.*

CHAPTER 3

SOUTHWEST CROWN GRACES BROW OF PURPLE FROGS

By Flem Hall
Fort Worth Star-Telegram

Team	W	L	T	Pct.
TCU	4	0	1	.900
SMU	3	0	2	.800

FT. WORTH, NOV. 30, 1929 — The dream of years has been realized. Texas Christian University has won a Southwest Conference football championship. The Fighting Frogs slashed their way to a touchdown in the fourth quarter

| TCU | 0 | 0 | 0 | 7 | 7 |
| SMU | 0 | 0 | 7 | 0 | 7 |

of a vivid, bristling battle at Clark Field Saturday and when the goal was kicked a richly deserved and more than earned 7-7 tie was achieved with Southern Methodist's mighty Mustangs. The draw gave the Christians a clear title to a crown they have eagerly sought since entering the conference in 1923.

In the massed presence of more than 21,000 people who crowded every inch of available seating space in the stands, the Purple and White made a great comeback in the closing minutes to come through a moral victor, and a champion. Owing to the fact the Methodists had previously tied a conference game, tying Saturday was the same as losing for it left them definitely behind the Frogs, who, until this last game, were untied as well as undefeated. The conference rule that counts a tie as a half game lost and a half game won makes the final standing:

Francis Schmidt's TCU teams won 46 games and a pair of SWC titles in five seasons (1929-33).

TCU tied because it had the better team. Howard Grubbs whirled through to a touchdown and Harlos Green kicked the extra point, and for all practical purposes that was enough to send the Mustangs back to Dallas empty handed.

Flare Into Action

The seven points came after SMU, stopped cold most of the afternoon, got away with a long pass that scored a touchdown in the third quarter. Stung by the sudden reverse that threatened to shatter all their hopes, the Frogs' flared into high power action and in a few minutes were pounding at the Methodist goal line. The big Red line stopped the mad charges on the 1-yard line, but the white-shirted Christians were not to be denied, and after another play Grubbs slanted off tackle with a vicious plunge that carried the ball the last needed yard. Green's place kick wasn't high but it was well over the bar and squarely between the posts.

A beautiful 40-yard run by Weldon (Speedy) Mason after catching a 16-yard pass from Bob Gilbert scored SMU's touchdown, and Alfred Neely was rushed in to kick the extra point.

Frogs Snap Into Life

The Methodist score came like a belt out of the blue. For all of the first two quarters and most of the third the Frogs had turned back every Methodist move towards a score. SMU had threatened mildly twice but had never come closer than the 20-yard line.

TCU had just punted, placing the ball on the SMU 44-yard line. It looked perfectly safe, but on first down

Harlos Green, an All-SWC fullback in 1929, booted the game-tying kick against SMU.

Weldon Mason raced far to the left, outran Grubbs and got in a partly clear field to take a long pass. As he caught it, it appeared that any one of three TCU tacklers would bring him down on the Christian 40-yard line, near the west sideline, but Cy Leland missed a flying tackle and Mason was now loose to travel the last 30 yards unmolested. Neeley, the guard who does the place kicking, was hurriedly put into the game, and kicked the extra point to put SMU ahead, 7-0.

SMU received the following kickoff, couldn't gain and punted. Leland then gathered in the ball on the 20-yard line and returned 20 more, barely missing getting away for a long run up the sideline. Grubbs carried once for 1 yard as the quarter ended. With that came a change in goals and a stiff south wind the Christians had to battle for 15 minutes.

Roberson Threatens

The first play in the last 15-minute period was a long pass that dribbled off Vance Woolwine's fingers. On the next play, Grubbs faked a pass and dashed through the middle of the line for a first down on the 50-yard marker. Grubbs then passed to Clyde Roberson for 16 yards. Three running plays with Grubbs and Green carrying netted 11 yards and another first down 23 yards from the goal line.

On the next play, Grubbs passed over the middle of the line to Roberson, who made a great leaping catch on about the 10-yard line. He came down running. Stumbled by a tackler as he took his first step, Roberson staggered on to the 5-yard line, where he fell. Not giving up, Roberson scrambled desperately for the goal line, and he was about there when a hurtling Mustang drove a knee into his back and stopped him on the 2-yard line. These were foul tactics, but the resulting penalty, of half the distance to the goal, did little damage.

Then and there, on the 1-yard line, the Methodist line made a great stand. On the first plunge Green carried to the 1-foot line and on the second lunge it looked like he dived over, but the officials ruled he had been stopped an inch or two short of the mark. On third down Green was clearly stopped with no gain, the line piling up in front of his charge. Leland carried off tackle on fourth down but was stopped just short of the goal. The ball then went over to SMU and Mason punted out to the TCU 25-yard line.

Swarm to Succeed

Undismayed by the failure of their previous bid the Christians swarmed back to the attack, this time to succeed. Grubbs opened with a pass to Leland, who skirted right end for 14 yards, placing the ball on the 11-yard line. Grubbs drove off tackle for 4 yards, Green added 2, and on two smashes Grubbs made a first down at the 1-yard line. He let Green carry twice and when he failed to gain Grubbs took the ball and carried it over, smashing behind Mike Brumbelow and Green.

SMU came back with a desperate bid for victory, completed one long pass, but Grubbs broke up the party by intercepting a pass on the TCU 30-yard line.

From there the Frogs opened another drive that threatened to score. Grubbs was the leader, making one 20-yard run and another for 15, but nothing came of them except Methodist was shoved into a hole and held there. As the last two minutes rolled around TCU accepted the championship winning tie — played for it rather than take a chance on losing while bidding for another score — by keeping the ball on the ground. And when the last gun barked the Frogs had the ball on the SMU 25-yard line.

Wind Brings Discomfort

In some ways the game was disappointing. It did not produce the abundance of sparkling, scoring play that was expected and until the last 20 minutes was too even to be exciting. A stiff, chilly wind that swept steadily out of the south, lengthwise up the field, was largely to blame for the turn of events. It changed the whole complexion of the game, ruining it nearly as completely as it did the spectators' comfort. All day, until a little

Grassy Hinton did it all for the Frogs, playing halfback, quarterback, passer and punter on the 1929-31 TCU teams.

Howard Grubbs, an All-SWC quarterback in 1929.

while before the game, the sun beamed brightly and there was no wind. Everything was perfect. Then a biting wind blew up from the south. It freshened, brought leaden clouds that blotted out the sun, and sent thousands into spells of shivering to the tune of chattering teeth. The wind was so strong at 2:30 p.m. that it was quite evident it would be almost impossible to score against it. As it turned out neither team did.

Brumbelow, the TCU captain, won the opening toss for TCU and chose the south goal with the wind to his back. It looked like a great break, but the advantage was taken away on the kickoff. SMU used a short kick, and when Ralph Walker fumbled, Malcolm Powell recovered on the TCU 49-yard line. That one play enabled the Ponies to push into the Frogs' end of the field, and when Walker and Grassy Hinton failed to use the aid of the wind to get off any exceptionally long punts, the 15 minutes passed without the Frogs profiting by their advantage.

Christians Win Decisively

At the end of the first quarter the sides exchanged goals and during all the middle 30 minutes of the game TCU fought the wind as well as the Mustangs. In the second quarter they more than held their own, and in the third quarter they held the upper hand until the one pass reached Mason.

When TCU got the wind to its back in the last quarter and set sail toward the goal nothing could stop the Frogs.

Except for that one long pass, the Christians whipped the Ponies decisively, as the statistics show. TCU made 16 first downs to SMU's six, and gained 179 yards to 75 on running plays. That 56-yard gain on the pass gave SMU a big margin in that department, but without it the Ponies gained only 16 more yards through the air than TCU.

Grubbs Outstanding Star

Howard Grubbs was the outstanding star of the game, but his unwillingness to call his own signal nearly cost the Frogs the ball game, and probably did keep them from winning. It wasn't until after SMU took the lead that he called on himself to carry the ball, and then when it was in easy striking distance he tried to give the scoring honor to his mates. It was only after Green and Leland had failed in six efforts to get the last few inches that he took the ball. Then, with one plunge Grubbs went over. Had he carried the ball the first time his team got within striking distance, another touchdown very probably would have been scored. However, it is to the great little quarterback's lasting personal credit that he, playing in his last college game, tried to give Green and Leland the scoring honor.

It was odd how Green could smash the line for steady gains any place on the field until on the 1-yard line. He could make 2, 3 and 4 yards against the SMU defense inside the 10-yard line, but he could not muster the power to gain the final inches.

CHAPTER 4

TCU's First All-American

BY WHIT CANNING
Fort Worth Star-Telegram

It was late in the day, and the Texas Aggies — hopeful of finally breaking a scoreless tie — were busily plotting strategy in their huddle.

Suddenly, an alien voice inquired, "Y'all got the guts to run my way?"

Startled, the Aggies looked up to see TCU end Raymond (Rags) Matthews, wearing an impish smile and standing in the middle of their huddle.

It was Oct. 22, 1927 — and the man confronting the unbeaten and seemingly invincible Texas A&M team was one of the first all-Americans in the Southwest Conference.

Foreshadowing a later era, he was not above tossing a little in-your-face chit-chat at the foe.

Sitting at the TCU 2-yard line with a first down, the Aggies accepted the challenge and sent their own superstar, three-time All-SWC tailback Joel Hunt, straight at Matthews, who stacked the play. After another run and an incomplete pass — both foiled by Matthews — the ball was still at the 2 on fourth down.

Matthews wandered across the line and repeated his challenge. He recalls that Hunt's reply was, "Get ready, you S.O.B. — here I come."

One collision later, the ball was still at the 2. For the Aggies, the resulting 0-0 tie was the only blemish in an 8-0-1 campaign in which they outscored their foes, 262-32.

"I always did some talking out on the field," said Matthews, who celebrated his 91st birthday on Aug. 17, 1996, "but I usually did a little more in the big games."

A good receiver and an absolute terror on defense, Matthews played for Dutch Meyer at Polytechnic High and Matty Bell at TCU — where Meyer had become an assistant. He was an All-SWC selection in 1926-27 and the first TCU player to make the national all-America teams.

Some researchers now believe he is the oldest living all-American.

"That's probably true," Matthews said, chuckling. "I can't think of anyone (older) than me who's still around.

"All the big media coverage back then was up in the East, so the all-American teams were filled with players from the East and West coast and the area around Chicago, because of Michigan and Notre Dame. The SWC didn't get much attention.

"Then somebody talked Grantland Rice into coming down here and watching a couple of games, and interest began to pick up."

After the 1927 season, Matthews was invited to play in the East-West Shrine Game in San Francisco, which was the only postseason game at that time other than the Rose Bowl.

There, Matthews was reunited with a pair of old foes. Hunt and Gerald Mann, SMU's "Little Red Arrow." They turned it into an All-SWC show, leading the West to a 16-6 victory against a heavily favored East squad.

On the game's first scrimmage play, Matthews hit Nebraska star Glenn Presnell so hard that he fumbled and left the game with a broken collarbone.

"They lined up in a Double-Wing T, and when the quarterback tried to hand off, me and Presnell got to the ball at the same time," Matthews says. "After I hit him, I recovered the fumble.

"On the next play, Hunt ran 20 yards for a touchdown, and later on, Mann caught a flat pass for another. I got the other points when I tackled a guy in the end zone for a safety. I think I had about 25 tackles that day."

Matthews spent the rest of the game issuing his "run my way" challenge to Yale star Bruce Caldwell, with the usual results. The next day, the headline in one San Francisco paper read, "Matthews Beats East."

Despite the rivalry between them, Matthews regards Hunt — who set a SWC scoring record (128 points in nine games) that stood for 62 years and remains only six points off the modern 11-game record — as the greatest back in SWC history.

"He could do anything," Matthews says. "One year, we were chasing him on the sideline with about a minute to play, when he suddenly veered out to the center of the field and (drop-kicked) a 50-yard field goal to tie the game."

They were almost teammates. Matthews enrolled briefly at

A&M but called Meyer and Bell to come get him after discovering that, "the place was out in the middle of a prairie and there were no women."

After a brief fling in pro ball, Matthews returned home and embarked on a successful career in the oil business.

*Rags Matthews,
an all-American end
in 1927.*

CHAPTER 5

Ben Boswell, an all-America tackle, in 1932.

HORNED FROGS WIN FRAY WITH LONGHORNS

By Leroy Menzing
Fort Worth Star-Telegram

Ft. Worth, Nov. 4, 1932— Texas Christian University threw the full fury of its mighty forward wall against Texas University before 20,000 fanatic fans at the TCU Stadium yesterday afternoon. The Horned Frog backfield put

TCU	7	0	0	7	14
Texas	0	0	0	0	0

on a two-touchdown scoring spree that carried them to a 14-0 victory and ridded their championship path of one of their most formidable foes. Now, only Rice Institute and Southern Methodist University remain on the schedule.

The 20,000 cheering fans — filling the TCU Stadium with Ft. Worth's largest football crowd in history — saw one of the most exciting and thrilling games since Southwest Conference football was brought here by the Frogs. Thrill and suspense came with the very first play and lasted through the sound of the final gun, which found Jack Langdon pulling Bohn Hilliard down 3 yards from the Frog goal line.

It was one of two times the Longhorns ever came close to a touchdown, the other being at the close of the first half when Harrison Stafford took a long pass from Ernie Koy, only to be dragged down by Blanard Spearman on TCU's 3-yard line. A few seconds later, Red Oliver intercepted an intended pass for Stafford and raced to midfield as the gun sounded.

TCU line play was so great from the very start that the Longhorns soon gave up on trying to gain on running plays and took to the air. The Frogs kept the Longhorns' three-star backfield of Stafford, Hilliard and Koy so bottled up they had a hard time

Francis Schmidt's 1932 Horned Frogs won the Southwest Conference with a 10-0-1 record.

gaining more yards than they lost.

Koy was the Longhorns' most productive back, turning in 50 yards. The majority of this was picked up on passing plays, but when he found himself trapped and was forced to run with the ball this turned into the Longhorns' best offensive play.

While picking up 50 yards, Koy lost 20. Hilliard was far from the sensational back of the Rice, SMU, Baylor and Oklahoma games, gaining only 20 yards, while losing 18. He even lost yardage returning punts — running long distances, but not goalward. Stafford gained no yards and lost 5.

For the afternoon, Texas gained only 71 yards on running plays and picked up 115 more on passes for a total of 186.

While Texas' great array of backfield talent was feeling the full fury of what probably is the greatest line that ever has been in the conference, the Frog backs were ripping the Longhorns defense for 227 yards on running plays and 13 first downs against eight for Texas. With their running attack clicking so well the Frogs did not need the air and tried only four passes, completing one for 10 yards.

Scintillating in the TCU backfield were Red Oliver and Blanard Spearman with some great help from Johnny Kitchen and Buster Brannon. Oliver scored both of the Frogs' touchdowns and drove well all afternoon. He appeared loose on the interception of Koy's pass at the close of the first half but was nailed by the Longhorns' Hank Clewis.

Again the TCU line must be credited when the success of the Frog backfield is discussed. Both of the Frogs' touchdowns were made on the right side of the line through gaping holes by Foster Howell, who starred on the offense all afternoon. He was not the

Blanard Spearman, an All-SWC halfback in 1931 and 1932.

star; there were others, all who played on the line. Madison Pruitt at end was a thorn to the Longhorns' ground attack all afternoon and received a great ovation when forced from the game in the fourth quarter by injuries. Jack Langdon stepped into his place and carried on. Ben Boswell was another reason that the Longhorns' attack was stopped, so were team captain Johnny Vaught, J.W. Townsend, Lon Evans, Jack Graves and Wallace Myers. Myers was forced out in the first quarter because of an injured leg and Graves played the reminder of the game.

TCU backs struck for their touchdowns in the first and fourth quarters with the wind to their backs, but the wind made no difference to them, as they gained more yards on running plays against the wind than they did with it. It was late in the first quarter when TCU gained the ball on Texas' 27-yard line for their first touchdown after they had just been stopped on the six-inch line.

On the first play, Spearman cut over his own left tackle to the Texas 2-yard line, where he was hit by Hilliard. Oliver then raced over right tackle for the touchdown. Otha Tiner rushed in the game for his specialty, field goal and extra-point kicking, and booted the ball squarely through the uprights.

The Frogs plowed from the Longhorns' 24-yard line near the middle of the fourth quarter for their second touchdown. Brannon picked up 2 yards and then Oliver added 11 for a first down. It was on this play that Pruitt was hurt, as was Coates, the Texas center, who was carried from the field.

An offside penalty set the Frogs back 5 yards, but Oliver came back with 18 more to carry it to Texas' 2-yard line. He went over right tackle once more for a touchdown, assuring him of the conference scoring lead. Again Tiner was rushed in and he put the ball through the posts and trotted off the field.

Thrills came within a few seconds after the opening kickoff when Spearman burst through the Longhorns from his own 22-yard line to midfield where he fumbled when tackled and the ball bounded into Hilliard's arms. However, the Frog line held and the danger was over for the time at least.

Townsend later intercepted one of Koy's passes to stop a threatening Longhorn march on the Texas 35-yard line. It was then that the

Frogs seemed touchdown bound, only to be stopped on the six-inch line. A Hubert Dennis to Pruitt pass went for 10 yards, but another to Oliver was incomplete. Then Kitchen took the ball, spun, handed it to Spearman, who tossed a lateral to Dennis for 18 yards. Oliver made 4 over right tackle and two more at the same spot, but one-half yard was the best that he and Kitchen could do in the next two tries.

The Frogs came right back for their first touchdown.

The second quarter was packed with just as many thrills, with the Texas rooters coming to their feet near the close. Texas had gained the ball on its own 39-yard line as a starter. Koy, trapped on a pass, broke away and ran to midfield. He then dropped back and shot a pass to Stafford for 46 yards with Spearman saving the Frogs from a possible tie when he nailed Stafford on the 3-yard line. Texas drew 5 yards for excessive time out and then Stafford floated wide for a pass, but Oliver was there and ended the threat by tackling him at midfield as the gun sounded.

Although the Frogs were facing a stiff wind in the third quarter, they drove through the Longhorns. However, the Longhorns were not without their

J.W. Townsend, the All-SWC center in 1932.

Fullback Johnny Kitchen plows into the line in the 14-0 win against Texas.

threats. They blocked one of Brannon's punts near the start of the period to gain the ball on the Frogs' 31-yard line. However, Hilliard lost 6 yards and failed to gain a second trip. Then Koy passed to Sears Earle for 15 yards just short of a first down, and he failed in his effort to plow the center of the Frog line.

The fourth quarter for the whole also was fought in Texas' territory, but the Longhorns threw a scare near the close when Brannon fumbled the ball when attempting to punt on fourth down and the ball went to Texas on TCU's 26-yard line.

A pass, Koy to Earle, netted 11 yards and a first down. Koy gained 8 at the line, but was checked for no gain on his next attempt. On a fake pass, he made a first down on the Frogs' 3-yard line. Twice Koy tried the line without gaining and then Hilliard tried a cutback at his left tackle, but Langdon dragged him down as the game ended.

Although the Frogs' forward wall almost completely checked the Longhorns, they, too, had their stars and the greatest of them was Stafford. He didn't gain any ground running with the ball, but he was everywhere all afternoon, and showed himself to be truly a great back. Once he jarred Vaught so hard when Vaught was attempting to tackle Hilliard on a punt that it was feared that the Frog leader

Johnny Vaught, an all-America guard in 1932.

would not be able to get up, but he did, yelling for time out.

CHAPTER 6

TCU's All-SWC Line

By WHIT CANNING
Fort Worth Star-Telegram

At a distance of 64 years, Johnny Vaught still remembers the hit.

It was at Amon Carter Stadium by Harrison Stafford of Texas, in front of what was then the largest crowd (20,000) ever to watch a football game in Ft. Worth.

The date was Nov. 11, 1932 — three days after a Depression-racked nation had voted Franklin Delano Roosevelt into the White House for what would be a lengthy stay.

The occasion was a collision of juggernauts — unbeaten TCU and once-beaten Texas battling for supremacy of the Southwest Conference, and maybe even a shot at the Rose Bowl.

It was also possibly the most unique matchup in SWC history. On one side was the TCU line — ends Dan Salkeld and Madison Pruitt, tackles Foster Howell and Ben Boswell, guards Vaught and Lon Evans, and center J.W. Townsend. In keeping with the custom of the day, all played offense and defense.

And at the end of the season, six of those seven were chosen to the All-SWC team, led by Vaught, who was also an all-American. The only exclusion was Salkeld, who missed some playing time with an injury and was beaten out by Baylor's Frank James.

On the other side of the ball was a Texas team that contained three-fourths of the All-SWC backfield — Stafford, Ernie Koy and Bohn Hilliard.

It was the only game in SWC history matching, essentially, the all-conference line against the all-conference backfield. Actually, 10 of the 11 All-SWC choices were on the field that day, since TCU's Blanard Spearman was the fourth back.

Eventually, defensive might prevailed, as the Frogs won, 14-0. But for a while, Vaught wasn't sure he would be around for the finish.

"They always let me release early on punts so I could go down with the coverage," he said. "One time, I went down there and the return man (Hilliard) suddenly veered sharply to the right, and I swerved to meet him.

"That's when Stafford hit me — about as hard as you can hit somebody. Knocked me clear across the field.

"I wasn't really hurt, but it knocked the breath out of me and I couldn't talk. So I signaled for Lon Evans (future Tarrant County sheriff) to call time out so I could catch my breath. I didn't want to go out of the game, because in those days you couldn't come back in until the next quarter."

Vaught recovered, but Stafford's hit became one of those legendary moments that was still talked about and written about 30 years later.

Of greater significance to the outcome, however, was Spearman's tackle of Stafford at the TCU 3-yard line after a 46-yard pass reception by Hilliard just before the half. On the next play, Red Oliver intercepted a pass in the end zone, ending Texas' only meaningful threat of the day. The Longhorns were also stopped at the 3 on the game's final play.

Oliver scored twice, at the end of drives in the first and fourth quarters, and another TCU drive was stopped at the Longhorns' 1-yard line. Texas made eight first downs and was forced to throw most of the day because the Big Three managed only 27 rushing yards against the formidable TCU front wall.

It was the only SWC defeat for the Longhorns, who finished 8-2 overall. The Horned Frogs finished 10-0-1 and outscored their collective foes 283-23.

"The only game we didn't win was a 3-3 tie with LSU down in Baton Rouge," Vaught said. "Red Oliver ran wild down there, but we just couldn't push the ball over the goal line.

"When we finished the season unbeaten, we were kinda hoping we might get a bid (to the Rose Bowl), but it didn't happen (Pitt was selected to meet USC)."

A graduate of Polytechnic High School ("My idol was Rags Matthews"), Vaught was destined for fame as the head coach at Ole Miss (1947-70,73) — where he won 190 games and six Southeastern Conference titles, and had 18 bowl teams.

Now retired, Vaught, 87, lives in Oxford, Miss., and is an avid golfer.

"At Ole Miss, I always had good luck with quarterbacks," he said. "I started out with Charlie Conerly and finished up with Archie Manning.

"But in all those years, I don't think I ever had a line as strong as the one I played on at TCU."

TCU's Purple Wall in 1932: (left to right) Dan Salkend, Fostor Howell, Johnny Vaught, J.W. Townsend, Lon Evans, Ben Boswell and Pappy Pruitt.

CHAPTER 7

FROGS KNOCK OWLS OFF UNBEATEN ROOST

BY FLEM HALL
Fort Worth Star-Telegram

HOUSTON, NOV. 24, 1934 — True to their pre-game promise those fightin' TCU Frogs "Yaled" those Rice Institute Owls here Saturday afternoon.

TCU	7	0	0	0	7
Rice	0	0	0	2	2

Although they weren't rated a chance, the Christians, playing gloriously, defeated the unbeaten Birds, 7-2, in a game that started with an amazing rush and ended in a riot, a game that promoted standing hair, backbone chills and goose pimples that stood out like asparagus sprouts all over the 14,000 astonished spectators.

The victory — although it did not wipe out Rice's chances to win her first Southwest Conference championship — did throw its dream of playing in either the Rose Bowl or the Sugar Bowl into the old soup bowl. It left them with only one objective — the conference championship, which they can still capture by winning over the Baylor Bears in Waco next weekend.

TCU won the game in the first eight minutes of play. The first time they were given the ball, they marched 80 yards straight down the field to the lone touchdown of the game.

Lawrence the Mainspring

Jimmy Lawrence, the hard running junior halfback who rushed off the bench at the end of the game to slug field judge Sergeant Fischer, was the mainspring of the drive. Ripping and tearing the sturdy Owl line to shreds on reverses to the left, and with valuable help from Taldon Manton and George Kline, the 180-pound pride of Harlingen carried the ball the great majority of the 74-yard drive to the Rice 6. From there he passed to Joe Coleman, the Frogs' captain, for a touchdown.

Jimmy Lawrence, an All-SWC halfback in 1933 and 1935.

The scoring play was a most peculiar one — partly a lucky one and partly the result of fast thinking and beautiful running. Swarmed over by three Rice linemen, it appeared that Lawrence was stopped for a 10-yard loss. Spotting Coleman just a few yards away Lawrence tore loose and tossed. Coleman gathered the ball in on the 13-yard line right up against the south goal line and took off. With the aid of one lone blocker he sidestepped, whirled and smashed his way over the goal line. Manton place kicked for the extra point.

The drive was made in the teeth of a stiff wind that swept lengthwise of the field against the Christians in the first and fourth quarters. With a seven-point lead, the Frogs dug in for their most determined, effective and spectacular defensive effort of the season.

Face-to-face with an offense that hadn't been stopped this year, with an attack that had power, speed and passing, the Christians, who had stopped few major opponents from scoring this season, rose to meet the challenge. Led by Walter Roach and Darrell Lester, who turned in all-around performances that stamped them as the equal of any end or center in the land, the entire line charged fast and hard, blocked and tackled, and thwarted the maddest and fiercest dashes of Bill Wallace and John McCauley, the Rice all-American touchdown twins and all their mates.

Riotous Conclusion

Although penalized to within a shorter distance, the Frogs never let the Owls power or pass the ball inside their 13-yard line.

Once, after TCU had deliberately given Rice a safety and 2 points in the fourth quarter to keep from trying to punt out against the wind after a Rice punt had been killed on the two-yard line, the Owls got inside the Frog 10. That was because Fischer, the field judge, had ruled a 31-yard Rice pass complete on the TCU 9-yard line due to pass interference. From there the Owls pushed 5 yards, but couldn't get over. It was the interference penalty that caused Lawrence to come off the bench as the final gun sounded and knock Fischer cold with a terrific swinging punch to the jaw. That started a large uproar on the field that continued for 15 minutes.

There was a great deal of excitement and some pushing and punching but no one was hurt and police finally cleared the gridiron.

After they scored their seven points, the Frogs made no serious attempt to add to their advantage. They frequently punted on second and third down and threw only three passes, all of which were long and deep in the Owl end of the field.

Wallace, McCauley, Albert Metzler, and numerous other Rice backs made ardent gallops, sweeps and smashes to gain quite a few yards in the middle of the field but they couldn't get anywhere near the Purple goal. Most of the time when they started a series of downs near the TCU goal they ended up a greater distance from their objective than when they started.

Dutch Meyer's first TCU squad in 1934 won 8 games and lost 4.

CHAPTER 8

Jimmy Lawrence (8) races upfield for big yardage against SMU.

SMU TAKES THRILLING GAME FROM TCU, 20-14

BY FLEM HALL
Fort Worth Star-Telegram

FT. WORTH, NOV. 30, 1935 — In a game that sizzled and crackled with all the fierce fire of roaring Southwest football, the militant Mustangs of Southern Methodist University Saturday defeated a gallant Texas Christian University, 20-14, at TCU Stadium. The second largest crowd (36,000) that ever saw a football game in Texas gasped at the bold, daring and audacious play of the two magnificent gridiron brigades.

With all the football world looking on or listening

SMU	14	0	0	6	20
TCU	0	7	0	7	14

through the eyes and ears of a multitude of national critics and radio announcers, the Pony Express and the Horned Frogs put on a grand show — a typical open, free-scoring Southwest conflict — a game worthy of the position it held in national attention.

Although they threw only six passes the Mustangs snatched victory out of the sunlit skies that canopied the perfect scene. With the score tied, 14-14, in the fourth quarter, with the ball on the TCU 37-yard line, Robert Finley, on fourth down with 4 yards to for a first, flung a long, true pass straight down the east sideline toward the north goal. Rambling Robert Wilson evaded the defensive left halfback (Harold McClure) and made a marvelous catch on about the 4-yard line and recovering from a stumble, crossed the goal line for the winning six points.

Ponies Score Early

Starting the conflict as sharp as tacks the Ponies whipped over a touchdown in the first four minutes of play and added another seven points in the early part of the second quarter. The dauntless Christians fought back with fierce and deadly effectiveness. They scored once before halftime and tied the count 14-all in the early minutes of the fourth quarter.

SMU gave a clear impression that it was the better team for the day and deserved to win by receiving the next kickoff and scoring without losing possession. Maurice Orr, who converted after the first two touchdowns,

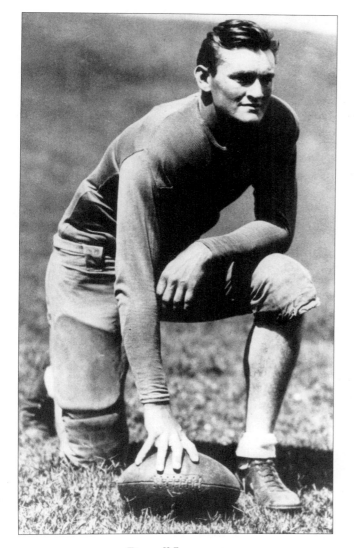

Darrell Lester, an
all-America center in 1934 and 1935.

failed in his third attempt and hope still burned brightly in the breasts of TCU supporters. And not without reason. Twice within the remaining six minutes the white-shirted forces swept into threatening position. They were stopped once on the SMU 28-yard line, and the final gun found them completing pass after pass that had carried them to the Methodist 35.

The Blue and Red played without the services of its star fullback, Harry Shuford, but TCU lost Rex Clark, ace left halfback, on the second play of the game, and lost only after Jarring Jimmy Lawrence, who scored both touchdowns, was forced from the game by injuries.

Stars Numerous

The swirling five-touchdown conflict was so studded with blazing individual effort that stars were almost as numerous as were players in the game, but when it was all over the numbers that burned most brightly in the spectator's memories were 27, 23, 47, 20, 11 and 21 of SMU; 45, 8, and 22 of TCU.

No. 27 was Finley, the substitute back who threw the deciding touchdown pass, the 185-pounder from Corsicana, who whipped another tremendous pass (33 yards) that set the stage for a 9-yard touchdown gallop by Wilson, No. 11, who played a full 60 minutes of brilliant football. No. 23 was Maco Stewart, who caught the first Finley pass and played a fine game. No. 47 was Truman Spain, who proved his all-America worth by playing the finest game at tackle seen here this season. No. 20 was Shelley Burt, the rugged right halfback, who bowled his way through the TCU line for 51 yards in 11 attempts. No. 21 was Bill Tipton, the left end, who twice helped the Blue and Red out of trouble. He made the first touchdown possible by recovering a Wilson fumble for a 7-yard gain on the TCU 13-yard line.

No. 45, 8 and 22 for TCU were Sam Baugh, Jimmy Lawrence and Darrell Lester, respectively. Slinging Sam, shooting with all of his accuracy, completed 17 of 44 passes and would have a much better average if his usually sure-handed receivers had been catching the ball as well as they ordinarily do. Time after time he laid the leather to the right spot, through the most excellent defense TCU has opposed, only to have his receivers muff the pitches.

Sammy Baugh — the greatest passer to ever play college football — shows the proper technique.

As it was he accounted for 180 yards of ground gaining on passes. He punted magnificently, averaging 48 yards from the line of scrimmage and he did as swell a job of running and on defense.

Lawrence was as fine a running back as there was on the field, and he did more than his share of the receiving. As stated before, it wasn't until he had to leave the game that SMU was able to win by passing over his position.

Lester was his all-American self at center, and nothing less. He did everything a center should do just as it should have been done.

80 Yards on Five Plays

SMU marched 73 yards in the first four minutes for its first touchdown. Starting from their own 27, the Mustangs ripped 19 yards on running plays with Burt passes to Sprague. Finley led another running assault that made a first on the 20. Then Wilson fumbled on an end sweep and Tipton recovered on the TCU 13. Burt burst through for a first down on the 1-yard line and Finley carried it over in one try. Maurice Orr converted.

The next scoring jaunt traveled 80 yards on just six plays. Wilson started it with a 22-yard jaunt around TCU's left end. Burt got three at tackle and Finley broke through for a first on the Frog 42. Burt made a yard and then Finley shot a long pass over George Kline to Stewart, who made an unbelievable catch on the TCU 9-yard line. On the next play, Wil-

Tears in One Dressing Room, Shouts From the Other After Big Game

Fort Worth Star-Telegram

The dressing room that a week ago resounded with hearty slaps on backs and the babble of congratulatory comment presented a different picture yesterday afternoon as the weary, beaten Horned Frogs of Texas Christian University went about the task of removing their uniforms.

And not so many steps away in another dressing room that last week saw a dejected Rice University team wondering dazily what had happened, there was shouting and laughter and a snatch of song. Here the elated Mustangs of Southern Methodist University pranced and pranked.

There were tears in the TCU room, tears that welled from the eyes of men, but there were words of praise for the victors.

"We were beaten by a great team," Coach L.R. (Dutch) Meyer declared. "But our boys played a grand ball game — a damned fine ball game."

The Frog captain, Darrell Lester, steadied himself as a trainer removed adhesive tape from his legs.

"They've got a fine ball club," he said. "They've got a couple of great guards. They've got a well-rounded offense as well as defense. In fact, they've just got a real, good ball club."

Jimmy Lawrence, the TCU co-captain, bending over as the injury that took him from the game was treated, looked up to say, "The best team won."

Surrounded by a milling mass of SMU ex-students and supporters, Coach Matty Bell paused frequently to pat one of his players or to laud their work.

"I'm mighty glad we won," he asserted. "It was a great ball game. We were lucky. Either team would have been lucky to win

"TCU has a fine ball club. It was a hard fought, clean game throughout. Of course I'm very proud of the way my boys came through."

Bobby Wilson, Mustang halfback, whose performance won him loud praise from Bell, glanced toward the door where a crowd was clamoring to enter the room. He grinned. "It was a fine game. Everybody came through in great shape. There's no doubt about Sam Baugh and Lester being great players."

son again swept left end and this time for a touchdown to the northeast corner. Orr again converted.

Just previous to that swift flight, TCU had made a 74-yard drive only to be stopped on the SMU 16.

A great punt by Baugh, one that sailed 50 yards and out of bounds on the SMU 4, started the first successful bid for points. The punt out was only to the Mustang 26. From there they went to the 5. A penalty against Sprague for interfering with a pass receiver gave TCU a first down on the 2-yard line and from there Lawrence drove over. Walter Roach converted to make it 14-7 and the half ended that way.

SMU Gambles, Wins

The third period was scoreless but, as the teams battled madly between the 30-yard lines, the play was marked by teeth-rattling tackles and brutal blocking. Just before the period closed Roach intercepted a Mustang pass on the TCU 44 and Baugh passed to Lawrence for a first on SMU's 43.

On the first play of the final period, Baugh again tossed short to Lawrence, who tore off a 17-yard gain. Two plays later Baugh passed to Willie Walls for a first down on the Pony 8. Two passes failed to click, but on the third Lawrence made connections and went over. It was on that play that we was hurt so he had to retire. Roach converted to knot the score at 14-all.

Then came the winning assault.

Roach's kickoff was short and J.R. Smith, who was the star of the remainder of the game, returned to his own 47. Two plays made a first down on the Frog 43 for SMU. When the next three plays netted only 6 yards, it appeared that the Ponies would have to kick. But, gambling boldly for victory, Finley passed instead and it worked for the score that's likely to put SMU in the Rose Bowl.

CHAPTER 9

A Nation Discovers
the Southwest Conference

By Whit Canning
Fort Worth Star-Telegram

In the rather florid style of the day, the climactic moment appears to have transpired something like this:

"Streaking like a brown blur across the brown gridiron and arched in soaring flight against the blue background of bright Texas skies, a spiraling football sped on its meteoric way here this afternoon to give the wild Mustangs of Southern Methodist a 20-14 victory over Texas Christian.

"Thrown long and far and with unerring accuracy by Bob Finley, the right halfback of the Dallas team, the ball zoomed like a projectile down from its airway flight into the hands of Bobby Wilson, Southern Methodist's brilliant 147-pound candidate for a backfield berth on the 1935 all-America. Wilson caught the ball while he was in the grasp of a Christian tackler. He whirled like a dervish and spun over the goal line."

Thus began one account of a game played between two undefeated rivals before an overflow crowd at Amon Carter Stadium on Nov. 30, 1935. It was a day on which the attention of an entire nation focused — for the first time — on the Southwest Conference.

The protagonists were two 10-0 teams each led by an all-American back — Wilson for the Mustangs and Sammy Baugh for TCU. Linemen Darrell Lester (TCU), and Truman Spain and J.C. Wetsel (SMU) were also all-Americans. The coaches were Matty Bell and Dutch Meyer — close friends and bitter rivals.

Awaiting the victor was the greatest prize in football at that time, pro or college: a trip to the Rose Bowl.

The above account appeared in a Los Angeles newspaper; its author, Maxwell Stiles, sat in a press box where Grantland Rice and Joe Williams filed stories back to New York. Bill Cunningham, filing for The Boston Globe, dubbed Wilson a "lizard-legged little

bundle of mobile murder" and declared, "brethren and beloved, Mr. Slingin' Samuel Baugh can chunk that cabbage." The writer from Kansas City called it a "heroic battle that has captured the fancy of the nation."

Almost all agreed that both teams — victor and vanquished — were better than anything else they had seen that year.

And so, a struggling, 20-year-old conference suddenly stepped into a limelight that would last nearly a half-century.

"It was really something," says Wilson, 82, now retired and living in Brenham. "As far as it being a real head-knocking game, that it wasn't. But it was really and truly a great game for the spectators because it had a lot of scoring."

It therefore justified the immense weeklong buildup that had surfaced even during a time out in the Princeton-Dartmouth game, when Steven Cullinam — center for the unbeaten and possibly Rose Bowl-bound Tigers — approached an official and said, "Know who the best team in the country is? Texas Christian."

Indeed, The Associated Press rankings the week of the game featured a three-way tie for first between Minnesota, Princeton and TCU. SMU was fourth, LSU fifth, Alabama sixth and Stanford, the eventual host team in the Rose Bowl, seventh. The Williamson Rating System had LSU first, followed by Minnesota, TCU and SMU.

As the week progressed, celebrities arrived — MGM casting director Rufus LeMaire, Columbia Pictures director Ralph Kohn with a party of six — and a Who's Who of coaching, led by Francis Schmidt of Ohio State, Bernie Bierman of Minnesota, Lynn (Pappy) Waldorf of Northwestern, Ray Morrison of Vanderbilt and D.X. Bible of Nebraska. Tickets sold for $1.65 each.

To accommodate the growing throng, 3,500 seats were hastily added, bringing the stadium capacity to 31,000. It is estimated that on the day of the game, nearly 40,000 jammed themselves into the facility. By the time the game started at 2 p.m., some had been there six hours.

"By the time we arrived," Wilson says, "they were just driving up to the fence and climbing over. I don't know how they all made it inside.

"That was during the depression, you know, and I think those people just wanted something to feel happy about. And this was it."

On Friday night, the Fort Worth Chamber of Commerce was host to visiting journalists at a dinner at the Worth Hotel. At game time, there were cars in the parking lot with plates from California, Pennsylvania, Florida and Michigan.

By the time Kern Tips and Cy Leland began a coast-to-coast radio broadcast originating on WBAP, the Frogs had been installed as slight favorites based on three factors: the home-field advantage, a slightly better showing against common foes, and knee injuries that rendered SMU fullback Harry Shuford (twice All-SWC) and Wetsel unavailable for combat.

"Actually," Wilson recalls, "J.C. inserted himself into the game once, but he wasn't much use, 'cause he couldn't bend over."

No matter. After being led onto the field by their "midget horse," as The Star-Telegram reported, the Mustangs wasted little time marching 73 and 80 yards to build a 14-0 lead, with Wilson scoring the second touchdown.

After one aborted 74-yard drive, TCU scored on a short march late in the second quarter. At halftime, Taps was played and, in the midst of the Depression, fans came up with $1,400 for a memorial for the recently deceased Will Rogers.

Baugh, whose receivers were having problems hanging onto his bulletlike deliveries, threw a touchdown pass to Jimmy Lawrence early in the fourth quarter to tie the game at 14-14.

But Lawrence, a top defensive back and the team's rushing leader, was injured on the play and left the game, helping set the stage for a memorable finish.

Wilson and Finley, Shuford's replacement, drove SMU downfield again, until the Mustangs faced a fourth-and 4 at the TCU 37.

SMU then lined up in punt formation, but Finley instead lofted a deep pass down the left sideline for Wilson, who caught it and went over the goal line with

what proved to be the winning score. TCU drove into SMU territory twice more, but failed to score.

For 60 years, the fake-punt pass has remained one of the most famous plays in SWC history — and, in the view of Baugh and Wilson, a little over-hyped.

"I thought SMU deserved to win," says Baugh, 82 and retired, living on his ranch in Rotan. "For one thing, they defensed us better than anyone else did all year. The reason I was throwing the ball so hard is because they dropped people back into our short passing lanes and closed the gaps. I had to throw the ball so hard to keep it from being intercepted that the receivers couldn't catch it."

Baugh finished the game 17-of-44 for 180 yards with eight dropped passes.

"But what galled us was, they won on a (fake punt) play we were expecting; we just didn't stop it," Baugh said. "Then, it was reported as a daring gamble, which it wasn't.

"See, there was a rule back then that if you threw an incomplete pass into the end zone on fourth down, it was just like a touchback — the ball came out to the 20. So if you were close enough, you might as well try it, because you might score."

In other words, an incomplete pass into the end zone was just as effective as a punt into the end zone.

Afterward, Wilson says, he and Finley laughed about it.

"Everyone kept congratulating us on this great gamble," Wilson says, "so Bob and I agreed in the shower that we wouldn't tell anyone about the rule because nobody mentioned it. Finally, some guy doing some research about 20 years later discovered it and wrote a story about it.

"We had planned to use the play on Lawrence because he came up so fast on coverage, but it turned out he wasn't in there when we called it. The two guys closest to me when I caught the ball were Baugh (the safety), and the kid who replaced Lawrence (Harold McClure). I remember it as a pretty routine catch; all that whirling dervish stuff was a bunch of hooey.

"As far as those dropped balls are concerned, I always thought they were catchable. Sam was throwing pretty hard, but he was right on target. With all due respect, I think Sam Baugh was the greatest passer we've ever had."

Tillie Manton (33) scrambles for extra yardage against SMU in 1935.

But in the end, SMU won with TCU's weapon — and the Mustangs band marched off the field playing *California Here We Come.*

The following week, SMU finished a 12-0 season with a victory against Texas A&M and received the bid to play Stanford in the Rose Bowl. TCU (11-1) went to the West Coast and beat a strong Santa Clara team and was invited to play LSU in the second Sugar Bowl.

So, at the end of the 1935 season, each of the two major bowls had an SWC team in it.

For the Mustangs, who had earlier whipped eventual Pacific Coast tri-champion UCLA, 21-0, to fan the flames of interest in Texas football on the West Coast, the second trip was a disappointment. Banged-up and uninspired, they lost to Stanford, 7-0, in the only Rose Bowl appearance by an SWC team.

Meanwhile, TCU used a Talden Manton field goal to defeat LSU, 3-2, in a driving rain in New Orleans,

thus replacing the Tigers as the No. 1 team in America, according to the Williamson Rating Service.

The trip West also earned SMU enough money to pay the mortgage on Ownby Stadium, and inspired Dallas oilman J. Curtis Sanford to create a Texas-based postseason game. The first Cotton Bowl game was played the next year.

And for Bobby Wilson, there remains one more vivid memory of the famous game.

"Toward the end," he says, "Matty sent in instructions for me to not carry the ball anymore, because I was getting tired. But we ignored him.

"I made a long run around end, but fumbled the ball away at about the TCU 18-yard line. Sammy brought 'em back downfield, but time ran out on 'em at about our 35. It was a pretty impressive drive for that day and time.

"And if Sammy had had a few more minutes, I might have been the goat instead of the hero."

The Game of the Century

BY GRANTLAND RICE
New York Sun

FT. WORTH, NOV. 30, 1935 — In the most desperate football this season has known from coast to coast, Southern Methodist beat Texas Christian, 20-14, Saturday and carved out a clear highway to the Rose Bowl beyond any argument or doubt.

In a TCU stadium that seated 30,000 spectators, over 36,000 wildly excited Texans and visitors from every corner of the map packed, jammed and fought their way into every square foot of standing and seating space to see one of the greatest football games ever played in the 67-year history of the nation's finest college sport.

This tense, keyed-up crowd even leaped the wire fences from the tops of automobiles to watch a 60-minute swirl of action that no other area of the country could even approach in the clash of two sectional teams.

Elusive running and forward passing that electrified the overflowing stadium — especially by TCU's all-American, Sammy Baugh — hard blocking and tackling, and magnificent kicking turned this climax game of 1935 into a combination of all-around skill and drama no other football crowd has seen this year.

With the Rose Bowl bid at stake, the Mustangs got the big jump by taking a 14-0 lead. In the first quarter, Bob Finley barged over the goal at the end of a 73-yard march that featured every known form and method of attack. In the second period, SMU struck again. A 33-yard pass from Finley to end Maco Stewart, who made a circus catch, set up a 9-yard dash around end by SMU's brilliant little Bobby Wilson, an all-America halfback if ever there was one.

Facing this smothering margin, Texas Christian came back from the middle of the second quarter with a counter charge that almost swept the Mustangs off the field.

TCU's attack was highlighted by the incredible passing of Sammy Baugh and driving runs of Jimmy Lawrence, a truly great all-around back. The Horned Frogs, with savage drive, repeatedly knocked on the Mustang goal and finally scored as Lawrence bulled his way across from the 4-yard line.

Trailing, 14-7, near the end of the third quarter, Lawrence again climaxed a long passing and running march with a tying score on the first play of the fourth quarter as Baugh whipped the ball into his open arms from 6 yards out.

Tied, 14-14, the big crowd sensed a TCU victory against a fading Mustang team, but it was SMU that had the winning trick left. Halfway through the last period, the Mustangs moved across midfield on three runs by J.R. (Jackrabbit) Smith and a 10-yard reverse by Wilson.

But TCU's defense, led by all-America center Darrell Lester, stiffened and SMU faced a fourth down and 7 yards at the Horned Frogs' 37-yard line. That was when Southern Methodist pulled the most daring play of a daring game.

From punt formation, Bob Finley suddenly dropped back to midfield and pegged a 50-yard pass toward the northeast corner of the end zone where Wilson, the greatest running back of 1935, was racing for the goal line.

As the ball cleared Wilson's shoulder, the 150-pound back made a jumping, twisting catch that swept him over the line for the winning touchdown.

It was a great pass but an even greater catch.

In its excitement over the touchdown, SMU flubbed the conversion try, leaving TCU clinging to some hope for a one-point victory. There were still seven minutes left to play.

Baugh drove TCU to SMU's 30-yard line and again to SMU's 25-yard line but couldn't score, and Baugh was eating up ground in the Mustangs' end of the field again when the final whistle blew and SMU supporters were almost in panic from Baugh's deathly machine-gun fire.

By its victory over Texas Christian, SMU's fine squad picked up the Rose Bowl challenge. TCU is headed for the Sugar Bowl. The foes of both the Mustangs and Horned Frogs better be ready, for they proved that they are the most spectacular, all-around teams I have seen this year.

CHAPTER 10

Darrell Lester was injured in the first quarter against LSU and unable to finish the game.

FROGS WIN NATIONAL TITLE

By Flem Hall
Fort Worth Star-Telegram

NEW ORLEANS, JAN. 1, 1936 — Playing as glorious a game as ever a Texas Christian University team turned in, the purple-clad Horned Frogs defeated the Terrible Tigers of Louisiana State University, champions of the Southeastern Conference, 3-2, here this New Year's afternoon in the second annual feature of the Sugar Bowl's Midwinter Sports Carnival. An astounding 36-yard

TCU	0	3	0	0	3
LSU	0	2	0	0	2

field goal by fullback Tillie Manton won the ball game.

TCU's win, combined with Southern Methodist's loss to Stanford in the Rose Bowl, put the Frogs No. 1 in the final Williamson national rankings.

Dark and cold from the start, the afternoon turned rainy at the half and gridiron was a veritable morass before the end. Heavy rains Saturday, Tuesday, and Wednesday morning had the gridiron soggy and slippery before it became steadily worse as the play progressed. A cold wind out of the northwest swept the rain in slanting sheets diagonally across the field.

It was the consensus of the press box after the game that the better team won, that TCU outgained the

Tigers, who started the game an 8 to 5 favorite; outfought, outthought and outplayed the Bengals from Baton Rouge to gain the victory.

In spite of the terrible weather, the game was witnessed by approximately 37,000 fans, who occupied nearly every available seat in the bowl to form the largest crowd ever to witness a sporting event in the Deep South. And the customers stuck right down to the last play. So intense was the interest in the desperate play that discomfort was disregarded until the timekeeper's clock stopped the fray with TCU in possession of the ball on the LSU 23-yard line.

All points of the ball game were scored in the second quarter. LSU got two on an automatic safety to draw first blood, and then the Frogs, stung into action, whipped across three points within two minutes.

The Winning Kick

The safety was called after Sam Baugh, the No. 1 player of the game, accidently stepped back over his own end zone line while trying to launch a pass. He was hard rushed by Paul Carroll, the Tiger right tackle, and managed to get the ball off only after he had retreated a step too far, and an alert official called the automatic scoring foul.

The ball was put in play by a free kick from the 20-yard line. Walter Roach got off a long boot to the LSU 40-yard line. On the first play from there Bill Crass fumbled, and Willie Walls, who played a marvelous game throughout, recovered for TCU. From there Jimmy Lawrence, who played most of the game brilliantly in spite of a severe leg injury, passed to Walls for a first down on the 16-yard line. The next three plays netted a 3-yard loss, but left the ball only about 10 yards from the middle of the field. Center Jack Tittle passed the wet, slick, heavy ball back perfectly to Baugh, who set it down on the 26-yard line. Manton drove his right toe into the leather and it took off like a perfect golf approach shot and sailed squarely between the uprights and well over the crossbar for what proved to be the ball game.

Common Theme

It was the third time in as many meetings that field goals have figured vitally in TCU-LSU football games. In 1931, the Frogs defeated the Tigers, 3-0, and the fol-

On a rain-soaked field, Sammy Baugh punted 14 times against LSU for a 45-yard average.

lowing season they tied, 3-3. Today's game was the only other gridiron contest between the two.

No more spectacular and engrossing football was ever played under such adverse conditions as existed here Wednesday. Ordinarily, mud battles are dull shoving contests, but that was not the case in this Sugar Bowl scrap. Both teams tried everything in the book. There were three hair-raising goal-line stands — two by TCU and one by LSU; there was plenty of passing, especially by LSU; as sensational punting a game as was ever produced; a half dozen long and dazzling runs; daring and gambling play; and a field goal that'll go down in football history as one of the finest.

Three Stars Out

TCU played most of the game minus the services of three of her brightest stars — left halfback George Kline, all-American center Darrell Lester and halfback Rex Clark Kline went out early in the first quarter, never to return. On account of his peculiar eye trouble Lester suffered an injured right arm stopping a crashing plunge by Bill Crass on the goal line in the second quarter and had to leave the game. Clark played only one down and that was only by the courtesy of Coaches Dutch Meyer and Sidney Wolf who wanted the injured senior star to be able to say he played in the 1936 Sugar Bowl game.

Sophomore Bob Harrell played most of the time in the place of injured Kline and gave a good account of himself. Another sophomore, Jack Tittle, filled in for Lester and delivered an outstanding performance. So brilliant was he that the Frogs did not miss their captain. Tittle played the ball back accurately all afternoon, blocked well on offense, stopped all LSU plays

that came his way and batted down two passes.

Tinsley Good On Defense

Gaynell Tinsley, LSU's all-American left end, was all of that on defense, but just so-so on offense. Abe Mickal, Rock Reed, Bill Crass and Jess Fatheree took turns in turning loose their versatile skill at the embattled Christians, and although they flashed time and time again, they could never put together enough consecutive plays to cross the valiantly defended TCU goal line. Tracy Kellow, Wilson Groseclose, Drew Ellis, Glynn Rogers, Walls, Tittle and Walter Roach saw to that. Those linemen were given invaluable help by Manton, who just about proved himself the finest fullback in the South, backing up the TCU line so well that the Tigers were prevented from scoring a touchdown for the only time during the long season. He also distinguished himself by his sure-handed work on handling the ball on the intricate reverses and spinners that the Frogs persisted in using with success in spite of the treacherous slipperiness of the leather.

Jimmy Lawrence gave a great demonstration of determination and courage by playing most of the game despite his bad ankle. He did not just stand out there; he played as well as any back on the field, save

Tillie Manton boots the game-winning field goal against LSU.

SUGAR BOWL CLASSIC JAN. 1, 1936
Crass Misses Touchdown by Inches in Third Quarter

TCU's tough defense stopped the attempted touchdown dive of LSU's Bill Crass at the 1-yard line.

Sammy Baugh looks for an open receiver while being pressured by LSU's Gaynell Tinsley.

one — that one exception was Sam Baugh — that junior quarterback did the greatest job of punting this old writer ever saw, and not one, of the scores of veteran football observers who saw the game could recall a contest that produced kicking to compare with it. LSU had three really fine punters in "Honest Abe" Mickal, Bill Crass and Jess Fatheree, and they each did marvelous work; but Baugh outlasted and outkicked them all. Not only that, he made the longest run of the day — a 44-yard gallop off tackle that just lacked 2 yards of scoring a touchdown in the final minutes of the game. It was the run that made the one-point margin safe in the last three minutes.

CHAPTER 11

BAUGH'S PASSING TOPPLES UNDEFEATED BRONCOS, 9-0

Sammy Baugh lived up to his legend in the 9-0 win over Santa Clara.

BY AMOS MELTON
Fort Worth Star-Telegram

SAN FRANCISCO, DEC. 12, 1936 — Those TCU Horned Frogs, God bless 'em, are the guttiest, most magnificent gang of football players that ever came down any pike.

TCU	0	6	0	3	9
Santa Clara	0	0	0	0	0

All of Texas and the Southwest would have swelled with pride to see their own boys batter into defeat the last untied and undefeated major team in the nation here Saturday afternoon — Santa Clara, 9-0.

Yes, sir, the Texans had a good reputation, they had a great band and they were all fine folks — but defeat the mighty Santa Clara Broncos? TCU couldn't win.

The sportswriters all said so, the coaches over this way were certain of the outcome and the California fans had only pity for the boys from Texas.

40,000 Fans See Upset of Their Lives

Well, those fightin' battling, rootin'-tootin' boys from the cow country gave 40,000 in Kezar Stadium the jolt of their lives. They not only won, but decisively. The score might have been bigger had the Purple not been content to sit back and hold its safe lead in the final quarter.

The Texans were in a hole most of the first quarter. Once, the great Nello Falaschi intercepted one of Sammy Baugh's slips and returned it to the Frog 3-yard line before he was tackled from behind. But the Broncos couldn't make an inch running and two pass-

Walter Roach snags Sammy Baugh's touchdown pass.

es into the end zone ended the threat.

Then, early in the second quarter, the Frog fans got a big scare. From his 47, Baugh launched a perfect pass to Walter Roach. But the ball popped out of Roach's arms and fell into the hands of Harold Seramin, a fast little back. The Bronco took off. Twice it appeared that he would be bagged, but each time he broke free and continued his journey. Finally he raced across the goal untouched. But on the play, an alert official caught a Bronco blocker clipping on the Frog 14. Three plays made only 3 yards and then Bruno Pellegrini was rushed in to try a field goal from the 26-yard line. It was short.

Line Holds Broncos to 4 First Downs

And that was the last serious Bronco threat. The Purple line halted the famous Santa Clara running game to four first downs. When the Broncos tried to pass in a pinch, the Purple secondary either knocked them down or intercepted. Vic Montgomery, Glen Roberts and Baugh intercepted four enemy passes and only one toss was completed by the Broncos.

The Frogs didn't have much luck running against the best line they've seen in many a moon, but their passes did all right, although the Broncos remained in a five-man line most of the afternoon. After Baugh found the range, he was just as deadly as ever. To say that had those 40,000 fans with him when the game ended would be a gross understatement.

The winners scored with such suddenness that most of the crowd didn't know what was happening. Roberts, who played the game of his career, intercepted a Bronco heave on the Frog 15 and returned it to the Purple 33. After a shovel pass to Montgomery made 2, Baugh rifled to Roach, who made a great catch between two defenders. Roach flipped a back pass to Roberts and the play carried to the Santa Clara 47.

Then Baugh called on an old favorite — a pass that scored twice on Baylor. It was a deep shot to McCall behind the Bronco right half. The ball arched up perfectly and came down softly into McCall's arms on the Santa Clara 9. Again Baugh called a pass but his receivers were covered. So he tucked the leather under his arm and battled to the 5-yard line.

Then, Baugh dropped back and his famous arm uncoiled. In the end zone, Roach was traveling at full speed between the secondary. The ball hit him like a bullet and he hugged it to his stomach for the touchdown. L.D. Meyer's extra-point kick was high enough but just to the left of the uprights.

Baugh's Toe Deals Out Misery

That would have won for the Frogs but they weren't done. Baugh, who outpunted several Broncos all day, pushed the California boys into a hole early in the third stanza. A short return punt gave the Frogs the ball on the enemy 42. A shovel pass to McCall and a bullet pass to Roach made a new try on the Bronco 22. A shovel pass to McCall made 9 yards but two other passes misfired.

Then Meyer stepped backed and from the 21-yard line, arched a perfect boot through the goal posts to give TCU a 9-0 lead.

Baugh was everything the Southwest has been claiming. There wasn't a fan or sportswriter who didn't know they had seen an all-American in action when this games was over.

CHAPTER 12

Sammy Baugh: College Football's Greatest Passer

By Whit Canning
Fort Worth Star-Telegram

Standing under a backyard tree on an early autumn afternoon, a tall, affable rancher who could reach back and grasp a thousand memories settles quickly on one:

"The first time I came here," he says, gazing at two huge landmarks in the distance, "I fell in love with those mountains."

They are called the Double Mountains, and they form the back gate to the sprawling ranch, halfway between Rotan and Aspermont, that Sam Baugh and his wife, Edmonia, bought here more than half a century ago.

"We bought the place in 1941," says Baugh, now 82 and retired. "Borrowed the money from a lady over in Eastland that I never even met. It was arranged through someone else, but we paid her back."

They settled in raising cattle and children (Todd, David, Bruce, Stephen, Frances). They had known each other since their high school days in Sweetwater, and when Edmonia died six years ago, they had been married 52 years.

"The place looked a little different back then," he says. "The house was about four rooms and there was no electricity. We got water from a cistern, and when it was low, we just used the trough out there."

By 1941, however, there was considerable electricity connected with the name "Sammy Baugh," since it identified a man who was perhaps the most famous football player in the nation. He was a towering (6-foot-2) leader known from coast to coast by a catchy nickname he despised: "Slingin' Sam."

It was a clumsy alliterative ploy, perhaps, but an apt description of the former TCU all-American's passing skills, by then being used in the service of the Washington Redskins.

Multiple Talents

In truth, Baugh was the consummate athlete: a fine runner, outstanding defensive back and brilliant punter, as well as captain of his high school basketball team and a baseball player courted by the St. Louis Cardinals.

But more than that, he was a passer whose performances often left observers — and opponents — awestruck.

After watching Baugh in a losing performance against SMU in 1935, a Boston writer filed a report calling him "better even than Michigan's great Benny Friedman."

And Bobby Wilson, the star who led the Mustangs to victory that day, still maintains that, "With all due respect, Sam Baugh was the greatest passer we've ever played."

In Baugh's case, it was a skill with inauspicious beginnings.

"I grew up in Temple, where my dad worked for the Santa Fe railroad," he said. "All through junior high, I played end, but when I got to high school, I wound up playing on about the sorriest team Temple ever had.

"We couldn't beat anyone, and one day the coach, Bill Henderson, came over and said, 'We can't run on anybody and we can't stop anybody. Maybe we can throw on 'em. I'm puttin' you in at tailback.

"Didn't make a damn bit of difference that I could tell — we just kept right on losing.

"But then my daddy got bumped to a job in Sweetwater. It was the Depression then, and a lot of people were gettin' laid off and moving around, and you went wherever there was work. When I went out for the high school team, they automatically put me at tailback (quarterback) because that was where I played at Temple."

Although he twice led Sweetwater to the state playoffs, Baugh was considered a better baseball prospect (third base) coming out of high school. That's how he met Dutch Meyer, the man he would soon become

Slingin' Sammy Baugh led TCU to a national championship in 1935.

famous playing football for at TCU.

"Francis Schmidt was still the football coach, and Dutch was the baseball coach," Baugh recalled. "So Dutch recruited me for baseball with the idea that I could also play football.

"Uncle Billy Disch was also recruiting me for Texas, but it was a baseball only deal. I went down there and I was tempted. But then I sat down in the stadium and watched the football team working out, and I realized how much I still wanted to play.

"So I came to TCU, and when I was a sophomore, Dutch became the head coach."

At TCU, It Came to Pass

It was a fortuitous convergence.

Under Schmidt, the Frogs had had great teams but little national recognition. Meyer's teams, with their wide-open, pass-oriented offenses, gathered headlines as well as victories.

"Everything I learned about football, I learned from Dutch Meyer," Baugh said. "Back in those days, most teams — even in the pros — would only throw on third down, and then they always tried a deep pass.

"Dutch taught us a short passing game, and early on he told me, 'You can throw from your own 1-yard line, if you see an opening.' We were doing a lot of things nobody else had thought of."

In three seasons (1934-36), Baugh completed 270 passes for 3,384 yards and 39 touchdowns, leading TCU to an overall 29-7-2 record with victories in the Sugar and Cotton bowls. He was a two-time all-American.

In 1935, the Frogs finished 12-1 and — despite the loss to SMU, which later lost in the Rose Bowl — wound up the season ranked No.1 in the Williamson Rating Service after defeating LSU in the Sugar Bowl.

The next year, in the final two games of his career, Baugh directed victories against Santa Clara, the eventual Sugar Bowl champion, and Marquette, in the inaugural Cotton Bowl.

On to the NFL

During the summer after his graduation, Baugh played in the College All-Star Game and flirted with the idea of becoming a pro baseball player (he discussed it with Rogers Hornsby and Branch Rickey). He got a job with a lumber company and played for

Washington coach Ray Flaherty watches as Baugh signs a pro football contract to play for the Redskins.

a semi-pro team called the Pampa Roadrunners in a memorable game against a black barnstorming team that featured Josh Gibson, Satchel Paige and Cool Papa Bell.

He also received an offer from Redskins owner George Marshall, at which he was not immediately inclined to jump.

"I think he was offering something like $5,000 and it was worth considering," Baugh said, "but I already had a job — and jobs were very important at that time. I didn't know who the damn teams were 'cause I'd never paid any attention to the pros. I didn't care much about playing up there."

"I asked Dutch about it, and he said, 'Well, if they'll pay that, why not ask for $8,000?'

"So I did, and they accepted. To me, it looked like a million bucks."

In a way, it was.

"After I'd been on the team awhile, I discovered that we had three All-Pros making $2,700 a year each,"

Baugh makes his way through the Texas defense in TCU's 28-0 win over the Longhorns in 1935.

Baugh said. "And there were a lot of other guys making $150-$200 a game.

"It scared the livin' hell out of me, because I thought someone might find out how much I was making. It really gave me a strange feeling to know I was so overpaid when we had guys doing their job as well as I making less than $200 a game.

"We won the (NFL) championship that year, and Cliff Battles led the league in rushing. The next year, he asked for a $250 raise up to $3,000 a year, and Marshall wouldn't give it to him, so he quit," Baugh said.

"If I'd known what they were doing, I would have given him the $250 myself, because after that first year, I was making $12,000."

Not that there was any doubt about Baugh's worth to the team: In the title game the franchise won its first championship when the rookie quarterback threw for 354 yards and three touchdowns on any icy field to lead a 28-21 victory against the Chicago Bears.

He did it again five years later, throwing a TD pass and coming up with a crucial interception on defense to lead Washington past the Bears, 14-6.

During much of a then-record 16-year career (1937-52), Baugh was the league's leading passer, punter, or both — and one of the top defensive backs.

During his first nine seasons, he led the Redskins to five divisional titles and two NFL championships. In 1945, the last of those teams lost the title to the Cleveland Rams, 15-14, when Baugh, passing out of his end zone, hit the goal-post (then situated on the goal line). Under the rules of the day, it was a safety and provided the Rams with the winning points.

He also became involved, unfortunately, in the most hideous championship game in NFL history: the Bears' famous 73-0 massacre of the Redskins in 1940.

It was an event Baugh blames largely on Marshall, who ridiculed the Bears and called them "cry babies" after Washington had beaten them during the regular season.

"He just kept it up after that, making fun of them every chance he got," Baugh said. "It was ridiculous for anyone to say stuff like that about a team that was as powerful as they were back then.

"Every time he opened his mouth, they got madder and madder, and our morale got lower and lower. He basically destroyed his own team, but George was kind of like that. I never knew anyone who liked him much.

In 1969, Baugh was named to the All-Time all-America team during college football's centennial.

"Anyway, they started scoring early and never let up, and we couldn't do anything right," Baugh said. "When it got to be 28-0, I went over to our coach (Ray Flaherty) and told him we might as well go for broke, because we didn't have a chance anyway. So we started throwing on fourth-and-10 instead of punting, and things just got worse.

"I remember saying, 'Hell, we may get beat, 60-0, but we've got to try it.' Well, we sure didn't get beat, 60-0."

Early in the game, a Washington receiver dropped a sure touchdown pass in the end zone. Sensing a "momentum shift," reporters trooped into the locker room afterward to ask Baugh how he thought the game might have come out if the receiver had held onto the ball. Said Baugh, "73 to 6."

Settling in Rotan

After his retirement as a player, Baugh coached for 16 years, including stretches with Hardin-Simmons, Tulsa, Oklahoma State and the Detroit Lions, and a brief stint as head coach of the debt-plagued New York Titans, who subsequently became the Jets.

About 25 years ago, he finally settled in full time on the place at the foot of the Double Mountains. He has seldom left it since.

"I've never been back to Washington," he said. "They've been trying to get me to come up there so they can retire my jersey or something, but I don't think I'm going.

"I don't like flying and I don't like big cities. Never have.

"We started out to raise two boys and a girl ... but we had the four boys before the girl ever came along. Those two youngest boys, whenever I had trouble with them, I used to tell them, 'Just remember, you're lucky she (Frances) didn't come right after David, or you two wouldn't even be here.'

"Several years ago, we put the place and the cattle and everything in the kids' names, so I don't have to worry about much anymore. I don't have many hobbies. I've never shot a bird on this place," Baugh said.

"I roped all the time I was playing ball and kept it up for about 25 years, until I couldn't get on and off the horse anymore. Then I took up golf."

Every year on Labor Day, he plays in the Sam Baugh Classic in Rotan, where the main street is now named "Sam Baugh Avenue." He can handle all that pretty well, because no one asks him to make a speech and it doesn't interfere with his main rule:

"I don't like to be anywhere," he said, "that I can't get back from by sundown."

Reflecting for a moment upon life's enjoyments, his eye falls upon a rocking chair sitting in front of the television set.

"If I sit in that damned thing and don't do anything else for about a week or two," he said, "I get sick.

"Old people need something to do — a reason to get up every day. They need exercise, and that's why I play 18 holes whenever I can.

"So, I guess you could say I'm happy as I can be, right where I am, doing what I want to do."

Baugh completed 285 of 597 passes for 3,471 yards and 39 touchdowns in his career at TCU.

Baugh, right, starred in the movie serial "King of the Texas Rangers."

Hollywood a Baugh for Slingin' Sammy

BY ELSTON BROOKS
Fort Worth Star-Telegram

FT. WORTH, JUNE 9, 1974 — Everybody remembers Slingin' Sammy Baugh for his TCU all-America days and his later exploits in pro football, but leave it to Les Adams, the movie buff extraordinaire, to hunt up Sam and talk to him about his days as a movie star.

All right, so it was only one Saturday matinee serial called *King of the Texas Rangers*, but who besides Adams would remember even that?

"Sam Baugh isn't hard to find," Adams reports after riding the dusty highway trails of West Texas. "His name is right there on the mailbox. Finding the mailbox is the problem."

Adams found it in a 40-mile triangle bounded by the West Texas towns of Rotan, Clairemont and Aspermont, where Baugh has his spread in the shadows of the Double Mountains, rusting Clabber Girl Baking Powder signs, and fenced-in-three-grave cemeteries.

The Samuel Adrian Baugh who answered the door at his 8,000-acre ranch is little changed from the tall, lanky youngster from Sweetwater who led TCU to all those victories in the mid-1930's, Adams reports.

Writing in *Those Enduring Matinee Idols*, a magazine devoted to the old Saturday serials, Adams discovered that Baugh hadn't even been told the plot as he plodded his way through the 12 chapters of *King of the Texas Rangers* back in 1941. Adams refreshed his memory by bringing along some old scene stills of the serial. Their exchange went this way:

S.B.: You gotta remember, though, this was all over 30 years ago, and I was there only six weeks and I've been run over by a lot of Chicago Bears in between.

L.A.: Fair enough, Sam. But first one question that has little to do with the serial itself: What did Redskins owner George Preston Marshall think about his highly prized quarterback, probably representing 90 percent of the value of his franchise, going off to Hollywood and possibly breaking his neck doing a serial?

S.B.: Lord, he was tickled to death. It was good publicity for him, the Redskins and me. In those days, pro football did good to get the game scores in the papers and anything — short of going to jail — that got publicity pleased everybody.

L.A.: Okay. Sam, it's your ball. Run to daylight.

S.B.: Some guy from Republic called me here at the ranch shortly after the 1940 season and said they wanted to fly me out there and talk about making a movie. I went out to see them. Just me. No agent. No lawyer. We talked and they told me it wouldn't take over six weeks. Offered me $4,500. I signed the contract and came on back home to the ranch.

I have never been around a nicer bunch of people to work with than that whole crew at the studio — the actors, the directors, the crew, all of 'em.

L.A.: Who are the ones you remember the best?

S.B.: Monte Blue, because I knew him from movies I watched as a kid. And Pauline Moore, who was a very sweet person. I remember Kermit Maynard as a very friendly guy and guess I was impressed with him at first just because he was Ken Maynard's brother.

Duncan Renaldo I'll never forget. He helped me more than anybody. The first day at the studio the director handed me some paper and said it was my lines for the next day, and to study them that night. I did. And if they used those lines the next day someone else did them 'cause I never heard them. Then they gave me some more to learn that night that I haven't heard yet, either. The next day I told Duncan I had three days of lines memorized I still hadn't used.

He laughed and said, "Sam, you don't need to learn those lines at night. They'll tell you what to say."

I didn't waste any more nights studying those lines!

L.A.: Who impressed you the most?

S.B.: Tom Steele. I guess there wasn't anything he couldn't do ... or wouldn't. If the NFL would have let us use doubles, he's the one I would have picked.

Not having ever worked on a picture before, I can't really say whether or not I did more of my own stunts and things than they might have had somebody else doing. As far as I know I did all of my own riding but could be wrong because there were a lot of scenes filmed without me being around and Steele or somebody could have doubled for me without my knowing it.

For some reason they gave me a couple of horses to ride, but the one I remember the best was a big black with a blaze face. He was a fine animal but I would have hated to have to work cattle with him. He was trained for movies and I mean he was trained. I'd be on him going down a road behind the camera car and the minute somebody hollered "Action!" that old blaze was long gone — whether I was ready or not.

L.A.: Were you ever asked to make another serial?

S.B.: No, and if they had I don't know when in later years I would have ever had the time.

Looking back, though, I think I would have made an effort to find the time because I can truthfully say that I can recall no other six-week period in my life that I so thoroughly enjoyed as the time I spent on that picture. No way I can tell you just how great those people at Republic treated me, or just how great I thought they were.

After a long day of filming, Baugh teaches Republic Studio actress Judy Canova how to punt a football.

CHAPTER 13

FROGS TOPPLE MARQUETTE, 16-6

By Flem Hall
Fort Worth Star-Telegram

DALLAS, JAN. 1, 1937 — With a sling-bang attack that whipped over a field goal and two touchdowns in the first 25 minutes of play, and with a sturdy defense that piled up the Marquette Golden Avalanche, Texas Christian University captured a spectacular football game here this New Year's Day. The score in the Cotton Bowl classic was 16-6.

TCU	10	6	0	0	16
Marquette	6	0	0	0	6

So sudden, sharp and dazzling was the sweep of action, that 15,000 spectators, who braved threatening weather, forgot the gray gloom of the afternoon.

Led by Sammy Baugh, who outpassed and outplayed "Buzz" Buivid, the Texans uncorked a flamming offense that flared into long gains both on the ground and in the air.

Although it was Baugh who paced the attack and won the attention of the crowd, it was L.D. Meyer who did the real damage to the cause of the Golden Invaders from Milwaukee. He scored all of TCU's 16 points. He kicked a 33-yard field goal for the first three points in the opening minutes. Before the first quarter ended, he collaborated with Baugh on a 55-yard pass-and-run gain for the first Frog touchdown, and in the second quarter he took an 18-yard pass from Vic Montgomery for the second score. He even converted the extra point after the first touchdown. His second attempt was blocked.

All the Horned Frogs Contribute to Victory

A 60-yard punt return by Art Guepe in the first quarter accounted for all of Marquette's points.

The game was played under almost perfect football conditions and those timid souls who stayed away

L.D. Meyer scored all of TCU's points against Marquette.

for fear of getting wet, or being bored with a mud battle, will be eligible for a nice lifelong regret.

A drizzling rain that had fallen most of the day stopped 30 minutes before the 2 p.m. kickoff and when the field covering was removed the grassless turf was dry and firm except for small and widely separated spots.

Both surprised, the two great exponents of offensive football set out to celebrate by showing the folks something.

They did. Pulling the throttle wide open, they scored 16 points in the first 15 minutes. The premises were lathered with the old razz-mu-dazz in the most approved unorthodox fashion.

The party cooled down after TCU scored again in the second quarter, but there was no scoring at all in the second half. The ball, however, continued at all times to move up and down the field with rare speed and quick exchanges of possession.

Not only was Buivid overshadowed by Baugh for the day, but he was outsparkled by his teammate, Art Guepe. In addition to making the Marquette touchdown, the cocky little quarterback sparked the Gold's attack all afternoon.

Before the game was half over, Coach Dutch Meyer, feeling safe behind the 10-point lead, sent in most of his reserves. Every one of the 28 members of the squad (except Willie Walls, who was so ill he could not attend the game) took part in the engagement, and at no time after the first 25 minutes was the full first string TCU team on the field. Baugh was on the bench for nearly a quarter and was only reinserted in the closing minutes when the crowd howled to see him one last time.

From start to finish, the TCU line outcharged and outfought the smaller Marquette forwards. Cotton Harrison, Ki Aldrich, I.B. Hale, Forrest Kline, Solon Holt, Drew Ellis and Bull Rogers were most in evidence as Marquette plays were wrecked before they started, and as big holes opened up for Frog ball car-

TCU's starting backfield for the inaugural Cotton Bowl in 1937: (left to right) all-America quarterback Sam Baugh, halfback Harold McClure, halfback Scott McCall, and fullback Glen Roberts.

riers swinging around on reverses.

While the first string was on the field, TCU was in command of the game, but for a time in the third quarter, against the reserves, Marquette took the offensive. The Avalanche threatened twice, but each time the utility boys had the stuff to break up the drives and get the ball.

In the matter of passes completed, Marquette shaded TCU, 10-9, but the Frogs threw two for touchdowns, and gained more yards. Most of Buivid's were for short gains and not one of them did any real damage.

Unconscious Player Preserves TCU Victory

By Don L. Wulffsen

Amazing True Stories
Cobblehill Books, 1991

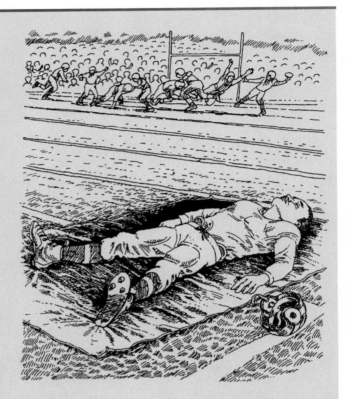

It was November 1923. The Texas Christian University freshman team was playing Terrel Prep. TCU beat Terrel by a score of 63-0. However, they would have lost if they had not had the help of an unconscious player.

TCU had only 20 players on its team. By the fourth quarter many of them had been injured. Finally, with only a couple of minutes left in the game, the coach looked around for a substitute. But there was no one left to send in!

TCU had only 10 men on the field, but the rules say there must be 11. The referees told the TCU coach that his team would forfeit the game unless they had the right number of players.

Just then, Ernest Lowry, who had been hurt on the opening kickoff, struggled up off a blanket and said "I'm all right, coach. I'll go in." But the effort to sit up was too much for the boy and he passed out.

Suddenly, the frantic coach had an idea. He placed Lowry's blanket on the field just inbounds, and the unconscious boy was laid on it. He was far away from any action, but he was a legal eleventh man.

"We were on defense," the coach explained, "so Lowry could be any place back of the line of scrimmage. And he lay there during the final plays of the game. He gave us our 11th man. It's the only time an unconscious player ever won a football game."

CHAPTER 14

Johnny Hall sweeps around left end against Carnegie Tech in the 1939 Sugar Bowl.

NO. 1 TCU TOPS CARNEGIE TECH

By Flem Hall
Fort Worth Star-Telegram

NEW ORLEANS, JAN. 2, 1939 — With a versatile attack, Texas Christian University defeated the game and gallant Tartans of Carnegie Tech Monday in the fifth edition of the Sugar Bowl, thus earning the No. 1 ranking of sports-writers around the country.

TCU	0	6	6	3	15
Carnegie Tech	0	7	0	0	7

It was with power, passes and kicking that the Christians made the two touchdowns and one field goal that enabled them to win, 15-7. Carnegie's most consistent method of attack was a bristling, quick-starting and hard-hitting attack, but it was with a brilliant 38-yard pass in the last seconds of the first half that the Tartans scored.

Trail at Halftime

To win this, the Frogs' second Sugar Bowl triumph, the great TCU team, which rolled undefeated and untied through a regular season schedule of 10 games, displayed the true championship quality — the one quality that was left open to questions until Monday. The Frogs got off the floor to win.

For the first time, they found themselves behind when Carnegie Tech scored and kicked the extra point.

The second half started with the Pittsburghers leading, 7-6. The first time they got possession of the hoghide, the Frogs could not be stopped. Moving with great strides they went 80 yards for a touchdown on five plays without losing possession.

Just to take all the pressure off, Davey O'Brien, who showed 'em by gum, again today, kicked a fourth-quar-

*Davey O'Brien had just one Christmas wish
for Santa Claus in 1938.*

ter field goal from the 9-yard line.

Frogs Punt But Once

They had to put the sideboards on this 50,000-seat gridiron palace to hold the crowd that turned out to see the fifth renewal of the classic, and not a spectator failed to develop an uncontrolled crop of goose pimples as the two brilliant rivals cut loose on one of the most glittering offensive games of the fall and winter.

TCU punted one time. That fact alone indicates accurately how fearfully effective the ground-gaining maneuvers of the big white-shirted representatives from Fort Worth were.

When they got the ball, the Frogs took it or threw it places.

The one punt was by the second string in the second quarter and it figured in making TCU's first touchdown. Jack Odle kicked the ball 40 yards out of

bounds in the coffin corner, just six yards from the goal line.

When Tech punted out, the TCU regulars took over and went 48 yards on 11 plays to take a 6-0 lead.

O'Brien had no excuses for failing to convert after the touchdowns. His placekicks were wide.

Weather Near Perfect

Monday was the first dry day in the history of this young but husky bowl game.

For four consecutive years, rain and mud prevailed. Monday it was different. It was warm and clear. A fog held the field until noon but it gave way to a golden hazy sunshine an hour before the kickoff at 1:15 p.m. and the conditions held until the final play — the one that saw Ward Wilkinson making 4 yards to retain possession of the ball for TCU.

In the middle of the field, the turf, still tinged with green, was just soft enough to suit the churning cleated feet of the embattled forces.

There wasn't a dull minute in the bristling play that cracked and exploded with dazzling brilliance and astounding force on every down.

Best Team Frogs Played

Because they kept the ball most of the time and were rarely stopped except deep in the enemy end of the field, the Christians built up a big advantage in all the statistics. TCU was in the driver's seat practically all afternoon, but Tech had a fine team and was very much in the ball game until O'Brien booted that field goal with seven minutes left to play.

The team that beat mighty Pittsburgh, 20-10, and which bowed only to Notre Dame, 7-0, was the best team the Frogs had played, and the eight-point margin of victory was completely satisfactory to the Frogs and their supporters.

TCU turned on the heat at the very outset.

In the first quarter the Frogs made marches of 43 and 32 yards, only to be stopped on the Carnegie 12- and 24-yard lines.

At the start of the second quarter both coaches sent complete new teams on the field. TCU's seconds pushed the Carnegie reserves back across the middle of the field and Coach Bill Kern got his regulars into

Davey O'Brien adds a fourth-quarter field goal to boost TCU's lead to 15-7.

action. Odle kicked them to their own six and Coach Dutch Meyer turned the situation back to the "A" squad.

Hall Stars on Drive

The Carnegie punt out was to the Tech 48. O'Brien passed to Johnny Hall for 13 yards. Hall raced for nine yards. Those two plays made a first down on the 24. Three smashes shoved inside the 20. On fourth down, O'Brien passed to Hall for 16 yards. From there, on three plays the Christians scored, Sparks making the last yard.

Carnegie took the next kickoff and went to town with big, fast and tough George Muha doing most of the dirty work.

Merlin Condit started the 64-yard advance by throwing a 21-yard pass to Ted Fisher. The next two plays gained only three yards and on third down Earl Clark intercepted a pass and ran 25 yards to the Carnegie 35-yard line, but Durwood Horner, the TCU end, had been offside so the play was called back

and the Frogs were penalized 5 yards.

Moroz Connects

It was on fourth down of this series that Petey Moroz cut loose with a long pass to Muha for the Carnegie touchdown.

The play originated on the 37-yard line. Moroz dropped back to the 50 to throw and Muha made a fine running catch as he was racing across the goal line. It was a perfectly timed heave that neither Hall nor O'Brien, both of whom were right with Muha, had a chance to break up without fouling the receiver.

Muha converted with a placekick.

Only seconds remained in the half and it was just as well for TCU as O'Brien fumbled the kickoff and Carnegie recovered on the TCU 19. Two plays later the half ended with the Tartans shoved back to the 34-yard marker.

Long Passes Bring Score

That third-quarter drive of the Christians to get

Davey O'Brien attracts a crowd of Carnegie Tech tacklers as he dives for extra yardage.

back in front was probably the most pleasing thing about the whole game to the thousands of Texans in the crowd. The Frogs had to start from their own 20. O'Brien passed to Clark for 35 yards, and a play or two later from the 44, O'Brien pegged a pass to Horner down the middle. The big end caught the ball almost between two Tech players but evaded both of them and ran 24 yards across the goal line.

That was really the ball game but no one was sure of it until many minutes later.

In this same period, Carnegie staged its most inspiring parade of power. For 48 yards, the Tartans ripped and roared and bumped their way through the stalwart TCU defense. The drive carried to the Frog 28. Then the quarterback switched to passing. Two shots missed and Ki Aldrich intercepted the third one.

Frogs Wrap Up Win

That was all for Carnegie. The Tartans were through.

The Frogs whirled down the field 70 yards only to be stopped inside the 10.

In the first part of the fourth quarter they marched 49 yards to the Tech 1, and kicked the clinching field goal on fourth down.

TCU and her stars, individually, disappointed no one here.

Aldrich and O'Brien were all-American in every way, and as a team the Christians did all that anyone could have asked of, even the team that has been called the finest in Southwest annals.

The prestige of the passing game and the Southwest was upheld.

CHAPTER 15

Frogs of '38 Were a Group to Respect

BY WHIT CANNING
Fort Worth Star-Telegram

As the TCU Horned Frogs rolled through the 1935 season, the impression grew that they could probably whip just about any team in the country.

Except one.

"Every week, we'd scrimmage against the freshmen," recalls Sammy Baugh, the team's legendary tailback. "And we couldn't handle them.

"We used to sit around and talk about it, and we figured that by the time they were seniors, they'd have a good chance to win it all."

Baugh and his varsity teammates were a pretty salty crowd themselves — finishing 12-1 after a narrow loss to SMU (which went to the Rose Bowl) and a Sugar Bowl victory against Louisiana State.

They were also skilled prophets: When those freshmen were seniors in 1938, they won a national championship, and their leader — tailback Davey O'Brien — won the Heisman Trophy.

As a senior in 1936, the 6-foot-2 Baugh helped coach his 5-7 sophomore understudy, in keeping with Coach Dutch Meyer's system of enlisting seniors to serve as part-time assistants.

"Davey was always real smart, and he picked things up quickly — in the classroom or on the field," Baugh says. "As for his size, I never thought of Davey as small, because he was big-boned and stocky. He was just kind of short."

But the most awesome player in the bunch, Baugh says, was the team's other 1938 consensus all-American, Ki Aldrich. A two-way terror (center, linebacker), Aldrich was described by many opponents in that era as the best player they had ever faced. Aldrich, who

*Don Looney, an All-SWC end
in 1938 and 1939.*

The Horned Frogs in 1938 posted an 11-0 record and were voted national champions in all polls following the season.

is deceased, was recently inducted into the Southwest Conference Hall of Honor.

"I never saw anybody else like Ki Aldrich," Baugh says.

"When we went out to the West Coast and beat Santa Clara in 1936, he was just a sophomore. But he was all pumped up, and he was out there yellin' at people to do this or watch that and just jabberin' away."

"Finally, one of the seniors turned to me and said, 'Who is that guy?'

"I had to laugh, because I had known Ki since we were kids growing up in Temple, before my family moved to Sweetwater. We just lived a couple of doors away from each other," Baugh says.

"Every day after football practice, Ki would take his shoulder pads home with him. They had this old tin garage then, and he would go out there and get into one corner and just start banging into the wall.

"Pretty soon, everything in that garage was loose — things that had been hanging up on nails had fallen down onto the ground."

Ki Aldrich anchored the great TCU lines in 1936-1938.

CHAPTER 16

Davey O'Brien:
All He Did Was Win

BY WHIT CANNING
Fort Worth Star-Telegram

It was halftime at the Sugar Bowl — Jan. 2, 1939 — and TCU coach Dutch Meyer was fuming.

"We were playing Carnegie Tech," recalls Allie White, one of the Frog tackles that day, "and they had scored right before the half to go ahead of us. Dutch was fit to be tied.

"Just before they scored, we had an interception nullified by a penalty, and Dutch was demanding to know which one of us jumped offside.

"So I told him it was me. Actually, it was (end) Durwood Horner, who played next to me, but the official called it on me. And Dutch says, 'Well, congratulations — you just got us behind for the first time all year!' He was really upset."

Fortunately, a handy savior was present.

"Starting out in the second half," White says, "Davey just opened up the passing game and we went 80 yards in about five plays and scored — and went on to win the game. And that took care of that."

It was also the recurring theme of the magical autumn of 1938 — when for the first time in history, a team from the Southwest Conference won the national championship.

It was a team of notable and diverse talent; but its rise to perfection came clearly through the exploits of its remarkable leader — a gritty giant-killer aptly named Davey O'Brien.

He stood 5-foot-7 and weighed 150 pounds — and when he drew back his slingshot, it fired flying footballs in a manner that astonished foes and witnesses alike.

"We were a good team," White says. "And some of us, I felt, realized how lucky we were to be playing together at TCU at that time. And we had a lot of heart.

"But the thing that made us great was Davey's passing, and his leadership. That gave us an edge over everyone we played. The thing that really stands out about him is . . . determination.

"I felt he could have been a great guard, if that's what he had wanted to be. He was just so determined to succeed at whatever he tried to do."

O'Brien arrived at TCU in 1935 after an outstanding high school career at Woodrow Wilson in Dallas, which is where he was when White first saw him.

"We played 'em when I was at Masonic Home, and he was zig-zagging around the field," White says. "Someone said he was going to TCU, and I said, 'So what?'

"I wasn't much impressed until I tried to tackle him. He ran right underneath my arm and just kept going."

After understudying Sam Baugh as a sophomore in 1936, O'Brien ranked second nationally in total offense (1,411 yards) in '37 and led the nation in punt returns and passing — but the Frogs finished 4-4-2, and Meyer commented at one point that their weakness was an inability to throw the long ball.

"So, during the off-season, Davey worked on that real hard," White says. "I guess he threw every day. And he came up with something that solved the problem.

"He had thrown the javelin in high school, and he

Davey O'Brien looks for an opening in the Rice defensive line in 1938.

Known for his giant-killing performances, O'Brien poses for a gridiron version of "David and Goliath."

developed this little crow-hop when he wanted something extra on the ball. It added about 20 yards to the ball, and it made a big difference."

In 1938, O'Brien completed 94 of 167 passes for 1,457 yards and 19 touchdowns. He led the nation in passing and total offense (1,847 yards) and directed 10 consecutive regular-season victories in which only one game was as close as seven points.

Nationally, the Frogs ranked first in passing and second in total offense and were invited to the Sugar Bowl to face Carnegie Tech — conqueror of Notre Dame and defending national champ Pittsburgh, and the cream of the East.

O'Brien put on a stunning show in New Orleans — completing 17 of 27 passes for 224 yards and directing a 15-7 triumph that was far more lopsided than the score: TCU finished with a 365-168 edge in total yards.

When undefeated (and unscored-on) Duke fell in the Rose Bowl, the Frogs rose to the nation's highest rank.

By that time, O'Brien had become far more than just another spangled quarterback commanding an invincible legion: an entire nation had become enthralled with "Little Davey" and his pass-happy teammates.

It began early in the year when the Frogs travelled to Philadelphia and demolished a Temple team coached by Pop Warner, and continued through the Sugar Bowl victory — by which time fabled New York sportswriter Grantland Rice had declared, "That boy must be stuffed with scrap iron."

O'Brien became the first player in SWC history to win the Heisman Trophy, and the only SWC player to win the Heisman, Maxwell Trophy and Walter Camp Award in the same year.

In an era when most teams threw only under the threat of utter oblivion, Meyer's TCU teams were almost unique in their reliance on the pass as the primary weapon — and his first two tailbacks (quarterbacks) became football legends.

A towering, 6-foot-2 star with a rifle arm, Baugh was the physical opposite of O'Brien, but in terms of results, they were nearly identical.

"Well, I never really thought of Davey as being small," Baugh says. "He was short, yeah — but he had wide shoulders and a lot of muscle packed into that body. And he was tough as a boot.

"He was also well-suited for that short passing game

O'Brien rushed for 109 yards and hurled 3 TD passes against Rice in 1938.

that Dutch taught us. He let us throw the ball from anywhere on the field, and that was perfect for Davey.

"We had a lot of success with it when I was there, but when I left I could tell that that bunch Davey came in with was going to be even better than we were. One of 'em was Ki Aldrich, who I had grown up with in Temple before we moved to West Texas.

"I remember in high school, Ki would go home after practice and spend about an hour banging into the side of the garage, toughening himself up. They had some tin hanging up in the garage there, and every afternoon you could hear that tin rattling for miles around.

"We scrimmaged those guys every week when they were freshmen — and they were the toughest team we played all year."

In this atmosphere, says Mason Mayne, who played with both quarterbacks at TCU from 1935-37, O'Brien quickly emerged as the team leader.

"He was really a great athlete," says Mayne, who was TCU's Most Valuable Player in '37, when O'Brien averaged 30 yards on eight kickoff returns, ran back 58 punts, and directed three closing victories to launch what would become a 14-game winning streak. "He seemed to have an ability — or determination — to make himself excel at anything he really wanted to.

"He was an outstanding baseball player, and I think

O'Brien arrives by stagecoach at City Hall in New York City after a parade down Broadway.

he could have had a successful career as a professional golfer, if that's what he had wanted to do.

"He wasn't the punter Sam was — but like Sam, he was a great defensive player (O'Brien still ranks second in TCU annals with 16 career interceptions). He couldn't stand to watch a punt roll — he'd pick it up and run with it, and he gained a lot of yardage that way.

"He was a quiet, reserved type of person, but everyone respected and admired him. He had a command about him in the huddle — and he became a natural leader.

Although O'Brien was also a good runner, he possessed another talent that became extremely useful.

"He was one of the first players I ever saw who had that knack for being able to stay in the pocket and concentrate on throwing the ball despite the rush," Mayne says. "He used to say he didn't want to get away from his friends.

"The type of game we played then, we would throw from inside our own 10-yard line to get out of trouble. Dutch reasoned that we were safer throwing the short pass than trying to run and maybe fumbling the ball.

"So Davey threw whenever he felt like it. He had confidence in us, and we had confidence in him."

Nevertheless, White believes that Meyer may have originally had misgivings about O'Brien's size.

"Davey grew up in a foster home in Dallas," White recalls, "and I think someone in that family was connected with a TCU trustee — and that's how he got into school. He had been a big star in high school, but I'm still not sure Dutch would have taken him if it hadn't been for that connection."

But Don Looney, a favorite O'Brien receiver both at TCU and later with the Philadelphia Eagles, disagrees.

"I really think there was an affinity between Dutch and Davey," he says, smiling, "because they were both

Davey O'Brien was college football's most honored player in the 1930's.
(Top left) O'Brien enjoys his stagecoach ride down Broadway with Amon Carter.
(Top right) O'Brien receives the Heisman Trophy,
(bottom right) the Maxwell Trophy,
(bottom left) and the Walter Camp Trophy.

such short little guys.

"I know that there were a lot of times that I would go out for a pass and look back for Davey — and I couldn't see him. Then all of a sudden the ball would come flying out of nowhere — right into my arms.

"But he was also built like a weightlifter, and by 1938 he could put a lot of distance on it.

"I remember one game where I went out on a deep route — and I ran past this defensive back, who looked at me kinda bored, like he thought I was crazy. A few yards downfield I looked up, and here it came — spiraling right down on top of me.

"And all of a sudden that defensive back yelled, 'Sonofabitch!' and started chasing me — but it was too late. I was behind him for a touchdown."

A not uncommon occurrence, White recalls.

"We ran everything you could think of back then — single wing, double wing, box, spread," he says, "and a lot of teams had problems defensing us.

"When we went up there and played Temple, they were finally reduced to just trying to grab our receivers and hold 'em, 'cause they couldn't cover 'em. And Davey was just sitting back there calm as could be, pickin' 'em to pieces."

When O'Brien graduated, the Eagles were standing by with a contract and a $12,000 bonus, so he played two years in the NFL before quitting to join the FBI along with former teammate I.B. Hale.

On the final day of the 1940 season, Baugh and O'Brien met on the field for the final time, as the Redskins faced the Eagles.

"We were standing on the field talking before the game," Baugh says, "and Davey told me it was going to be his last game. He wasn't getting much protection, and he was getting banged up pretty good and he was ready to get out.

"Sure went out in style, though."

In the last game he ever played, O'Brien threw 60 passes and completed 33 of them — 14 to Looney, who says, "It's a game I'll always remember."

As for the memories of those who knew O'Brien best, images of the man supercede those of the foot-

O'Brien stands brave in the pocket against an onrushing Arkansas defense.

O'Brien (center) is joined (at left) by teammates I.B. Hale and Ki Aldrich and (at right) Boyd Keith and TCU President Dr. Edward Waits during a postseason trip to New York in 1938.

ball player.

"He was an excellent student," Mayne says, "and always well-liked and respected by everyone he met. But it was really uncanny the way that, anything he concentrated on, he seemed to excel at.

"After they joined the FBI, he and Hale both became superb marksmen, but some of the stuff Davey used to do really amazed me.

"We used to do the thing where you'd throw a rock in the air for someone to shoot at, and after awhile I was throwing small pebbles in the air — and he was shooting them.

"And he used to have this routine where he'd look into a mirror and shoot back over his shoulder at a piece of metal — and he had a couple of cow patties set up back there and the bullet would split and hit both patties. It was amazing."

"Davey was a smart person," Looney says. "I remember he studied geology, and I always felt he would have been successful in the oil business if he'd wanted to do that.

"He was such an honest person — and anytime you needed him, he was there."

"If everyone had Davey's character," Mayne says, "you wouldn't need laws or policemen."

After 10 years with the FBI, O'Brien returned to Fort Worth to go into private business. As the years passed, awards continued to pile up — induction into the National Football Foundation and Hall of Fame, induction into the Texas Sports Hall of Fame, and others.

In 1960, he was one of 25 players named to receive Sports Illustrated's Silver Anniversary All-American Award, based on lifetime achievement in addition to athletic exploits.

He died on Nov. 18, 1977, after a long battle with cancer. Even at the end, the indomitable spirit survived — along with a disarming sense of humor.

"He used to tell me, 'I'm going to beat this thing,' and he really fought it hard," Mayne says. "The only thing he complained about was the chemotherapy making his hair fall out. He had a thick head of hair and he was proud of it, and he used to kid me because I'd lost most of mine.

"I went up to see him in the hospital one day, and all his hair was gone, and he had saved it and put it in a box. And he handed it to me and said, 'Here, get yourself a toupee made.'"

In the years since O'Brien's death, his teammates have often spoken eloquently of his memory. But the feeling was probably best summed up recently by Allie White:

"I loved Davey."

CHAPTER 17

With an escort of blockers, TCU's Dean Bagley sprints for a 55-yard touchdown against Texas in 1941.

FROGS RIP TEXAS, 14-7

By Flem Hall
Fort Worth Star-Telegram

AUSTIN, NOV. 15, 1941 — It took the Christians to catch up with the Bible plan. They did it here this sunny Saturday afternoon. Incredible as it sounds, Texas Christian University's football team earned a 14-7 victory over the University of Texas Longhorns on the hallowed sod of Memorial Stadium.

TCU	0	7	0	7	14
Texas	7	0	0	0	7

The Christians did it in plain sight of at least 25,000 people, so there can be no mistake about it. The report of the score is correct.

What happened?

Well, broadly speaking, spirit matched spirit and a fierce, relentless line beat down speed.

Narrowing it down some, the truth is that smart defense caught up with the magnificent team that was No. 1 two weeks ago and the front-page subject of a national magazine this week.

Then, coming right down to cases, it was a dazzling 55-yard run by Dean Bagley and a Emery Nix to Van Hall 19-yard pass that did it. Those were the two plays that scored touchdowns. Phil Roach converted after each score, the last of which came at the end of a 72-yard march that was climaxed just eight seconds before the game-ending gun.

Texas had no excuse Saturday. Coach Dana X. Bible had every one of his stars ready physically. It was agreed that the great team was mentally tuned. The Orange was bouncing off a 7-7 tie at Baylor last week. The game was played here on the Longhorns' own pas-

One of the heroes of the 1941 Texas game, Emery Nix threw the winning pass to Van Hall.

Derrell Palmer, an all-America tackle in 1942.

Saturday. Rather it appeared that TCU, for the day at least was a throwback to those great Purple teams of '29, '32, '35, and '38 — years when they were the terror of opponents.

Every one of the two dozen boys whom Coaches Dutch Meyer and Mike Brumbelow craftily used in the game to overcome the greater Texas manpower was a hero, but the outstanding ones were Derrell Palmer, Bagley, Nix, Hall, Roach, Bruce Alford, Woody Adams, Bill Crawford, Mike Harter and Leonard Pugh.

It was Palmer, the 220-pound junior left tackle who led the line in its furious, never-ending effort to smash down the lancing of Pete Layden, the sweeps of Jack Crain and the power of Spec Sanders.

The 18-year old giant played the kind of football Saturday that his coaches have been saying will some day make him all-American. He literally picked up Texas forwards and tossed them back among the ball carriers.

TCU won the game in the statistics as well as on the scoreboard. The Frogs out first-downed Texas, and gained more yards both running and passing.

As in the Baylor game last week, the Texas first team ran out of gas, faltered and collapsed in the stretch drive of the fourth quarter. While it was Bagley's beautiful run, Nix's pass and Hall's catch that scored the points, it was the defensive play of the Frogs that really carried the day. Texas, the unstoppable Longhorns, were knocked out of the air and all but stalled on the ground.

Scout dope and smart coaching did as much to foil the Texas attack as the bristling play of the Frogs. It was figured out in advance exactly what had to be done to hold down Texas scoring: Layden had to be stopped on his famed thrusts through the middle of the line and the passing game had to be rushed and covered.

Coach Meyer cooked up an unorthodox line setup and a series of varied maneuvers that baffled the Texas blockers and rendered the running game less effec-

ture. The score was tied at the half and Texas had all the time any team needs to win, if it can. The game was truly played under ideal field and weather conditions.

Outstanding TCU Game Plan

Texas simply couldn't cut it.

Have the Longhorns lost some of the something that made them sensationally successful in the first six games of this season?

That was not the impression observers got here

tive than it has been since Layden, Crain and Company commenced to make life miserable for Longhorn rivals.

Texas wasn't unlucky Saturday. The Longhorns had every opportunity to score time after time. Once they were handed the ball through a fluke on the TCU nine-yard line. They ended up trying a field goal from the 9-yard line. Again they made a first down on the 8-yard line. That threat fell dead when Bagley (who was a ball of fire all afternoon) intercepted a pass.

For most of two quarters Texas, thanks to the great punting of Layden, kept TCU in the hole and had dozens of opportunities to strike with their long gainers that killed SMU, Rice, Oklahoma, LSU, Arkansas and Colorado.

TCU had few chances to score, but the Frogs never missed a trick.

Texas scored first, in the final minute of the opening quarter, when Layden (who played up to his all-American rating through the afternoon) took a lateral from Crain and dashed 36 yards down the sideline.

Bagley Makes Greatest Run of Southwest Season

TCU tied the score late in the second quarter when Bagley, subbing for Nix, struck like a bolt from the blue. TCU was back on its own 45. The 150-pound tailback took the snap, backed up as if to pass, scattered the rushers, broke into a run, stopped, reversed his field, got a great starting block from Bill Crawford and was on his way, swaying and weaving.

He side-stepped and side-

Van Hall caught the game-winning pass between two Texas defenders.

slipped a half dozen Longhorns who had good shots at him. He never went to the sideline. He ran almost down the middle of the greensward, northward. Finally, he came face-to-face with Crain on the 20-yard line. Then and there Bagley gave Crain some of his own medicine; a stop, a jiggle, a sidestep and a stiff arm. Crain grabbed an armful of air and the San Saba kid went on to finish the greatest broken field run of the Southwest season.

The final TCU drive to victory went this way: It started from the Purple 27 when Texas failed on fourth down to make first down. In 150 seconds it moved 72 yards on seven plays.

Nix faked a pass and broke through over the middle. He was finally nabbed after a 35-yard jaunt. That made it first down on the Texas 33. There was less than two minutes left to play.

Frank Medanich galloped 5 yards off tackle. Two more plays added 4. With fourth down and a yard needed for a first, Nix swept his right end for six and a first on the Texas 24.

Texas took too much time out and was penalized 5 yards to the 19.

With eight seconds left, Nix dropped back, took dead aim and fired down the slot to Hall, who made the catch between two Longhorns on the goal line. He tore over for the touchdown. Roach converted.

TCU kicked off short but time ran out while the Longhorns were scrambling frantically to lateral pass their way up the field. The return died 60 yards from the goal.

CHAPTER 18

GEORGIA OUTLASTS FROGS' COMEBACK, 40-26

BY AMOS MELTON
Fort Worth Star-Telegram

MIAMI, JAN. 1, 1942 — In the wildest, weirdest football battle ever waged in this corner of the country, the Georgia Bulldogs outscored the courageous TCU Horned Frogs here Thursday afternoon, 40-26.

TCU	7	0	7	12	26
Georgia	19	14	7	0	40

It was an Orange Bowl battle that will be long remembered. Some 35,500 gaily-clad fans turned out expecting a few well-spaced thrills. What they saw left them almost too excited to find their way to the exits. In fact, hundreds of them just sat still for 10 minutes when the hairy-chested affair finally concluded.

Georgia, with a fine team and certainly the best back of the 1941 season, richly deserved its victory. Coach Wally Butts' fast team, well equipped on the ground and in the air, almost chased the Frogs off the field for 35 minutes.

They had the Texans completely bewildered. Never has the Frog pass defense leaked so badly. Never did the Christians make such futile efforts at tackling and blocking. The score mounted to 40-7 with only a few minutes played in the second half and the crowd began to fear that it would be a slaughter.

But the Frogs are not quitters. They didn't quit once during the regular season and they didn't here. Everything was against them. They couldn't hold the enemy, they couldn't move themselves and they were battered and weary from their empty-handed efforts.

But there was too much tradition

Kyle Gillespie passed and ran for 128 yards against Georgia in the Orange Bowl.

behind those purple shirts. Suddenly, almost as if a fresh wind had blown into the stadium, the tide turned. Things began to happen. Battling as few Frog teams have under such circumstances, the boys came storming back. They knocked over three touchdowns in rapid order. They turned back every Georgia thrust. And at the end, they were only 5 yards from another score after little Beecher Montgomery had returned a punt 50 yards.

At the end, it was the Purple team for which the gathering stood and cheered. That great comeback in the last 25 minutes saved the Frogs, the Southwest and Coach Dutch Meyer from humiliation.

It was the first defeat suffered by a Meyer-coached team in a bowl game.

Frankie Sinkwich was the boy who sank the Frogs. A slim-looking boy in his big chin guard, Sinkwich didn't look impressive during the pre-game warm-up. But once the battle was joined, it was Sinkwich against the Frogs and the Christians came out second best.

The boy drives with unbelievable power. He made the Frogs look mighty bad at tackling. But he's just that good. And when he wasn't running, he was riddling the Purple pass defense with everything he threw. The Frogs just couldn't savvy the stuff and their secondary had the worst day in many years.

Along at the end, the Texans beat Sinkwich into submission. They cracked him with vicious tackles in the last quarter until he was forced to retire. But the damage was already done. It was then that the Frogs took command of the game, but too many points had already poured across the goal line.

Bruce Alford was the Frog star. The Waco boy, stout-hearted as a lion, fought to the last ditch. He blocked a punt, he made two great catches for touchdowns. He threw the most vicious tackles on the field. Ronnie Brumbaugh, Dean Bagley, Kyle Gillespie and Charley Conway all did well. But Alford was the leader.

Bruce Alford was voted the Most Valuable Player in the 1942 Orange Bowl.

Kyle Gillespie (40) looks for an opening in the Georgia defense near the goal line.

Scoring Starts Early

The Frog defense was inadequate from the start. For some time, they were unable to stop any drive Georgia started and the Bulldogs ran up the amazing total of 478 yards from scrimmage. The Frogs got only 202, which is about the true picture of the game. The ease with which Georgia scored at times was numbing. The Christians simply weren't there when Sinkwich took off on a run or flipped his famous jumping pass to a teammate who was wide open.

At times, the Frogs were entirely demoralized.

The scoring started almost before anybody was settled. The first time they got the leather, the Bulldogs went 64 yards in seven plays. The payoff was a pass from Sinkwich to Lamar Davis against the sideline. It carried to the Frog 10. From there, Sinkwich simply shot over the guards for 7 yards and big Kenneth Keuper made it from there.

TCU got a lucky break when Darrell Palmer recovered a fumble on the Bulldog 22. Three plays later, Gillespie hit through tackle with great force and drove 5 yards into the end zone. Frank Medanich kicked the extra point and TCU led, 7-6. But from there to the half, Georgia struck with a fury and efficiency rarely seen by veteran scribes. They scored quite easily as the Christians fell entirely to pieces.

Sinkwich Pass Scores

The next score resulted from a 67-yard drive that took only three plays. The payoff was another Sinkwich pass that came down in the arms of Melvin Conger. Gillespie stumbled over Medanich on the play and Conger completed the 62-yard jaunt all alone. Again the point-after kick was missed and it was 12-7.

The next thrust carried 60 yards and needed only one play. From his 40, Sinkwich passed to blocking back Cliff Kimsey, who wasn't touched as again the Frog secondary just seemed to disappear. This extra-point attempt was good and it was 19-7 after about 13 minutes of wild football.

As the second quarter opened, the Bulldogs went 37 yards, needing seven plays again. Sinkwich made an outstanding play for the score. It was a pass from the Frog 15. Rushed fast and apparently swarmed under by Purple shirts, Sinkwich reached up and threw a bullet pass. Keuper caught it on the Frog 5 and wasn't touched. That made it 26-7 as Leo Costa, the kicking artist who tried all extra-point kicks, made good.

By this stage, the Frogs appeared almost helpless. Replacements kept coming in but nothing seemed to halt the devastating Bulldog attack. The Purple tried to bring its passing game into play but it boomeranged. Clyde Erhardt, a fine center, intercepted a Gillespie toss to set up another Bulldog score. He got it on the Frog 23.

From there, only one play was needed as Jim Todd, Sinkwich's sub, passed to Davis on the 10. He simply stepped by Kring and went over. Costa made it 33-7 and so it remained to the half.

TCU's Rally

After halftime, Texas supporters half hoped for a rally. But Georgia stepped out and banged 80 yards for still another touchdown that promised to make it a rout. Again it was Sinkwich. Several times the Frogs seemed to hold for downs but each time Sinkwich just tore loose for enough to make a first. Finally, from the Frog 43, he dropped back to pass. A big hole appeared over the TCU middle and he put the ball under his arm and ran. Once by the line of scrimmage he cut out sharply toward the sideline, caught the Frog half-back coming in and went by him like a bullet. There wasn't anybody close when he crossed the goal line. Costa's kick made it 40-7.

Even a good Texan would have been excused for giving up at this stage. But the fans could hardly believe what happened. Groggy, beat up and badly outclassed if a team ever was, the Frogs suddenly took hold of themselves. From that moment to the final gun it was the Bulldogs who held on and the Frogs who ripped.

The first Purple thrust went 50 yards. Bill Ramsey was a big power, passing to Alford for a first on the Bulldog 31. Emery Nix then took over. First he ran for 6 yards, then passed to Fred Taylor for 20. Then he threw long into the end zone. Two Bulldog backs hit the ball and batted it into the air. The alert Alford grabbed it for a score. Roach added the extra point.

As the third quarter drew to a close, the Frogs went for another score. This drive was for 66 yards after Davis fumbled on a kickoff and Nix recovered. A Kring to Gillespie pass went to the 34. Conway and Bierman drove for a first on the 21. On the second play of the fourth quarter, Gillespie lofted a pass into the end zone and Alford took it behind two defenders for the score. Roach missed and it was 40-20 as the fans grew more and more excited.

To halt the rally, Sinkwich came back in for Georgia and led a drive that went to the Frog 7. But little Dean Bagley broke it up by intercepting a pass on the

The workhorse of the Georgia offense, Frank Sinkwich (wearing a plastic face mask) dives for extra yards.

goal line. On the impulse of that, the Frogs went 79 yards to score again.

The payoff play was a pass into the left flat, Gillespie to Kring. Kring, almost worn out from the bitter afternoon, took off at a half run. He got some explosive blocking downfield, finally broke into the clear about the Bulldog 20 and kept going. He was so worn he could hardly take the last step. The play carried 52 yards. Again Roach missed the extra-point kick and it was 40-26.

But the Frogs were still driving. One march went to the Georgia 36 where an intercepted pass killed it. And just before the end, Montgomery took a punt and raced through all but the last defender for 50 yards to the 10. He drove to the 5 as the game ended. Georgia was putting up feeble resistance at the end but the Frogs were also jaded. It was that kind of a game.

CHAPTER 19

Oklahoma A&M's powerful offense kept the TCU defense on the field most of the afternoon.

COWBOYS STUN FROGS, 34-0

BY FLEM HALL
Fort Worth Star-Telegram

DALLAS, JAN. 1, 1945 — With speed, spirit, and spiraling passes, the Cowboys of Oklahoma A&M completely outclassed the TCU Horned Frogs in the ninth annual Cotton Bowl New Year's afternoon to win, 34-0.

Okla. A&M	14	0	7	13	34
TCU	0	0	0	0	0

A crowd of 37,500, which paid more than $100,000 for the privilege, watched brilliant Bob Fenimore prove his all-America ability at the expense of the hapless Purple.

Except for the second quarter, when they staved off repeated threats, the Frogs were never able to cope with the double-pronged attack the Aggies launched behind a line that never failed to charge fast and fiercely.

The hard-driving Cowboys scored two touchdowns in the first quarter, one in the third and two in the fourth. All of the scores were earned. The first touchdown, scored in the fifth minute, climaxed a 58-yard

Norman Cox an All-SWC fullback in 1944.

Dutch (middle) visits with all-America tackle Clyde Flowers (left) and Zeke Chronister.

drive. The second whirled 61 yards, the third 62 yards, the fourth 40 yards and the fifth 66 yards.

More A&M Standouts

Fenimore wasn't the whole show. Backs Jim Spavital and Cecil Hankins starred on offense, and left tackle Ralph Foster led the defensive attack.

The kicking of Mack Creager converted after each of the touchdowns except the last one.

After the score reached 21-0, Coach Jim Lookabaugh of the Aggies threw in his second, third and fourth teams. They were not nearly as lethal as the starters but the undermanned and weary Frogs were not able to resist the fresh eagerness of the reserves and they scored both of the fourth-quarter touchdowns.

TCU was never able to throw so much as a genuine scoring threat. The Frogs moved on the ground several times when in their own territory, but after crossing the 50-yard line, they were always thwarted by the bulling tactics of the burly Aggie line, and the perfect work of the secondary in covering pass receivers.

Only once did the Frogs get inside the A&M 35-yard line and that was on an interception.

Frogs Are No Match

Clyde Flowers of TCU played his usual sturdy game, but only Jim Cooper, the center, could match his effort and the two of them were no match for the coordinated work of the visitors from Stillwater. Bob Ruff was the only TCU back able to gain yards with any consistency, although Jesse Mason did some good work for a short time. Marcell Smalley, a substitute tackle, was the third best TCU lineman on the field.

Evidently razor sharp for their first bowl game, the Aggies came out in a turf-tearing mood. Spavital took the kickoff and blasted his way to his 41. In just eight plays and in spite of a penalty that cost them 35 yards, the Black and Gold Missouri Valley champions were in the end zone. Fenimore flared forth in dazzling variety on that first march that was

The 1944 Horned Frogs won the Southwest Conference and finished 7-3-1.

typical of most of the other parades destined to flow.

With twinkle-toed swiftness, the tall kid moved toward a flank, waved a hip and cut back with smooth deceptive power which either fooled tacklers or bowled them over.

Fenimore Gains

Hankins, almost as fast and a deadly-accurate pass catcher, fitted hand in glove with Fenimore, while the slashing driving Spavital supplied the power.

Fenimore made 5 yards and then passed for a first down on the TCU 38. Spavital hit the middle for 5. Hankins added 2. Spavital made it first down on the 26. Fenimore feinted a pass and raced to the 7, but A&M was guilty of holding and was set back to the 43-yard line. That was no hill for the Cow-

boys. Fenimore passed to Hankins, who went to the 1. Fenimore sliced through for six points. Creager replaced Hankins and kicked the point after.

Time after time the same story with slight variations was repeated.

Fenimore made two of the touchdowns, Spavital one, Creager one and Joe Thomas, a substitute, the other one.

Coach Dutch Meyer tried all kinds of defenses against the Aggies, including a seven-man line that moved Norman Cox, the fullback, into the line. None of them worked for more than a few minutes. The Aggies were too good in too many different ways.

They worked principally from a single-wing-back formation, but they also operated from a modified-T and double-wing.

Halfback Bob Ruff was one of the few offensive stars for TCU.

97

CHAPTER 20

FROGS SMASH TEXAS HOPES

BY AMOS MELTON
Fort Worth Star-Telegram

FT. WORTH, NOV. 16, 1946 — If the Texas Longhorns never see the pesky TCU Horned Frogs again, it will be 10 years too soon. And it's most likely that D.X. Bible, due to end his active coaching career this season after 32 years, always will have a feeling of great respect for little Dutch Meyer.

TCU	0	7	7	0	14
Texas	0	0	0	0	0

For those rumors you've been hearing about what went on in the TCU Stadium Saturday afternoon are true. The Meyer coached Frogs, losers of five straight games and rated hardly good enough to get on the field with a major foe, rose right up and smacked over the mighty Longhorns, 14-0. It was one of the most startling believe-it-or-nots of a dippy season.

Back in 1941, D.X. Bible got his Bible-plan going and came up with a great ball club, but the Frogs beat him by a touch. In 1942, it was the same story when Little Beecher Montgomery had his three minutes of undying glory. Then in 1944, the Frogs did it again, nosing out a 7-6 triumph that gave them the conference title.

It seemed impossible that history could go right on repeating. There wasn't a reason in the world for the Steers being unwary. They still had a chance at a piece of the conference title and almost a sure shot at some bowl game. They had Bobby Layne and as fine an overall squad as the circuit has seen.

But as 21,000 fans who looked on will testify, it did happen again and there was no fluke about it. An amazingly efficient pass defense concocted by the Dutchman, plus a Purple squad free from injuries and spoiling for battle — that was the story.

The Christian team, made up for the most part of freshmen and sophomores, played one of the finest games in TCU history. The Frogs were alert, always in the right places, perfectly coached and ready for a supreme effort.

They made none of the mistakes that have hurt them so badly all season. And as even the most ardent Steer fan must concede, the youngsters richly deserved their triumph.

The result, of course, ruins what was to have been one of Texas' greatest seasons. They can't win any part of the conference title and it's hardly likely they'll be getting any letters from bowl committees. At the same time, the sparkling victory salvaged the Frogs' somewhat disappointing year and gave the young team new incentive for years to come.

In the final analysis, perhaps, it was the Frog pass defense plus outstanding individual play by a dozen that told the story against the Steer double-wing formation, Layne's favorite throwing setup.

The Frogs used a 6-1-4. From it they got terrific rushing with Fred Taylor, Dick Lipscomb, Alan Pike,

Pete Stout, an All-SWC fullback in 1947.

Dutch (right) instructs his quarterbacks in the fundamentals of passing.

Scratch Edwards and Harold Kilman giving any Steer passer time to set himself. At the same time, their deep secondary, led by Tommy Bishop, Charley Jackson, Dave Bloxom and Lindy Berry, covered the Steer receivers like a toupee covers a bald spot.

As a result, Texas completed only eight of 22 passes for the miserable total of 28 yards — by far the lowest to which the famed Texas air game has been held this season. And it put the kibosh on the mighty Layne.

Not only did Bob take some wearing punishment from the terrific rushing but he gained only 37 yards on 31 plays all afternoon. That wasn't much for the nation's top offensive hand and simply points out the efficiency and savagery of the Christian defense.

Not once did the Longhorns move into real scoring territory. They reached the Frog 17 early in the first quarter with the help of the wind. After that, they never came closer than the Purple 33 and managed to get into the Christian end of the field on only three other occasions.

The Frogs earned their scores and barely missed another. They went 52 yards on four pass plays mid-

way in the second for a score and pushed over from the 10 in the third after blocking a Steer kick. They missed a third touchdown soon after when they were unable to drive over from the 3-yard line.

So in the matter of scoring and scoring chances it was all TCU. Texas had a slight edge in the figures, thanks to their 120 yards rushing. Most of those went to big Bill Cromer, the newly found driving back who did a good job smashing the line when Layne's passing game completely stalled. In the air, the Frogs outgained the Steers with 55 yards on five completions while Texas completed only eight for its 28 yards.

There were no extenuating circumstances for the Longhorns. The field was dry and fast, skies were clear and the sun smiled. It is true that there was a whipping north wind that chilled the customers and greatly affected kicks. But it was as fair for one side as the other — in fact, the Frogs made some of the best gains into the breeze.

No, you can only say that a great young TCU team, playing that long-expected "perfect game," simply licked the Longhorns.

Texas won the toss and took the wind in the first quarter in an effort to count quickly. They got a good chance when Layne punted out on the Frog 13 and again on the 12, but each time, little Carl Knox kicked back fairly well.

Then one of Knox's punts drifted in the high wind and Layne returned it from the Frog 33 to the 28. Layne fired a pass to Max Bumgardner for a first down on the 17 and it looked like the Steers would follow the script to a quick tally.

But the Frog defense began to function and on four plays, Layne lost 1 yard. One was a run Pike stopped cold, two were passes slapped down by Pike and Jackson, and the fourth was a shovel pass.

Although nobody knew it at the time, that was the closest the Steers came to scoring.

The Frogs held on grimly until they got the wind at the start of the second and immediately teed off. Knox was the boy. The 150-pounder from Arlington, who has overcome a reluctant knee to skipper the Frog offensive backfield, got off a mighty quick-kick that sailed over Layne's head for 77 yards.

That set Texas back on its heels and set up the first score. Unable to gain, Frank Guess punted into the wind for only 12 yards, giving TCU the ball on its 48.

From there Knox started pitching. Taylor made a great catch — one for a first down on the Texas 24.

Three passes failed but on the fourth Knox hit Lipscomb on the Texas 11. From there on second down, Knox again faded to throw. Lipscomb, that agile Paschal grad who is going to be one of the sector's finest ends one day, cut out sharply behind Jim Canady, the defensive right half. Knox lofted into the end zone a perfect shot that Dick gathered in all alone on a dead run. Bishop, one of the game's greatest stars, kicked the extra point.

The Frogs continued to attack in the second period, reaching the Texas 19 once but couldn't keep going.

TCU elected to take the wind in the third quarter and the strategy paid off. The period had hardly opened when Layne tried to punt from his 20. The middle of the Christian line came crashing through to block the effort. Wayne Pitcock and Kilman were the leaders. The leather bounced back to the Texas 10 where Kilman fell on it for the Purple.

Berry was in at tailback and engineered his team to a tally in five plays. He first made 5 yards himself on two tackle tries. Then he sent big Bloxom barging into the guards to the 2-yard line. On fourth down, Berry powered at the middle, just missed a score but made a first down on the six-inch line.

From there, Bloxom blasted over in one try. Again Bishop kicked a perfect point and the surprised crowd could hardly believe the scoreboard's "TCU 14, Texas 0."

That ended the scoring but TCU had another chance a few minutes later. Knox, that versatile little man, set this one up with great help from Bishop and Lipscomb. He kicked from his 32, the ball bouncing out of Cromer's hands back to the Steer 10. There Cromer made the mistake of trying to pick it up and the vicious working Bishop, down fast, hit him hard. Cromer lost the ball and Lipscomb made a diving recovery on the Texas 3-yard line.

It looked like another Frog score but this time Texas didn't yield. Bloxom got only 1 yard on two runs and Lindy couldn't gain at tackle. On fourth down, Berry tried to pass over the middle and big Hub Bechtol intercepted it in the end zone for a touchback.

There were a few more thrills. On one, Charley Jackson broke into the clear around the Texas left end and raced 34 yards before he was collared. It came in the fourth when the Frogs were fighting the wind and was a great help. Pete Stout kept the attack going by moving the ball to the Texas 30 but from there Knox punted into the end zone.

There was no question of Texas scoring after that. The Frog rushers had Layne on the ground every pass he tried and the Purple secondary latched on to the Steer receivers like long lost brothers. You got the impression Texas couldn't score in a year.

Lindy Berry led the Frogs in total offense, punt returns and kickoff returns as a freshman in 1946.

CHAPTER 21

FROGS STARTLE SMU WITH 19-19 TIE

By Amos Melton
Fort Worth Star-Telegram

FT. WORTH, NOV. 29, 1947 — Psychiatrists and steam-shovel operators are gonna have a big Christmas in these parts. By conservative estimate, the boys with the big scoops have a steady job for weeks shoveling the finger nails out of TCU Stadium.

SMU	0	6	7	6	19
TCU	6	6	0	7	19

As for the medics who take care of nervous breakdowns — they can just get their soft couches and dim lights all ready for 32,000 limp and babbling individuals who will be dropping around at any time.

The whacky folks will be the unfortunates — or fortunates — who sat on the slopes of Frog field Saturday afternoon and saw TCU and SMU dash and drive to a 19-19 tie in their traditional battle.

Without a single dissenting vote, the duel was voted the most hilarious, drama-dipped and nerve-shattering in the history of the long series. So throat-clutching were the goings-on that most folks won't be able to swallow until Monday.

With the kind assistance of a soda water boy (he's holding the still-quivering typewriter steady) here's a hazy account of what happened.

The Frogs, sharp and ready, roared to a 12-0 lead in the first 17 minutes. The Ponies, led by Doak Walker, who played one of the greatest games in conference history, came back strong and kept nibbling at

Morris Bailey caught the long pass in TCU's 90-yard, 2-play touchdown.

the lead until they finally shoved ahead late in the third at 13-12.

That brought things up to the last two minutes and those final 120 seconds were as wild as any in the memory of any living football fanatic. Everything happened.

The Christians, operating back of their 10-yard line, went 90 yards on two plays.

Yep, that's correct. The mighty little Lindy Berry hurled a pass and lank Morris Bailey, the sophomore end, reached up for a great catch near the Frog 40. Ponies were all about but Morris spun free, took off in an open field and seemed gone. Then as Walker and Paul Page began to converge on him about the Frog 20. Bailey cut across field and spied Charley Jackson coming up fast.

Just as he was tackled, Bailey flipped a backward pass that traveled 15 yards square into Jackson's eager hands and the halfback broke for the east sideline.

But he was finally collared on the Pony 8-yard line.

On first down, Lindy called signals and started what looked like a straight off-tackle play. But just as he was hit about the 5, the little man whirled and flipped a lateral out to big Pete Stout, who had floated wide.

It was a low toss but Stout scooped up the potato and there wasn't anything but daylight to six-point territory. He made it in a leap. Berry, the darling of the Frog fans, was hurt on the magnificent effort and received an echoing ovation as he left the field.

Then Wayne Pitcock kicked the extra point to make it 19-13, and the 32,000 booby-hatch candidates were sure the Frogs had won since there was only a minute

Lindy Berry led the nation in punt returning as a sophomore in 1947. He was selected as an all-America in 1949.

40 seconds to play.

But they reckoned without darting Doak Walker, who wasn't gonna take a licking. He took the kickoff, faked a handoff and then shot up the east sideline in a whiteshirted blur.

The Frogs converged valiantly but were blocked or just missed tackles. Walker broke into the open spaces and seemed gone, but the Frogs' Randy Rogers had held back as safety man and he finally shoved Walker over the sideline on the Frog 36.

Matty Bell rushed Gilbert Johnson, his ace hurler, to the mound but his first two efforts were high. Then Walker got in the act again. He sneaked out, made a fine jumping snatch of Johnson's pass on the Frog 15, and was dropped on the 10. There was 20 seconds to play.

While the ushers rushed to the aid of fainting old ladies and swooning co-eds, Johnson started a run as if to sweep the Frog left end. Then he planted his feet and passed.

It was a rifle shot of some 12 yards that plugged Sid Halliday right on the goal line.

Halliday was hit hard by two Frogs as the ball arrived but he held to the precious leather like a mamma kangaroo pocketing a youngun. It was a touchdown and tied the count at 19-all.

Then in a mighty hush — while the 32,000 hardly dared breathe, Walker made his try for the all-important point-after kick. It was wide to the left and as referee Jack Sisco brushed the grass with his "no good" sign, the throng roared with the thunder of a 105-mm barrage.

That ended it. Carl Knox, playing his last second for the Frogs, tried mightily to return the kickoff for another score but he was dropped on the Frog 14, and the tremendous battle ended before another play.

Thus, the Frogs put the only blemish on SMU's record for the season and prevented them from earning their second perfect year in history.

And nobody could say either side was lucky. They

deserved just that — a tie. The Ponies had an edge in the statistics, but in a way they were fortunate to count again in so little time.

One thing is sure, the Ponies had it when they had to have it. Or rather, you could say Doak Walker had it. He was the difference all afternoon.

So both teams go to bowls — SMU to the Cotton and TCU to the Delta. If it were possible, the best game might be a rematch of the old rivals. Surely few in this sector were as good as this one. Even veteran writers thought it more exciting than that legendary 1935 duel between undefeated teams. This one was a honey.

The deadlock gives SMU a clear title with only a half-game lost while the Frogs won fourth place.

From the outset, it was evident that the Frogs were ready. After five minutes of play they blasted 50 yards on seven plays for the first score. Bailey and Stout were the heroes. Bailey made his first terrific pass catch for a first on the Pony 13.

From there, the bull rush of Stout scored in just four plays. He blasted two steps for the counter. Pitcock missed the extra-point attempt.

Walker almost scored on the ensuing kickoff (the guy was dynamite all day), but was stopped on the Frog 23, after 77 yards. But the threat died on the Frog 4.

On the last play of the first quarter, Johnson's pass bounced off Walker's shoulder and the Frogs' Orien Browning intercepted in a flash and broke into the open, picking up great blocking.

He was forced finally to cut back on the 12 and was dropped on the 8 after 56 yards.

Berry made it to the 2 on three tries and on fourth down the ever-ready Stout just went over the top at the middle for his second touchdown. This time Pitcock's point try was blocked. The crowd could hardly believe what it had seen.

The Mustangs then settled to complete their chores. Just before the half, they were messing around on their 38, where it was second and 11. Walker dropped back to pass, wasn't rushed too fast and took off around the Frog left end.

He turned the corner at the sideline, paced himself for blockers around the Frog 40, then soared into the open and went 61 yards for SMU's first tally.

Walker also kicked the extra point, his 18th in 20 tries for the season. But it was his last for the day.

The Frogs probably will be kicking themselves in their old age for missing two fine opportunities early in the third. Randy Rogers covered a fumble by Dick McKissick on the Pony 17, but the chance died with Paul Page intercepting Berry's pass in the end zone on fourth down.

Two Mustang plays later, a low pass-kick skidded between Walker and McKissack, and the Frogs' Wayne Rogers bounced on the leather only 5 yards from the Pony goal. But even this great opportunity died when three runs and a pass failed.

SMU took the lead just as the third ended. The Ponies went 51 yards on 13 plays, the most damaging being passes from Walker to "hooking" ends.

From the 3-yard line on second down, Walker raced wide to his right and as David Bloxom missed a tackle on the 5-yard line, went over the corner. Walker missed the extra point to make the score 13-12 — which is where the real excitement began down there at the end.

Pete Stout (left) and Al Vaiani formed a rugged backfield duo for the Horned Frogs in 1947. Vaiani was stricken with polio following the season and was unable to return to the team.

CHAPTER 22

REBS' LATE PASSES TRIP FROGS, 13-9

BY AMOS MELTON
Fort Worth Star-Telegram

MEMPHIS, JAN. 1, 1948 — After stumbling around the frigid premises for three quarters like a ham actor living in the past, the Old Miss Rebels suddenly remembered the script here Thursday afternoon.

TCU	0	9	0	0	9
Ole Miss	0	0	0	13	13

Trailing a hard-trying and vicious TCU team by nine points, the great Charley Conerly suddenly soared to the dramatic heights of football. In just five minutes his rifle arm accounted for two touchdowns as the Confederates defeated the Christians in the first Delta Bowl game, 13-9.

For 45 minutes, the 28,600 partisan fans shivered in the 30-degree weather — and thrilled to the great work of a Frog team that seemed several touchdowns better than the Southeastern Conference champs.

As a matter of fact, the Purple line was so superior to the Rebel line for those first chapters that it was hard to believe. Sportswriters in the press box found themselves feeling a bit sorry for Johnny Vaught and wondering if Ole Miss was that poor or TCU was that good.

But nobody needed to fret.

In the closing minutes of the third quarter, Conerly launched a passing flurry that carried exactly 80 yards in eight plays for a touchdown. The extra point, however, was missed and the Texans still led, 9-6.

The Frogs, still going strong, marched right back to the Rebel 37 where an intercepted pass sat Conerly up in business again. This time he threw only two passes — and they ate up 63 yards — to win the ball game.

It was that easy. The strange thing about it was that up to that time, Conerly had looked like just another thrower — many of his efforts sailing wide, others

Otis McKelvey proved to be one of the heroes for TCU against Ole Miss.

plunging into the ground short of receivers.

Four of his passes had been intercepted by the alert Christians.

But when he did remember that he was the nation's greatest passer — Charley the Great — his tosses were perfect and, while it must be admitted that faulty tackling by the Frogs contributed most of the distance gained, you couldn't take anything away from that passing.

In more ways than one, it was a tough game for the Frogs to lose. They were sharp and powerful most of the day — and put on a great final display by marching from their 1 to the Old Miss 38 just before the gun sounded.

But they fumbled badly, losing the ball twice at cru-

Quarterback Lindy Berry rips for big yardage through the Rebels' secondary.

The 1947 Horned Frogs finished the season with a record of 4 wins, 5 losses and 2 ties.

cial moments. And they never seemed able to cash in all the way on their obvious superiority in the line.

Both teams rolled up 15 first downs but Ole Miss had an advantage in total yardage, 297 to 196. The figures are a bit deceiving as a true picture of the rough-and-tumble in-fighting. On just head-to-head stuff, the Frogs were much better, blocking huge holes for their backs and limiting the Rebs to a scant 10 yards running in the first half.

But as they always have, they paid off on the score again. And it would be unfair to say the Rebs didn't deserve to win — but it's certainly hard to even suggest the Frogs should have lost.

The Mississippi folks started well enough, moving 60 yards to the Frog 10 the first time they got the ball. But Charley Jackson snared a Conerly pass to end it. From there on the game belonged to TCU until that last period.

With Lindy Berry and Pete Stout roaring and racing for fine yardage — and Stout hitting a fine new jump pass to Morris Bailey every now and then, the Frogs paraded 76 yards to the Rebel 14 the first time they tried the offense.

The Frog attack moved so easily and steadily the Ole Miss folks were amazed.

Early in the second quarter, after Carl Knox had punted over the enemy goal, Bobby Wilson, subbing in for Conerly, tried an ill-advised pass from his 20. The shot was in the deep right flat where Charley Jackson had the receiver covered. The ball was batted up and Berry flashed in to intercept on the Reb 30.

He was against the north sideline in the clear and with some fine blocking, was over the goal line before anybody could even launch a tackle. Wayne Pitcock, who kicked beautifully all afternoon, pounded through a perfect extra-point kick.

Just four plays later, the score mounted, 9-0. From his 13-yard line, Conerly tried a punt. Big Scratch Edwards came roaring in, ran over the fullback and breasted the ball squarely.

The bounding leather skittered to the goal line in the southeast corner, rolled over and out of the end zone as three Frogs pursued it. Referee Harry Viner immediately signaled the automatic safety.

At this stage, it looked like an easy Texas victory while the Ole Miss folks sat stunned. And it kept right on looking that way.

Great rushing by Bob and Bill Moorman, Bailey, George Boal, Harold Kilman and Alan Pike, who was a standout all day in his last game, had Conerly throwing the ball like a junior high chunker. And the Ole Miss run game wasn't effective.

The Frogs continued to move at will. They advanced to the Ole Miss 12 after Bull Hicks recovered a fumble on the 23-yard line, but a fourth-down pass to Kilman was fumbled and the threat died. The Rebs' best effort before the half carried only to the Frog 40.

Starting the third period, TCU took the stiff northwest wind figuring to tally again. But a fumble cost the Purple the ball once and a fine Conerly kick set them back to their 2 another time.

The next Reb hope for a score was killed by Dave Bloxom, who intercepted a quick pass over the middle on the Frog 22. Jackson got another Conerly effort on the 33 and things looked fairly safe with a minute to go in the third quarter. Then it happened.

From their 20, the Rebs decided to run, and reverses by little Farley Salmon and Jack Stribling made a first down at the Frog 40. A short pass and defensive holding penalty on the Frogs (trying to hold a receiver) carried the ball to the 23.

Conerly then ran for 2 yards and on the next down, dropped for a deep pass. End Joe Johnson circled down behind Al Vaiani, took the perfect toss at the goal line and fell over. Bob Oswalt missed the extra point but Ole Miss began to take hope.

They didn't have long to wait. Again the Frogs moved up the field but a Berry to Bailey pass was tipped and sailed squarely into the hands of the Rebs' Wilson, who was on his knees on his own 37.

From there, only two plays were needed. Conerly hit Johnson about 15 yards deep over the middle. The Frog safety was close but he slipped and Johnson just kept running. He was wide open but Randy Rogers pulled up on him fast and finally made a sure tackle on the Frog 13.

On the very next play, Conerly flipped to fullback Earl Howell in the right flat at the line of scrimmage. Three Frogs had clean shots at him but they missed and he emerged from the stack still running about the 5 and went over easily. This time Oswalt's kick was good.

There were nine minutes to play and the Frogs gave the enemy fans heart attacks by holding the ball for six of them. From their 1-yard line, where Otis McKelvey was dropped on the kickoff, the Christians powered upfield for 59 yards.

Carl Knox and McKelvey were the heroes of this dying effort.

Both of them ran for miles from the spread formation. But the last threat died when Knox's pass was batted up and intercepted by the Ole Miss linebacker on the Reb 38. The victors froze the ball the last three minutes.

Pete Stout had over 100 yards in total offense against Ole Miss.

Chapter 23

Lindy Berry, a two-time All-SWC quarterback, cuts back against the grain on a long run back against Texas in 1949.

Berry Outduels Walker in Final Meeting

By Whit Canning
Fort Worth Star Telegram

When it was over, Doak Walker hugged Lindy Berry and Dutch Meyer cried.

It was Nov. 26, 1949, a day when two brilliant collegiate careers came to a close and another went into temporary hiding.

As a backdrop, a capacity crowd of 33,000 filed into Amon Carter Stadium to view the last of three memorable duels between TCU's Berry and SMU's Walker, a duo of opposing tailbacks who amassed more than

8,000 total yards in their careers, not to mention about 2,000 in punt returns.

In each of the two previous meetings, Walker — SMU's three-time all-American and Heisman Trophy winner — had engineered last-gasp touchdown drives enabling Cotton Bowl-bound Mustangs teams to come away with 19-19 and 7-7 ties against the upset-minded Frogs.

This time, there was no Cotton Bowl bid waiting, and the two heroes looked a bit the worse for wear — Walker hobbling on a severe cramp and Berry wearing a plaster mask to protect a broken jaw suffered in a victory against Texas two weeks earlier.

But these ailments paled in comparison to the wounded heart of Meyer, who was about to face his old friend, former coaching companion and spirited adversary, Matty Bell, for the final time.

Bell was scheduled to retire after SMU's final game the next week against Notre Dame. Not to be out-done, Meyer was playing the situation for all it was worth in the dressing room.

"We were in there before the game," Berry recalls, "and Dutch came in, kinda shuffling around and mum-bling and gettin' weepy and all, and finally he says, 'Well boys, I ... I guess this is gonna be my last game,' and his voice started cracking, and he says, 'They haven't renewed my contract ... so I guess this is it.'

"Then he looks up at us with tears in his eyes and he says, 'Boy, I sure would love to beat Matty one more time.'

"Well, I was the captain, so I held a quick team meeting and I told 'em, 'Look, we've just got to go out there and win this game for Dutch,' and every-body agreed and we went out there all fired up."

SMU quickly took a 7-0 lead on a 37-yard run by Kyle Rote, but in the second quarter, Berry moved the Frogs 87 yards in three plays, including a 56-yard pass and run to George Boal and a 29-yard scoring pass to Jimmy Hickey.

Berry, who also intercepted a pass during the game, then scored the go-ahead touchdown after setting it up with a razzle-dazzle pass and lateral play.

But late in the third quarter, SMU's Fred Benners threw 57 yards to Rusty Russell Jr. to cut the lead to 14-13. Rote tried, and missed, the extra point because Walker was unavailable. He had been injured again on a third-quarter hit by TCU's Orein Browning, who had just spent six weeks recovering from a broken jaw.

It was to be the last play of a legendary career. Walk-er never returned to the game, and was unable to play the next week against Notre Dame.

Berry then clinched a 21-13 TCU victory with a 21-yard touchdown pass to John Archer. Berry threw for 250 yards in the game, concluding his career with 4,452 total yards — nearly 900 more than Walker, his famous all-American opponent.

Rote had 162 yards for SMU on rushes and pass recep-tions.

TCU had a 351-312 edge in total yards and beat

Berry (right) visits with his idol, Davey O'Brien, before practice during the 1949 season.

SMU for the first time in seven years. Meyer was cry-ing again. So were Mr. and Mrs. Charles Berry, Lindy's parents.

At midfield, Walker limped out, hugged Berry and said, "You were great."

In the locker room, Meyer used a towel to wipe the tears from his face and played coy with reporters ask-ing if this had been his last game. He never actually gave a straight answer.

The next week, Berry sat in the Cotton Bowl and watched Rote — filling in for Walker because of Brown-ing's hit — play the game of his career in a thrilling 27-20 loss to Notre Dame's national champions.

"By that time," Berry said laughing, "we had found out that two days before we played SMU, Dutch had signed a new three-year contract."

CHAPTER 24

TCU Upsets Sixth-ranked Texas A&M

BY WHIT CANNING
Fort Worth Star-Telegram

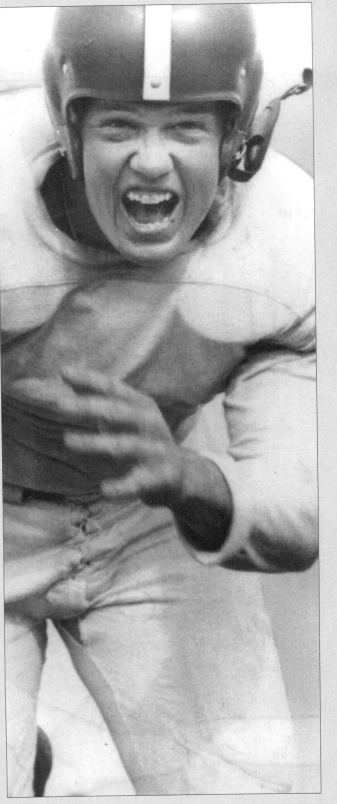

Doug Conaway, an all-America tackle in 1951.

I t was midseason, and Dutch Meyer was crying again.

As the years passed, it seemed, the longtime TCU coach was becoming more and more emotional. After every big victory, he wept.

And this one was big.

"This was the sweetest victory of my coaching career," Meyer said, sobbing, "and the most courageous comeback I've ever witnessed."

It was Oct. 20, 1951, and Meyer and a capacity crowd of 35,794 at Amon Carter Stadium had just watched TCU torch undefeated, sixth-ranked Texas A&M, 20-14.

On a day that began with three Southwest Conference teams ranked in the Top 10 — Texas was fourth, Texas A&M sixth, Baylor 10th — it was a momentous event. Because at the end of the season, it would be the Horned Frogs who would roll into the Cotton Bowl on a ride that began with the victory against A&M.

What made it worse for the Aggies was that they were felled by a crippled TCU team that wiped out a 14-point deficit by rallying around a third-string sophomore tailback in the fourth quarter.

And a key play was an onside kick that was, well, a little strange.

Coming in, the possibility of all this occurring seemed remote in the extreme. The Aggies, led by halfback Glenn Lippman and their great fullback, Bob Smith, were 4-0, averaging 377 yards per game, and had beaten Oklahoma, the defending national champion. They seemed to be rolling easily toward a three-way title fight with Baylor and Texas.

By contrast, the Frogs (2-2) had just been ripped, 33-19, by Texas Tech and had lost their preseason all-

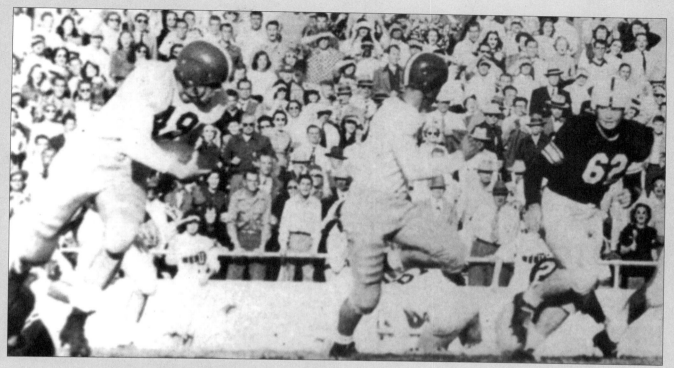

Ray McKown picks up interference as he turns the corner against Texas A&M.

America candidate Gilbert Bartosh, in the process.

In fact, the Frogs' top three offensive threats — Bartosh, backup tailback Mal Fowler and fullback Bobby Jack Floyd — were hobbled with a sprained ankle, knee injury and broken hand, respectively.

This dropped the mantle of leadership on the gangly shoulders of Ray McKown, a sophomore from Dumas. After this day, they would call him "The Dumas Dandy."

But for 51 minutes, the dandiest folks on the field were the Aggies — who led, 14-0, after scoring passes of 55 yards to Smith and 11 yards, early in the fourth quarter, to Billy Tidwell.

But with nine minutes to play, McKown took the deep snap in the spread, sliced through a hole in the left side of the line, broke away from a crowd of Aggies, veered toward the right sideline and raced 49 yards for a score. The "courageous comeback" had begun.

"On the extra-point attempt," said Allie White, then a TCU assistant coach, "they roughed our kicker and got assessed a 15-yard penalty on the kickoff, so me and Dutch figured it would be a good time for an onside kick.

"We wanted to line it up on one side of the field and kick to the other sideline, but we didn't know how far from the middle of the field we could set up, to get the angle we wanted.

"The rule book said the ball had to be inside the 'inbounds line' (hash mark), but we figured that must be the same as the 'out-of-bounds line,' so we set it up way over next to the sideline. It turned out we were doing something illegal, but the officials didn't realize it, and neither did we.

"There was a brief discussion after the kick, but Dutch assured everyone that he had looked it up in the rule book, and everyone just accepted that."

The ensuing kick, from the A&M 45, was recovered at the 30 by TCU's Wayne Martin, and the Frogs drove in for another score, but missed the extra point to trail 14-13.

The Frogs still needed a break, and got it when Roy Pitcock recovered a Tidwell fumble at the A&M 22 on the second play after the kickoff. McKown scored the winning touchdown with 1:35 left.

The next week, TCU's confidence in McKown solidified when he piled up 340 yards in a 28-26 loss to an unbeaten Southern California team led by Frank Gifford.

From there, as the Aggies, Bears and Longhorns faltered, Meyer's battered Frogs became a Cinderella champion.

CHAPTER 25

WILDCATS CASH CHANCES, ROMP OVER FROGS, 20-7

By Lorin McMullen
Fort Worth Star-Telegram

DALLAS, JAN. 1, 1952 — Kentucky had the bounce, the zest, the knack for doing it when it counted in the 16th annual Cotton Bowl classic here Tuesday. Texas Christian University, distressingly flat except for one magnificent minute-and-half surge late in the third quarter, succeeded only in making it a masterpiece of frustration.

Kentucky	7	6	0	7	20
TCU	0	0	7	0	7

And so the four-times beaten Wildcats from the Bluegrass thoroughly trounced the Southwest Conference champions before a capacity throng of 75,349 who shivered in 40-degree weather, 20-7.

Kentucky scored on two surges of 53 and 57 yards in the first and second quarters to post its 13-0 halftime lead.

With two minutes and 49 seconds remaining in the third quarter TCU sent in quarterback Gilbert Bartosh for his first offensive chance of the day. In four plays that required only one minute 37 seconds, he registered a touchdown, achieved on a tremendous 43-yard run by the bruising fullback, Bobby Jack Floyd.

After Keith Flowers' point-after it was a ball game and set the gigantic crowd a-cheering that the Frogs at last had found their groove and were ready to unleash an offensive more in keeping with their reputation.

Keith Flowers, an all-America linebacker in 1951.

Going against the wind as they changed ends for the last quarter, the Frogs bogged after a 40-yard advance. Ray McKown made a superb 32-yard kick-out on the 8, for what loomed as the break TCU needed for another chance.

Here, however, Kentucky's offense made the move that quite likely saved the victory. For it squirmed out to the Kentucky 36, Vito (Babe) Parilli kicked deep into TCU territory and the Frogs never threatened again.

Their desperation here led directly to Kentucky finding itself in scoring position and the Wildcats, characteristic of their conduct here Tuesday, capitalized for the third touchdown.

That, definitely, was Kentucky's nature — capitalizing.

In contrast, the Frogs drove 70 yards to the 4, 59 yards to the 24; 48 to the 5, and 51 to the 1 — missing them all by various and sundry methods.

In the Beginning

The Wildcats had the ball only twice in the first quarter — and made it good for a 7-0 lead. Starting from the 47, Larry Jones lugged for 11 yards in two tries. Allen Felch added four and Vito Parilli, who had missed on his first three passes, hit the great Kentucky end, Steve Meilinger, over the middle, for 31 yards and a first down on the 7.

After Emery Clark plunged for two yards and Parilli threw high to Meilinger, the Kentucky quarterback passed to Clark for the 5 yards and a touchdown. Bobby McFarland just missed breaking it up. Harry Jones kicked the extra point.

The Frogs, who had bogged once on the 4, wasted another a 59-yard

push to the 24 early in the second quarter. Here, Clark intercepted a Mal Fowler pass, returned to the Kentucky 43 and the Wildcats went 57 yards for another touchdown in 11 plays.

A Parilli pass to Meilinger for 23 yards set this one going, Harold Gruner chimed in with a timely 7-yard run and down on the 13, fourth down and 6 to go. Parilli fired over Ronald Fraley to Clark, who was deep in the end zone, for the 13-0 lead.

TCU made its 48-yard move to the 5 after this and came back later in the quarter with its 51-yard march to the 1 — all for nothing.

Floyd Scampers 43 Yards

The one time Kentucky was guilty of mis-using a long drive occurred just before TCU's lone score in the third. Expertly mixing runs and passes, Parilli guided the Wildcats 44 yards to the 23, where Fraley intercepted a third-down pass in the end zone.

And then, with 2:49 left in the third quarter, Bartosh drew his first chance of the game. On the first play he slashed off left tackle for 9, passed to John Medanich for 22, zipped up the middle for 6.

Here Bartosh called a direct snap-back to Floyd, who shot through left guard, swerved to the left sideline and went 43 yards for the touchdown on the longest run of the day.

When Flowers kicked goal there was just 1:32 remaining in the period.

Against the wind in the fourth period Bartosh guided the Frogs 40 yards to the 40, where it was a fourth down, 6 to go. The TCU command sent in McKown

Ray McKown, nicknamed " The Dumas Dandy," was a true triple-threat back who earned all-America honors as a sophomore.

to punt and he obliged with his neat kick-out on the 8.

But here, where holding 'em was imperative for TCU, Tom Fillon broke loose for 17 yards on a third-and-7.

That spoiled everything. For Kentucky held the ball, put TCU in the hole with the kick and Bartosh was spilled for losses of 14 and 11 yards trying to get off passes.

When Kentucky ran back McKown's kick to the 27, Ed Hamilton made 12 yards in two carries, Clark added 4. Fillon made 7 on that delayed buck at the middle, Parilli sneaked for 2 yards, Hamilton hurled himself over left tackle for 3 yards and the touchdown — 25 seconds before the end of the game. Harry Jones added his second conversion.

TCU fumbled the following kickoff, Don Dyer recovered and Kentucky had the ball on the 8-yard line at the final gun.

The first TCU mishap — coming as the Frogs had taken the first kickoff and marched down the field — sputtered on the 4-yard line, where Floyd fumbled and McKown recovered for a loss of 7. Here, on the 11, on fourth down, TCU sent in Fowler for an unsuccessful jump pass.

In the second quarter, Clark's interception of Fowler's pass spoiled the second long march, and after Kentucky scored TCU went to the 5 on a 15-yard piling-on penalty. This time John Harville lost three, McKown two, Bob Blair dropped a pass in the end zone, McKown's run lost six yards and Kentucky took over on the 10.

Near the end of the first half, TCU had a first down on the 1-yard line. Bill Doty, in the game for the injured Floyd at fullback, failed on a line play and TCU was penalized five yards for a slow substitution. McKown made four yards in two tries and then missed with a pass. Kentucky took over this time on the 2.

It was just that kind of day. The Frogs had spurts of efficiency but seemed to have snap, dash and coherence only in that brief third-quarter interlude that produced the score.

This was a shame, too, for it wasted so many good

Bobby Jack Floyd (32) darts through the middle of the Kentucky defense for a 43-yard gain.

midfield plays, including a 29-yard run by Floyd, who was the day's top rusher with 115 yards in 14 carries, and a 51-yard pass from McKown to Ted Vaught.

The statistics indicated TCU's need for goal-line punch.

The Frogs marked up 15 first downs and gained 300 yards — usually enough for three touchdowns — which slightly exceeded Kentucky's gains. But the Wildcats clicked when it counted, TCU faltered with the goal line in sight.

Parilli proved himself the superb ball-handler of his reputation, passing smartly for eight completions in 22 attempts for 85 yards and two touchdowns. The Kentucky backs — the Jones twins, Clark and Fillon — ran well, better than expected.

Doug Moseley, Kentucky's all-America linebacker, was hurt in the first half and didn't return.

CHAPTER 26

When Dutch Meyer's Frogs Were Princes

By Dan Jenkins
Sports Illustrated
September 1981

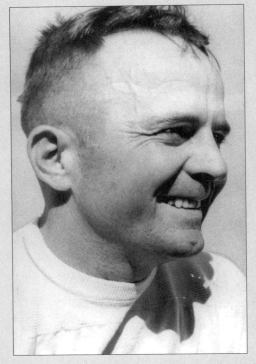

The canvas pants didn't look baggy then, not like they do now in the old photographs. They were the color of a manila envelope, and I thought they were as sleek as the long-sleeved white jerseys with purple numerals and the shiny black leather helmets. A wide purple knit stripe curved down the back of each canvas leg, and somehow the pants turned elegantly golden if the sunlight hit them just right on those Saturday afternoons when a TCU Horned Frog named Slingin' Sammy Baugh or Davey O'Brien would throw the football so hard at times, often so far and always so accurately that he would make another stumbling ignoramus out of a hated Longhorn, Bear, Owl, Razorback, Mustang or Aggie, whatever it was.

I speak wistfully of a time in the mid-to-late 1930's when practically everything seemed better to me than it does today except, of course, air conditioning.

Even gangsters were better in the 30's because you could tell them apart from the politicians. Gangsters put black shoe polish on their hair, wore pinstripe suits, packed heaters and talked about C-notes as they slapped their women around.

Cars were better because they were flashy roadsters with rumble seats and all kinds of wraparound chrome, and you could drive from Fort Worth, Texas, to Shreveport, La., on nine cents worth of gas.

People could dance to the music of the 1930's with-out hopping around like Siamese cats, or people could listen to the music without screaming at a teen-ager to turn down the heavy metal or put on earphones. Music was definitely better.

Food was better. You could almost always open the packages food came in. Or you could pull food out of the ground or wring food's neck in the backyard and then roll it in flour and pitch it in the frying pan. You could also get food at drugstores which, if they were good drugstores, sold comic books and strawberry milk shakes.

Comic books were better because they were serious. It was a sad day for America when comic books got funny.

Movies and novels were better because they had good guys and bad guys in them, and frequently had endings. Movies were also taller because the leading men were taller and pretty good sword fighters. In a 30's movie, Dustin Hoffman wouldn't get the girl. He'd get the luggage.

Staying home was better, even if you didn't read a book. You could listen to the *Amos and Andy Show* and *One Man's Family* and *I Love A Mystery* on the radio instead of hurling your house slipper at the TV when *The Love Boat* comes on, and then switching over to Alistair Cooke introducing Part 17 of *Kristin Lavransdatter*.

Presidents were better. There was never going to be but one president, and you could trust FDR.

All in all, trains were better in the 30's, and so were newspapers, swimming holes, cafeterias, shade trees, bicycles, cornbread, drive-ins, doughnuts, candy bars, picnics, oceans, skies, parades, dust storms, rodeos, Christmases and tap dancing.

Dutch enjoys a card game with his star quarterback, Davey O'Brien, while on a train in 1938.

And football.

Football was better because college football was the major league. Pro football consisted largely of a group of second-class citizens waddling around in the baseball parks of blue-collar cities.

The pros were already astute in the art of offensive holding, but they were pushovers for Sam Baugh, fresh out of TCU. He led the College All-Stars to victory over the Green Bay Packers, and then he became the All-Pro quarterback in his rookie year while taking the Washington Redskins to the NFL championship. Until Sam Baugh, pro football in Texas was a one-paragraph story on the third page of the Monday sports section.

Meanwhile, college football was glamorous, mysterious, *important*.

Every team in the country had its own look, and the players dressed properly. If a player had shown up for a game in a fishnet jersey cut off at the rib cage, he'd have been thrown in the slammer for indecent exposure.

Nobody wore a face mask, and the gladiators were expected to play offense and defense, quite often, like Sam Baugh, for 60 minutes.

No two college teams ran the same offense. Their coaches had names like Dutch, Jock, Tiny, Pop, Bernie, Biff, Stub, Clipper, Pappy and Slip, and they all developed a variation of the single wing, double wing, triple wing, spread, short punt and box formations. They used shifts, men in motion, unbalanced lines, tricky reverses, daring laterals, statues, flickers, shovel passes, buttonhooks and long passes, which weren't called "bombs" yet because World War II hadn't started.

The modern T formation was still an idea that Clark Shaughnessy would shape up when he was with the Chicago Bears and take with him to Frankie Albert and Stanford in 1940.

I wasn't old enough in those days for a grownup to let go of my hand at TCU's big concrete stadium on the campus, a stadium that held at least 24,000 camel's hair overcoats and Stetson hats at the time, but I was already aware of a phenomenal blessing.

I had been born in the football capital of the universe, South Bend, Ind., and Tuscaloosa, Ala., notwithstanding. Fort Worth was the home of Texas Christian University, and TCU was the dominant force in

Dutch played for the Horned Frogs in 1916-17 and 1920-21.

society known to sportswriters as the jinx-ridden, upset-prone, wild and woolly Southwest Conference.

All this was impressed upon me hundreds of times by my parents, grandparents, uncles, aunts and older cousins, all of whom had a habit of pinning a large souvenir button on my crocheted sweater when I would be taken to TCU's home games.

The button I prized the most was about three inches in diameter, ringed in purple and white, and featured in the center, the black and white photo of a wiry, bareheaded man poised to toss a football. The button proclaimed: I AM FOR SLINGIN' SAM BAUGH AND THE FIGHTIN' FROGS OF '35 — WE'RE NO. 1!

That particular souvenir may have been given to me by the uncle I overheard one Saturday as he remarked to my dad: "Our Frogs are gonna play some whup-ass with them Rice Owls some today."

And the Frogs did — then.

What has happened to them in the past couple of decades, after a 30-year reign as consistently the best team in the Southwest Conference — and one of the best in the country — shouldn't have happened to a University of Chicago. The Frogs couldn't have slipped any lower in the college ranks if the chancellor had built an underground stadium to avoid a nuclear holocaust.

It has occurred to me that there must be thousands of TCU graduates scattered among Dairy Queens everywhere who have no appreciation, no real understanding, of what the Frogs were. To most of these individuals, TCU is simply a cozy array of cream-colored buildings on a gentle hill near downtown Fort Worth where they spent a happy young adulthood going to Kappa Sig rushes and Tri Delt formals. And perhaps they giggled occasionally at an amusing little football team that has now won only nine games in the last seven years (14 games in the last nine years, 1973-81), and has not, in fact, beaten or even tied the Arkansas Razorbacks in 22 seasons (until 1981).

About seven years ago, I was loitering in the same stadium where I had marveled at the deft spirals of Sam Baugh and Davey O'Brien, where I had been dazzled by the scampers of men like Lindy Berry and Jim Swink, where I had actually felt sorry for the ball carriers who were struck down by such assassins as Ki Aldrich, Derrell Palmer and Bob Lilly. The stadium now holds 46,000, and it is still a pleasant old place surrounded by trees, a short walk from the dorms. It's a sturdy plant built strictly for football — no track around the playing field, the action up close — and I was suddenly compelled to join in some laughter. A cluster of TCU students in the east stands had unfurled a banner, which proclaimed: WE'RE NO. 113!

The students had timed the unfurling to coincide with the 81st point scored by the University of Texas Longhorns that crisp afternoon.

Maybe it is to such witty followers of present-day TCU football that I am basically addressing myself. They might better appreciate their own humor if they fully understood how far the Frogs had fallen.

Contrary to what most of these followers may believe, TCU once produced national champions in authentic polls in real newspapers, conference champions regularly, bowl teams in abundance, All-Americas by the gross and even a Heisman Trophy winner. Uh-huh. Just like your normal everyday Ohio State or Southern California. ...

★ ★ ★

The Southwest Conference to which I was blessedly born was organized in 1915, and for the first time in 25 years of its existence no football champion ever repeated, which was why sportscasters were inspired to label it a jinx-ridden, upset-prone, wild and woolly place. Incidentally, what generally passed for colorful sportswriting back then was a story that might well have begun:

COLLEGE STATION, Texas, Oct. 23 — Yippee-tie-yi-yee! Baylor's Bullet Billy Patterson, the Hillsboro Dilly, threw a green-and-gold lariat around the gallant but hapless Texas Aggies Saturday, and despite the dipsy-doodle footwork of A&M's Dick Todd, the Cromwell Cyclone, the hungry Bears corralled the

maroon-clad Farmers, 13-0, and kept alive their title hopes in the topsy-turvy, wild and woolly. ..."

TCU dipsy-doodled into the conference in 1923, and almost immediately the Frogs became a major contributor to its jinx-ridden, upset-prone reputation. On an average of every other season in their first 15 years as members, the Frogs either defeated or tied the team that won the championships. But it didn't stop there.

For close to 40 years, the Frogs repeatedly pulled off gigantic upsets, even in those seasons when they could do little else but provide an excuse for the Texas Christian University Swing Band to prance onto the field in policeman's caps and strike up a rendition of *Plenty of Money and You*.

A lot of legendary folks felt the sting of the TCU upset. Like Joel Hunt and the powerful Aggies of '25 and '27, and Bill Wallace and the powerful Owls of '34. Like Jack Crain, Mal Kutner and the powerful

Taking a break from a game, Dutch discusses strategy with Gilbert Bartosh.

Longhorns of '41, who went into the TCU game rated No. 1 and had just been splashed on the cover of Life magazine. The baggy pants knocked them off. And then there was Doak Walker, the best all-around football player anybody ever saw when he was at SMU. Doak never got better than a tie with the Frogs in the seasons of '47, '48 and '49 when he was college football's last three-year consensus all-America back.

But the Frogs were much more than spoilers. Upsets were just the comedy relief provided by Francis Schmidt, Dutch Meyer and Abe Martin, the three men who coached TCU through the glory years.

Those years began in 1929 when Cy Leland's breakaway running brought the Frogs their first conference championship and the glory ended with the last title in 1959 (shared with Texas and Arkansas), which was the result, by and large, of Bob Lilly's mayhem in the trenches, as the *Illustrated Football Annual* might have put it.

Over this span of 31 consecutive seasons, from '29 through '59, the Frogs were the best team in the Southwest Conference. I just happen to have proof. All TCU did was:

• Win more national championships (two — '35 and '38) than anybody else in the conference.

• Win more conference championships (eight) than anyone else.

• Go to more bowl games (11) than anybody else in the conference.

• Produce more all-Americas (16) than anybody else in the conference.

• Turn out the Southwest Conference's first Heisman Trophy winner, Davey O'Brien, in '38.

• Become the first team in the conference to go the Sugar Bowl, Cotton Bowl, Orange Bowl and Bluebonnet Bowl.

• Never let more than three years slide by without producing either a championship or a bowl team.

• Maintain a winning edge over all six of their conference opponents. Let the record show that the Frogs were 19-11-1 against Rice, 18-10-1 against Baylor, 18-11-2 against Texas A&M, 16-10-5 against SMU, 15-12-2 against Arkansas and 16-5 against Texas.

I should add that nearly all of these Frogs were wonderful human beings and great Americans, and only rarely did any of them get taken into custody for trying to kidnap the Baylor Bear.

The most impressive part of this period was the first 10 years, or pretty much throughout the Depression, that I thought was so fun-filled.

It so happens that TCU was the best football team in America from 1929 through 1938 because the Frogs won more games (90) than any other major college. Well, O.K., if you want to be picky and figure it by percentages, the Frogs were the fourth-best team in the nation behind Alabama, Pitt and Fordham, but not bad, huh?

I would also point out that only Pitt, USC and Notre Dame were awarded more mythical national titles over this arbitrary decade, and only Tennessee fielded more undefeated elevens.

Good company in other words.

In the seasons of 1935 and 1938, it is safe to say, TCU football did more for civic pride and the Fort Worth dateline than Sally Rand's Nude Ranch at the Texas Centennial celebration.

Not until my first car date years later did I experience anything as thrilling as the Saturday afternoon of Nov. 30, 1935. It was the day TCU and SMU played a football game of such monumental dimensions that my dad took the precaution of bringing an extra flask of "cough medicine" to the stadium.

Two prizes of unbearable importance were at stake in the game: The national collegiate championship and a bid to the Rose Bowl. Neither prize had ever been earned by a Texas team. To the fans of the two neighboring cities, Fort Worth and Dallas, the game meant something more: bragging rights for all eternity.

My relatives and everyone else began playing the game ahead of time, for it was evident that TCU and SMU were so talent-laden they were bound to arrive at their colossal meeting with unblemished (10-0) records, which they did.

I was accustomed then to being dragged to TCU workouts, and it was always fun to watch Sam Baugh

The Frogs' win over Carnegie Tech in the 1939 Sugar Bowl was the crowning moment in Dutch's career.

spit tobacco and lie on the grass when he wasn't knocking somebody down with the football. And it was terrifying at first to hear Dutch Meyer growl.

Dutch was almost a cartoon character of a football coach, a tough little man in a baseball cap with a whistle around his neck. When he spoke the word "football" it sounded like a volcano erupting, and all the words that followed in a sentence came out like the scratching of cleats on a sheet of rusty tin.

At some point during the week of preparations for that SMU game, Dutch no doubt said, "FOOTBALL ... is a game played by MEN! Not a bunch of damn sissies and city slickers from Dallas!"

There was a moment that week when I went over and stood as close as I could to Sam Baugh and center Darrell Lester, the all-Americas, and another of my heroes, Jimmy Lawrence, a great all-purpose half-

back. They were relaxing on the sideline.

To the group I inquired, "How do you get to be a TCU water boy?"

I won't swear it was Sam Baugh, but a voice replied: "First you go over there and ask the trainer if he's got anything to cure lice."

What nobody had been totally prepared for on the day of the game was 40,000 frenzied people trying to fit themselves into TCU's 24,000 seat stadium. Many without tickets leaped over fences from the tops of automobiles and many drove their cars through the fences. Some paid scalpers $100 for a ticket — at the height of the Depression, the equivalent of $4,000 now — but these weren't the ones who trampled policemen, climbed over the backs of each other and spilled onto the playing field.

I recall seeing hordes of strangers in slouch hats

Dutch enjoys visiting with his two greatest players, Sammy Baugh (left) and Davey O'Brien.

down on the field posing for pictures with Dutch Meyer and Matty Bell, the SMU coach, before the kickoff. I was older and well into the life of a sportswriter covering other TCU teams when I learned that some of the people my dad called celebrities that day were Grantland Rice, Paul Gallico, Bill Stern, Bernie Bierman, Pappy Waldorf and assorted Hollywood and Broadway types.

The TCU-SMU game of 1935 has been called various things by various historians. It has been written about under such chapter headings as *The Greatest Game Ever Played. The Aerial Circus and The $80,000 Forward Pass.* I once had a junior high school teacher who gave it even more significance. She put it first in the order of importance on a list of the five most memorable events in a history of Fort Worth. To her, it ranked ahead of Vernon Castle, a famous dancer, getting killed in the crash of his training plane in World War I, ahead of the Texas & Pacific Railroad coming to town, ahead of Swift and Armour putting meatpacking plants in the city and ahead of Major Ripley Arnold opening a fort called "Worth" on a bluff above the Trinity River to protect settlers from the Indians

in 1849.

What I mostly remember about the game itself was the noise in the stadium, SMU running sweeps and reverses in a blur of red and blue uniforms and the Frogs continually dropping Sam Baugh's passes, although he kept hitting his receivers in the chest and hands. Sam threw an amazing 43 passes that day, which was unheard of among civilized people, according to Granny Rice's game report.

I remember Jimmy Lawrence catching one of those passes for a touchdown late in the game and then being carried off the field with an injury. My dad and others were very sad to see TCU lose Jimmy Lawrence, but they were very happy that the Frogs had finally fought back from a 14-0 deficit and tied the game at 14-14 after a whole afternoon of swirling action.

With about four minutes left to play and SMU lined up on fourth down in punt formation near TCU's 40-yard line, my dad was sipping his "cough medicine" with some relief. The Frogs had gained far more yardage than the Mustangs, and they now looked like the better team, and the Rose Bowl would surely select TCU in the case of a tie. In our section, everyone seemed to agree on this.

Everyone was still agreeing on it when the SMU punter, fullback Bob Finley, didn't punt. Instead he dropped back and hauled off and lofted a desperate 50-yard pass toward the TCU goal line. The next thing anyone noticed was SMU's speedy all-America halfback, Bobby (Will-o'-the-Wisp) Wilson, was racing down the sideline trying to get there before the football.

Sam Baugh, playing safety, struggled to get there from the other side of the field. At about the 3-yard, line Bobby Wilson leaped high into the air and twisted around for the ball was arriving on his "wrong" side. The Will-o'-the-Wisp made a miraculous catch and stumbled into the end zone. The Mustangs won, 20-14.

Hundreds of TCU fans, including my dad, sat limply in the stands for more than an hour after the game and drank their "cough medicine" and stared at the spot where Bobby Wilson came down with the football. Fort Worth's heart was broken.

The broken hearts took little consolation later in the fact that TCU was chosen as the No. 1 team after the bowl games by the Williamson System, the only one of the syndicated ranking systems of the day (the AP inaugurated its weekly top 10 in 1936) to publish a ranking after the bowl games. This was after SMU was upset by a mediocre Stanford team in Pasadena on the same day that TCU defeated the highly regarded LSU team in the Sugar Bowl. It would only mean something in the brochures.

Years after the tragedy, Dutch Meyer said to me, "FOOTBALL taught me a lesson in '35. I sent our lads out there like it was a crusade. They had tears in their eyes when they left the dressing room ... and it give 'em butterfingers."

I asked my dad recently what he remembered best about the TCU-SMU game, other than Bobby Wilson catching that pass. He said, "That's the sickest I've ever been in my life, including illness."

You would think that in 1938 Davey O'Brien and his mates would have cured all the illness. I'm sure they cured some. But the Frogs were so good behind little Davey's passing and running and ball-handling magic, they throttled everyone

with ease. They never had a real scare in their 10-game schedule and a Sugar Bowl victory over Carnegie Tech. There was no drama.

They received all of the most enviable No. 1's and O'Brien swept the Heisman, Maxwell and Camp awards as the Player of the Year. He weighed only 150 pounds and stood only 5-7, but he bounced off tacklers like a rubber ball, skittered between them and flipped 20-yard laterals like a fastdraw gunslinger. His long passes were long spirals and they seemed to be guided by destiny into the arms of Don Looney, Earl Clark and Johnny Hall. In the meantime, Ki Aldrich and I.B. Hale blocked everybody and tackled everybody.

The only suspense about 1938 was whether any of the Frogs or their rich and intimate fans would get drunk enough to fall off the stagecoaches they had hired to parade themselves around New York City when O'Brien went East to collect his awards.

Those of us who stayed home scampered to the picture show downtown to see the newsreel of O'Brien in his tuxedo when he accepted the Heisman and later in the mayor's office shook hands with Fiorello LaGuardia. We saw our immortals and their friends in the cowboy hats riding on the stagecoaches in the newsreel. I assumed from the small gathering of bewildered New Yorkers on the sidewalks that our grid heroes were receiving what the Star-Telegram called a "grand welcome by the Great White Way."

Nobody fell off the stagecoaches. Our nobility was confirmed.

So much for national championships.

Dutch Meyer never found another Sam Baugh or Davey O'Brien, and he almost didn't find the T formation until just before he retired. But Lord love him. In 1951, when everybody but Ethiopia and TCU had gone to the split T, Dutch swiped one last conference title with the old spread and triple wing. A marvelous tailback named Ray McKown would take a long snap and either throw the ball into the unknown or run about 25 yards and hope to get back to the line of scrimmage.

Even Dutch knew it was time for a change.

Meyer Built a Winner, but Missed the Roses

BY DICK MOORE
Fort Worth Star-Telegram

FT. WORTH, DEC. 4, 1982 — Because of the great football teams Dutch Meyer built at TCU in the 1930's, Fort Worth became a star on the nation's road maps instead of an insignificant red dot.

Meyer, who died early Friday morning in a Fort Worth hospital at the age of 84, gave to Fort Worth two national championship teams, a Heisman Trophy winner, a couple of Sugar Bowl championships, a victory in the first Cotton Bowl, a handful of all-Americans and two of the country's most prolific passers in Sammy Baugh and Davey O'Brien.

Breakfast for many was not complete without reading daily of Dutch and his Horned Frogs and their practices or games. Even on the team's three-day railroad trips to California to play Santa Clara or to New York to challenge Fordham, daily reports were filed from where the special train braked to allow the Frogs to work out.

But the most cherished sports prize of all in the 1930s, an invitation to the Rose Bowl, escaped Meyer and his Frogs. Not once but twice.

In 1935, the nation's eyes riveted on Fort Worth where unbeaten TCU and SMU collided with the winner getting a Rose Bowl bid.

Allison Danzig, a New York Times sports columnist, who was raised in Waco, said: "All my life, I had dreamed of covering the Harvard-Yale game. And there I was, covering the Harvard-Yale game, but longing to be in Fort Worth for the TCU-SMU game."

SMU won a thriller from the Baugh-led Frogs, 20-14, and the tears from the TCU fans would have flooded the Trinity River.

"I just laid my head down in the press box and cried," said the late J. Williard Ridings, who was the sports information director for the Frogs.

"I know Dutch always said it was his fault that we lost because he got us too tight," said fullback Tillie

Manton. "But we dropped enough passes in the first quarter to have beaten them by three touchdowns. The clock caught us with the ball on SMU's 20. It wasn't Dutch's fault we lost."

SMU went to the Rose Bowl and lost to Stanford, 7-0, and TCU went to the then-young Sugar Bowl and out-mudded LSU, 3-2, on Manton's field goal.

The Dallas papers snickered at the Frogs' bowl victory, which prompted the late Winston Croslin to draw a sports cartoon in The Fort Worth Star-Telegram of a Frog sitting on top of a bowl of sugar cubes and a Mustang nipping at some roses from outside of a bowl.

The caption was: "A little sugar is better than no roses at all."

Meyer's 1938 team finished far in front in the final Associated Press poll, with 65 of the 87 sportswriters picking the Frogs as No. 1 over Tennessee. TCU topped the Williamson rating while Rose Bowl host Southern California was ranked ninth.

O'Brien and center Ki Aldrich were unanimous all-America choices and tackle I.B. Hale was honored on most of the second teams.

But the Rose Bowl bid that Meyer and his Frogs expected never came. USC, apparently awed by TCU's offensive power, opted for Duke on the basis of not having its goal line crossed that season.

When O'Brien and Meyer went to New York early in December for Davey to accept the Heisman award, Dutch fired from the hip at USC.

"They took a team that scored less points in a season than we did in one game," he growled.

Sports editor Flem Hall of The Star-Telegram wrote in his column of Dec. 6: "It is just as well that TCU didn't get the Rose Bowl bid. Not getting it leaves the Frogs something else for which to shoot in future years."

It never came in future years. And Meyer became the reason that the University of Texas didn't go to the Rose Bowl in 1941 when his Frogs shocked the Longhorns at Memorial Stadium, 14-7 — the week the Longhorn starters had made the cover of Life magazine.

"He could convince you that you were gonna beat someone who was much better than you were," said Fred Taylor, a member of that team and later head coach of the Frogs. "Like that stunning upset of Texas'

unbeaten team in 1941. He did a better job of coaching than the other people did. We were ready and they weren't."

Meyer didn't just aim for Texas. He zeroed in on SMU's great teams of 1947 and 1948 with Doak Walker and Kyle Rote. SMU tied TCU in 1947 in Fort Worth, 19-19, after Walker missed an extra point that would have won the game and tied the Frogs again the following year in the Cotton Bowl with Walker getting the tying touchdown late in the game.

Jack Gallagher, the sports columnist for The Houston Post, was writing for The Austin American in 1948, and he said, "I'll never forget how frustrated Dutch was at Doak in that 7-7 game. Late in the game, Doak, who had been injured, came into the game.

"The quarterback faked to Doak and the whole TCU team went with Doak. The quarterback then threw a touchdown and Walker kicked the extra point.

"I turned my glasses on Dutch on the touchdown pass. He threw that Stetson hat that he always wore off and jumped up and down on it.

"Dutch was such an emotional guy ... so enthusiastic about everything whether it was football or baseball or what. He seemed to transmit his enthusiasm to players and even to the writers. I really liked dealing with him. I can still remember his tears in the dressing room. He was really emotional."

After Meyer gave up his head coaching position to assistant Abe Martin, he was still in much demand as a speaker. When TCU played Ohio State in 1961, he spoke to more than 500 members of the Quarterback Club in Columbus, Ohio.

He closed his talk with a favorite story about Baugh in a game with Tulsa in 1936. Meyer said the TCU players were up in arms when they felt Baugh had scored from the 1. Meyer said Sammy, sizing up the situation and not wanting to anger the referee, pulled him aside and told him: "You're absolutely right, sir. I didn't score."

Meyer told the group that on the next play, Baugh again dove into the line and the referee's hands immediately shot upwards.

"And Baugh hasn't scored to this day," the Dutchman roared in his gravel-throated voice.

That Quarterback Club crowd came surging to its feet in a roaring ovation to Meyer.

CHAPTER 27

Junior Joe Williams (left) and senior Hugh Pitts gave TCU a double knockout punch at center against Texas.

SWINK STAMPEDES FOR 4 SCORES, FROGS WIN, 47-20

BY FLEM HALL
Fort Worth Star-Telegram

AUSTIN, NOV. 12, 1955 — In a record-smashing, never-to-be-forgotten exhibition of offensive power, the Horned Frogs of Texas Christian University

TCU	6	14	0	27	47
Texas	0	7	7	6	20

snuffed out an estimated 40,000 red candles, killed a traditional hex and blew the University of Texas Longhorns out of both tub and bowl, 47-20, in a spectacular football game in Memorial Stadium Saturday afternoon.

Jimmy Swink and Charles Curtis collaborated on putting on the largest scoring circus any Southwest Conference team ever marshalled against the Longhorns.

Swink ran for 235 yards and scored four touch-

downs, in one of the most brilliant one-man shows in conference history.

Curtis threw three touchdown passes, all of them long ones and each figured prominently in breaking Texas' resistance. They canceled out the effect of the biggest scoring spree the Longhorns ever put into a losing effort.

All week, thousands of Longhorn supporters burned red candles to put the Frogs under the spell that reportedly enabled Texas teams of the past to overcome formidable foes. The Frogs made shambles of the myth and scrambled the tradition that had Texas students and players on an unprecedented emotional binge since Baylor was defeated here last week.

The victory was not as easy as you might suspect from the final score. Although the Frogs led most of the way, after scoring in the seventh minute of the first quarter, they were only six points ahead when the

Jim Swink was carried off the field by TCU fans following the Horned Frogs' 47-20 victory over Texas.

fourth quarter opened.

It was then that Curtis dropped two of his most devastating bombs — two touchdown passes within two minutes.

The progressive score went like this, with TCU first, 6-0, 6-7, 13-7, 20-7, 20-14, 26-14, 33-14, 33-20, 40-20 and 47-20.

Swink ran for 1, 62, 57 and 34 yards for his touchdowns as the Frogs scored in every quarter except the third, when they appeared to take things easy and bide their time until they got the wind advantage.

Curtis' touchdown passes to Ken Wineburg, Bryan Engram and O'Day Williams, in that order, carried for 27, 30 and 30 yards respectively and, added to the runs of the receivers, made scoring plays of 44, 37 and 42 yards.

The game was played before 57,000 — the largest and literally most colorful and noisy crowd of the year — in 80 degree temperature on a fast field that was whipped by a gusty 18 mph breeze out of the south.

This was the occasion for the 20th annual band day and in addition to the universities, there were 140 high school bands present. The estimated 10,000 uniformed boys and girls massed in the north end of the stadium, splashed the scene with a vivid assortment of colors. Generally, the music making was left to the Texas and TCU bands, but the high schoolers got together on one number and constantly added volume to tumultuous clanging.

The result left Texas leading, 27-13-1, in the series that started in 1897 but it broke a six-year Texas winning streak.

None of the seven TCU touchdowns was a gift. The Frogs had to travel 83, 74, 62, 46, 42, 65 and 34 yards for them and all on plays launched from scrimmage.

The Longhorns, on the other hand, had to go only 18 yards for their first score, 37 for the second and returned an intercepted pass 83 yards for the third.

Delano Womack, the Longhorns' leading ground gainer, scored the first Texas touchdown from the 2-yard line, Charley Brewer got the second on a 1-yard plunge and Curtis Reeves got the third after plucking a Curtis pass out of the hands of a would-be TCU receiver on the Texas 13. He sailed all the way straight south along the east sideline without ever being threatened by a tackler.

In addition to piling up statistics and records to a depth that flabbergasted the press box, Swink ran with an artistry that wrung shouting applause from even the most loyal Texas fans. His 62-yard run late in the second quarter cut back and forth across a large part of the field and left would-be tacklers strewn like dead indians in a Western shoot 'em up movie chase.

The play started as a pitchout to the left, but the 185-pound junior from Rusk was forced, after clearing the line of scrimmage, to cut back to the middle of the field, and almost every step of the last 50 yards was on a zig-zag course that wasn't helped substantially by the confused blocking. Swink changed pace, cut back, faked, and side-stepped empty-armed tacklers so much that he was running back of three Longhorns as the covey crossed the 15-yard line.

Those who have watched Swink in every game thought the run was one of the two most sensational he has ever made.

Jim Swink's stellar performance in 1955 and 1956 earned him a spot on the cover of Sports Illustrated.

Although the wind played an important part in the fourth-quarter, four-touchdown attack the Frogs used to smash records, the gusts didn't influence things much at the start.

The first time TCU got the ball, Ray Taylor fumbled it away when he was hit hard by Womack, but the second time the Frogs moved 83 yards on seven plays into the teeth of the wind to score. The big gainers were a 34-yard gallop by Swink and a 41-yard pass, Curtis to Williams to the Texas 2.

A fumble by Hal Pollard that Mickey Smith recovered on the TCU 18 set up the first Texas touchdown. Joe Clements passed to Pat Tolar for a first down on the 4. From there, Womack scored.

TCU struck back within two minutes, on three plays after the kickoff. Swink made 30 yards on two plays and then Curtis hit Ken Wineburg for the touchdown. Wineburg was loose back of the Texas right halfback and made a beautiful catch while trotting between the 10- and 15-yard lines.

It was less than three minutes later that Swink made his 62-yard run, on the first play from scrimmage after a Texas punt.

TCU had the choice of goals at the start of the second half and elected to fight the wind. It looked like a poor choice when a series of errors resulted in Texas getting the ball on the TCU 37 and scoring in five plays. That made the score, 20-14.

All through the third quarter it looked as if the Frogs were in danger, but when the goals were exchanged at the start of the fourth quarter, the picture changed completely.

It was on the very first play with the wind at that point that Curtis dropped another long spiral perfectly into the arms of Engram in the open for a touchdown.

Just two minutes later the Frogs scored again, and again on a long pass that cleared the Texas secondary. O'Day Williams took it on the other side of the field, back of the Longhorn left half, to show there wasn't any partiality.

Texas injected Reeves' interception and that steamed Swink up for his last two runs — both on handoffs — from Curtis that were so slick the Texas defense didn't know where the ball was until Swink was well on his way to the goal line.

SWC Choices Help '55 Team Dominate Hook, Line and Sinker

BY WHIT CANNING
Ft. Worth Star-Telegram

Turning back the clock precisely four decades, we discover two members of the Pitts family making a name for themselves.

In the autumn of 1955, Hugh Pitts, a senior center/linebacker at TCU, was in the process of becoming an all-American while helping the Horned Frogs win the Southwest Conference championship.

Down in Austin, meanwhile, cousin H.K. Pitts was becoming a famous inventor.

On the eve of that year's TCU-Texas game, H.K. managed to galvanize the entire student body with a nifty new hand signal he had introduced at a pep rally. It has been known ever since as the "Hook 'Em Horns" sign.

"Yeah, that's true," Hugh Pitts said, laughing. "Ol' H.K. was the guy who came up with that, although he had some problems with it afterward.

"He gave it to one of the cheerleaders, and they introduced it at the pep rally. Then after it got to be a real popular thing, I think the cheerleader kind of appropriated the credit.

"But H.K. got it all documented about how he actually thought of it. I think he has a copyright on it, or something like that."

A lot of good it did the Longhorns at the time. They were buried, 47-20, by one of the strongest teams in TCU history.

It became the most famous game in the illustrious career of Jim Swink, who ran through the Longhorns for 235 yards on 15 carries, including touchdown runs of 1, 62, 57 and 34 yards. On one of those runs, the TCU all-American proved so adroit that for a few yards, he had two Longhorns turned around and actually running interference for him.

But the day's events were a familiar story dur-

Jim Swink ran for 235 yards and four touchdowns against the Longhorns.

ing the '55 season, when Swink was the runner-up in voting for the Heisman Trophy after a season in which he ran 157 times for 1,238 yards (an 8.2 average) and scored 20 touchdowns and 125 points.

The Frogs finished the regular season 9-1 and were ranked fifth in the nation, with a 293-91 scoring margin against their opponents. They were ranked second in the nation behind Oklahoma in rushing offense (285.7) and eighth in total offense (353.1).

It was a team with four All-SWC selections — Swink, Pitts, end Bryan Engram and tackle Norman Hamilton — and the two all-Americans. For Pitts and the other seniors, who had come in as freshmen under Dutch Meyer, the season was a culmination of a slow growth process.

"Well, I was recruited (out of Woodville) by Allie White, and when I got here, we were still running the spread," said Pitts, now in the real estate business in Brenham. "The next year (1953), Abe Martin switched to the T-formation, and that was probably the best thing that ever happened to me.

"If we'd stayed with the spread, where you had to deep-snap on every play, I would've been a sunk duck.

"The next year, Swink and that group came to the varsity, and things started getting a little better. By '55, things were poppin'.'

"We could see ourselves getting better every week, and we developed a lot of confidence in what we were doing. We pretty much had no problem till we got to the Cotton Bowl."

In the Cotton Bowl, the Frogs lost Chuck Curtis, the SWC's leading passer, on the opening kickoff, and eventually fell to Mississippi, 14-13. They were also victimized by a holding penalty that wiped out a successful extra-point kick (they missed the second one).

"Yeah, I guess you could say we lost because Chuck couldn't follow instructions," Pitts said, laughing. "I remember sitting there before the game listening to Abe specifically tell Chuck that if they kicked it to him, he was supposed to lateral to Swink.

"Then he went out and tried to run it back, and they hit him and busted his ribs.

"But for me, the worst part about it was that I had to get right on a plane and fly to Hawaii for the Hula Bowl — and when I boarded the plane, there sat Eagle Day, the Ole Miss quarterback. I had to listen to him crow about it all the way to Hawaii."

After his career at TCU, Pitts became the No. 2 draft choice of the Los Angeles Rams.

"It was kind of a different world back then," he said. "I weighed 210 pounds and signed for $9,500."

CHAPTER 28

Jim Swink cuts upfield on his 37-yard touchdown run against Ole Miss in the 1956 Cotton Bowl.

OLE MISS SLIPS PAST FROGS, 14-13

BY FLEM HALL
Fort Worth Star-Telegram

DALLAS, JAN. 2, 1956 — The University of Mississippi Rebels, champions of the Southeastern Conference, spotted the TCU Horned Frogs, champions of the Southwest Conference, 13 points in the 20th annual Cotton Bowl football game before 75,500 spectators here this warm and sunny Monday afternoon, and then swung back to win by the margin of a single point, 14-13.

Ole Miss	0	7	0	7	14
TCU	7	6	0	0	13

The Frogs tried to play the game under too many handicaps — largely mistakes of their own making.

They actually lost the game for being in motion on a conversion effort. They made the 14th point on the first try, but, because a player was in motion, they had to try again from five yards farther back, and missed.

TCU was dealt a damaging blow on the opening kickoff when quarterback Chuck Curtis made the mistake of receiving and running with the ball. He was so badly injured when tackled that he never returned to action. That loss forced the Frogs to play a one-sided running game and robbed them of the deception that aided them tremendously all season.

Richard Finney, a junior who had not played a down all season with the first team, replaced Curtis and turned in a better job than could have reasonably been expected, but his best effort wasn't good enough. He threw three passes, completed only one and had two intercepted. The TCU running game had little of its

After trailing, 13-7, at halftime, Ole Miss dominated the second half, keeping TCU on defense.

usual deception and variety.

In spite of the handicap, the Frogs scored a touchdowns in the first and second to lead, 13-0, before the Rebels got their first touchdown to make it 13-7 at the half.

TCU dominated the third quarter but couldn't score.

Mississippi won the game in the 11th minute of the fourth quarter when Paige Cothren kicked the extra point after a touchdown that Billy Lott scored on a 5-yard gallop around his right wing.

The Rebs' winning move traveled exactly the same distance as their first touchdown parade: 66 yards.

The first whirl was a fast-striking, yard-eating series that required only four plays, with Cothren cutting

through the line for the last 3 yards.

The winning march was slower, but just as brilliant. It used 10 plays. Twice it looked as if the Frogs might have the attack beaten, but each time the Mississippians slipped away for the first down needed to stay alive.

The key play of the drive came against the TCU reserves. It was a fourth-down play. Six minutes remained to be played. Mississippi had the ball on the TCU 45 and 4 yards were needed for a first.

Quarterback Eagle Day rolled out to the left and dropped a short delayed pass into the hands of Cothren, who made 13 yards before being stopped on the TCU 31.

Coach Abe Martin hustled his first string back into action. A long pass missed and a blast at the line made only 2. With third and 8, the situation didn't appear to be bad, but on the next play Day went 25 yards to the 5. He started the play as a back-up pass, but when the TCU line dropped off he ran up the middle. Two linemen had open tackles at him, but missed. Swink got him on the 5, but that was just a temporary delaying action. On the first play from there Lott took a pitchout and out-ran the weary TCU defenders to the right hand corner at the north goal.

All of the Mississippi action on the vital try for point, from the snap to the holder, Day, to the kick by Cothren was quick, slick and perfect.

A little over four minutes remained to be played. The Frogs received the kickoff and made a first down, but a Finney pass was picked off by Rebel Eddie Crawford and TCU was dead.

Swink made both of TCU's touchdowns and was the biggest ground gainer on the field with 107 yards on 19 carries, but the all-America was given a bad time all afternoon by the alert and rough Rebel defense.

The Frogs went 44 and 75 yards for their touchdowns.

The key play in the first six-play drive was a brilliant 34-yard run by Ray Taylor to the Mississippi 1. Two other backs tried and failed to make the needed yard before Finney called on Swink, who drove over on a handoff that sent him inside the Rebel right tackle.

Harold Pollard kicked the point and it was 7-0 with 54 seconds left in the quarter.

Swink raced 39 yards around right end on a pitchout

for the second TCU touchdown in the seventh minute of the second quarter. Eight plays and a penalty had pushed the Frogs to the Mississippi 39.

Pollard's first kick was true, but it was canceled by some foul that wasn't visible from the press box. The referee signaled "illegal procedure" and after the game the Frogs said their line was in motion. Coach Martin said he didn't know what happened. Anyway, the point was canceled and the Frogs were penalized 5 yards. Although

rushed, Pollard got off the next kick, but the ball sailed wide. The seed for ultimate defeat was planted. Mississippi had one 59-yard run by Crawford across the TCU goal line called back by a foul. TCU suffered a similar loss when a 34-yard scamper by Finney to the Mississippi 8 was canceled by holding.

There were no successful goal-line stands, no near misses. TCU made two good moves in the third quarter but was thwarted both times.

Curtis' Absence Hurt, Says Vaught

By George Kellam
Fort Worth Star-Telegram

In the happy confusion of the Mississippi dressing room you got the impression that three things helped end Rebel coach Johnny Vaught's bowl drought — a missing TCU quarterback, physical condition and one point.

Ex-Frog star Vaught's 1953 and 1955 Rebel teams played and lost in the Sugar Bowl, so it was with much relish that Mississippi players and fans Monday afternoon shouted, "I knew we could do it — yea, Rebels!"

Coach Vaught is a practical man.

"Losing Chuck Curtis (the starting TCU quarterback) on the kickoff hurt 'em of course, but I thought that (Dick) Finney boy did a fine job. Frankly, he played much better than we thought he could.

"Curtis not being in the game hurt their passing attack more than anything, I think.

"I contribute our victory to a group of boys who were determined to get it and never let down, even when they were two touchdowns behind.

"Our physical condition was good. Though we played less than 22 men, I think, we were still hitting hard at the end. It was pretty hot out there.

Hotter than we're used to at this time of year. I think our physical condition had a lot to do with our victory. But I'll tell you, it all gets back to morale. You've got to have that. We did."

Vaught was carried part way off the field by some of his players. As they neared midfield, Vaught asked to be put down and ran over to grab the hand of dejected Abe Martin, TCU coach and a former Frog teammate of Vaught's.

They exchanged routine congratulations and started the battle through well-wishers to their respective dressing rooms.

Jim Swink, the TCU all-America halfback, broke through a mob of autograph hounds to shake Vaught's hand and congratulate the Ole Miss coach.

Vaught retaliated with flattery about the Frogs' play and Swink replied: "Thank you, sir, but we just didn't seem to be the same without him (Curtis)."

Dick Goehe, big No. 71 who put the tackle on Curtis on the opening kickoff and sent the Frog quarterback to the hospital, said: "It wasn't intentional. But we've had those kind run back on us before for touchdowns and I wasn't going to let it happen if I could stop it. Someone slowed him down and flipped his back toward me as I was coming in from the side. I really let him have it."

CHAPTER 29

Frogs Edged in 'The Hurricane Game'

BY WHIT CANNING
Fort Worth Star-Telegram

On game day, the report from College Station presented TCU fans with the cheery prospect of absolutely perfect showdown weather.

"A slight possibility of rain," it said, "but the turf will be firm and fast and the temperature will be in the 80s."

Given the subsequent reality, this would have been tantamount to a message on the bridge of the *Titanic* reporting a small patch of ice ahead.

It was Oct. 20, 1956, a day on which the rain fell — horizontally — the wind blew — up to 90 mph — and darkness descended shortly after noon. By that time, about half of a capacity crowd of 42,000 at Kyle Field had fled in terror.

But as the stadium light standards swayed like palm trees and small planes overturned at the nearby airport, two fierce adversaries remained locked in a struggle for supremacy that no one present has ever forgotten: a battle that became permanently etched in Southwest Conference lore as "The Hurricane Game."

Texas A&M 7, TCU 6. For the Aggies, a triumph of indomitable spirit. For TCU supporters, a heartache that has never gone away, kept alive by a disputed call that has burned in the collective mind for 40 years.

It was a game with an immense buildup, which had begun in the preseason, when it was projected as a possible battle for the national championship (provided someone managed to knock off Oklahoma) between two teams loaded with stars (five all-Americans) and the necessary dramatic contrasts.

There were the coaches — folksy Abe (The Jacksboro Philosopher) Martin and irascible Paul (Bear) Bryant, the commander of the famed march to Junction.

There were the halfbacks, TCU's Jim Swink and A&M's John David Crow. In 1955, Swink had scored 20 touchdowns and rushed for 1,283 yards with an 8.2-yard average in actually overshadowing the man who beat him out for the Heisman Trophy, Ohio State's Howard (Hopalong) Cassady. Crow, a line-buster and defensive demon, was destined to win the Heisman in '57.

There was the offense-defense matchup: TCU would finish the season ranked seventh in the nation in total offense (after ranking second in '55); A&M would rank eighth in total defense. There was the rematch angle: When the Frogs had rolled to a 9-1 regular season record and No. 5 national ranking in '55, their only loss was to the Bryant's Texas Aggies.

TCU arrived with a No. 4 national ranking after brushing aside three foes (Kansas, Arkansas and Alabama) by a combined 96-12 margin. In addition to all-America tackle Norman Hamilton, they possessed a wide array of offensive weapons, including Swink, Chuck Curtis, Ken Wineburg and Buddy Dike.

Jim Swink, TCU's all-America halfback.

The Aggies, with a wrecking crew defense led by Crow, Jack Pardee, Charlie Krueger, John Tracey, Dennis Goehring and Bobby Marks, were also unbeaten, but had dropped from ninth to 14th in the rankings after a tie with Houston (then in the Missouri Valley Conference).

The day dawned bright and sunny, as expected. Then it got a little weird.

"Strangest game I ever played in," says Curtis, who somehow managed to complete 9 of 19 passes for 101 yards. "The day started off real nice, with the sun shining and everything. Then it started raining. Then it started hailing. Then it got dark, the wind came up, and we had a tornado.

"During one stretch, we'd come up to the line and I'd be calling signals, but no one could hear them because of the hail bouncing off their helmets."

By that time, an odd pattern had developed that would prevail from the opening series to a point midway through the fourth quarter: relentless thrusts deep into A&M territory by the Frogs, and the Aggies somehow turning them away.

While the Frogs were launching a 73-yard drive early in the second quarter, the storm hit. By the time they reached the A&M 3-yard line, the rain was coming in sheets parallel to the ground, and, Swink once recalled, "You had to turn your head to breathe."

At that point, Swink took a handoff and sliced into the end zone, but TCU was offside and the play was called back. When the Frogs reached the 2 on fourth down, the Aggies recovered a Wineburg fumble.

Not that it was much help. Hamilton soon recovered a Roddy Osborne fumble at the 8, and thus launched the series that has been a point of controversy since.

With the ball on the 3 on third down, Swink once again seemed to score, but the officials said no, and placed the ball an inch from the goal line. When A&M jumped offside on the next snap, there was no room to mark off a penalty.

Swink dived into the stack again on fourth down and was stopped by Pardee, short of the goal line once again, according to the officials. It remains a goal-line stand for the ages.

It is also a sore point with the Frogs, who believe that Swink scored at least once, and maybe twice on the series.

"The third-down play was the one where he actually scored," Dike says. "I know, because I led the play and I was lying in the end zone and Swink was lying there with me, clutching my shirttail."

Vernon Uecker, who later blocked a punt to set up yet another scoring opportunity, also thinks Swink scored.

"He was past me, and I was lying on the goal line," Uecker says. "The official who was standing there moved his arm in the direction we were going, indicating Swink was across the goal.

"But the official who made the call came running from across the field, with rain splattering all over his glasses, and indicated no score.

"I know it sounds like sour grapes at this point, but it's true."

Curtis, however, figures he could have saved everyone the trouble if he had called an audible on the fourth-down play.

"That's the play I would love to have back," he says. "They were massed to stop Swink, and when we broke the huddle I was going to tell him I would fake the handoff and run a bootleg. But the wind was blowing so hard — howling — I was afraid he wouldn't hear me and would try to grab for it or something. So we ran Swink and they stopped it. If I had kept it, I could have walked into the end zone."

In the second half, the storm had passed, and the Aggies rose from certain doom to improbable victory, with an 80-yard drive that rolled down the field as quickly as the storm had an hour earlier.

Crow launched it with a 21-yard end sweep, and two plays later Watson swept the opposite flank for 37 yards to the TCU 20. But after the Aggies reached the 5, the drive bogged down.

Facing third-and-goal at the 8 after a loss, Osborne pitched to Watson, who began a sweep to his left. Suddenly, he straightened up and threw the only pass A&M tried all day — and with it came victory.

Crow caught it all alone in the end zone, and Loyd Taylor kicked the point that sent the stunned Frogs to defeat.

CHAPTER 30

In a duel of all-Americans, Jim Swink (23) catches a pass in the territory of the immortal Jim Brown.

FROGS NIP SYRACUSE, 28-27

By Lorin McMullen
Ft. Worth Star-Telegram

DALLAS, JAN. 1, 1957 — Harold Pollard's four-for-four conversions and the blocking of Syracuse's third point-after touchdown attempt by Narcico (Chico)

Syracuse	0	14	0	13	27
TCU	7	7	7	7	28

Mendoza produced a 28-27 Cotton Bowl victory for Texas Christian University Tuesday after 18 years of waiting.

The Frogs had dropped five successive bowl appearances and had not recorded a post-season triumph since 1939, when their national champions beat Carnegie Tech, 15-7, at New Orleans.

This one, played in ideal 65-degree weather before 68,000, unfurled under patterns precisely predicted. It was a moving offensive show all the way with the TCU passing game Syracuse couldn't stop and the Saltine Warriors riding powerfully on a running game spearheaded by all-American halfback Jim Brown.

Brown, Hamilton Honored

Brown gained 132 yards and was voted the game's outstanding back. The Frogs' all-America tackle, Norman Hamilton, was the one defender who came nearest to stopping Brown consistently and he was chosen as the game's outstanding lineman over Dick Lasse, the Syracuse end.

Runner-up to Brown was TCU's Charles (Chuck) Curtis, who completed 12 of 15 passes for 174 yards and two touchdowns and scored a third time on a 7-yard keeper.

Syracuse scored in the last two minutes to give the game its touch of such hair-breadth closeness.

For much of the afternoon it was TCU's game and a couple of time seemed on the verge of turning decisive. The Orangeman rallied for a 14-14 tie at the half and, after again falling two touchdowns behind in the fourth quarter, scored the last two times to pull close.

The Warriors' final touchdown came under weird circumstances. TCU had the ball and a 28-20 lead with less than two minutes to play.

Mendoza Preserves Victory

Jimmy Shofner punted out. Syracuse punched to the 28 in two plays and quarterback Chuck Zimmerman dropped back to pass. Halfback Jim Ridlon raced down to the goal line, where Shofner and O'Day Williams had him tightly covered.

But Zimmerman fired anyway and Ridlon, incredibly, leaped and made the catch between them. Brown kicked the extra point but the damage had been done earlier in the quarter when Mendoza swooped in to get his hands on the ball. There was no mishandling of the snap-back and no delay in Brown's kick. Mendoza simply blew in there and made the play he wanted.

TCU had an overall edge in yards gained, 335 yards to 298, but Syracuse posted first-down superiority of 16-15. The figure break-downs tell well the teams' strengths with Syracuse hammering out 235 yards on the ground to 133 by TCU.

But the Frogs connected on 13 of 16 passes for 202 yards and two touchdowns whereas Syracuse hit only 3 of seven passes for 63 yards and one touchdown.

Both teams were hurt by mistakes and injuries. Fumbles stopped two Syracuse drives and the Frogs took possession and surged 60 and 69 yards for touchdowns. A fumble by the TCU second team set up the Warriors for a 24-yard touchdown move in the second quarter.

The Frogs' line was butchered by a Friday practice injury suffered by right guard Vernon Uecker. He limped on the field but made the starting lineup — his 30th in a row for TCU — and played intermittently. He was handicapped and the Frogs' precision was not quite right when he wasn't in there.

TCU halfback Jim Shofner leaps to make the catch for the Horned Frogs' second touchdown against Syracuse.

TCU's Net Bowl Take Expected to Reach $70,000

Texas Christian and Syracuse each will receive between $135,000 and $142,000 for playing in the Cotton Bowl Tuesday.

Howard Grubbs, secretary of the Cotton Bowl, said paid attendance was something more than 60,000 and total attendance was about 68,000 for the game in which TCU beat Syracuse, 28-27.

Texas Christian will keep $60,000 of its share and will distribute the remainder among other members of the Southwest Conference, with TCU also sharing in the distribution. This means that TCU will get more than $70,000.

Syracuse, which is not a member of a conference and does not have to share its bowl receipts, will keep the entire amount.

Announcement of the attendance and receipts was made at the awards dinner Tuesday night when TCU received the trophy for winning the Cotton Bowl game, for the second time.

Syracuse also lost its right halfback, Jim Ridlon, for much of the third quarter.

It's late in the story to be making the first mention of Jim Swink, who played a fine all-around ball game, gained 41 yards on 12 carries, was the game's leading pass receiver with four catches for 60 yards and several times demonstrated his remarkable ability for getting open.

Brown was the victim in the most impressive of these maneuvers, a 30-yard gainer that set up TCU's fourth touchdown and the Pollard conversion that proved the winning move.

The Frogs were on the Syracuse 45 where Swink went out on the left flank, raced down, cut across to his right, faked Brown away and took the pass in the clear and went on to the 15 where he was knocked out of bounds.

Brown retaliated once by faking Swink aside on an end sweep.

TCU's touchdowns were scored on runs of 70, 35,

60 and 69 yards. Syracuse connected on drives of 70, 24, 49 and 44 yards.

TCU's scoring came in this order: a 6-yard pass from Curtis to John Nikkel, an 8-yard pass from Curtis to Shofner, a 7-yard keeper by Curtis and a 3-yard plunge by Swink.

Syracuse's touchdowns came on plunges of 2, 4 and 1 yards and the final was made on the aforementioned 28-yard Zimmerman to Ridlon pass.

There was a unique twist to the first-half scoring in that each team intercepted passes and then drove 70 yards to score and each recovered fumbles and pushed out short yardage for second touchdowns.

In the last half two fumble recoveries set up both TCU goal marches but the Frogs had to go 60 and 69 yards. Syracuse's two second-half scores came after receiving kicks and making advances of 49 and 44 yards.

The game got out of hand insofar as Coach Abe Martin's plans were concerned for his second unit. The Dick Finney team, which had saved TCU honor by beating SMU, almost lost this contest after providing one thrilling high spot.

With the score, 14-7, for TCU in the second quarter, the second unit took over, gained on four straight plays and then uncorked a flashy screen-pass deal from Finney to little Carlos Vacek, who took off down the left sideline, butted Brown out of bounds to keep going at one juncture and stretched it into a 28-yard gainer.

On the next play, however, Ted Warholak jolted Finney as he attempted to pitch out and recovered the fumble. Syracuse went on to tie the game at 14-14.

The regulars, aided by Vernon Hallbeck and Jim Ozee, played all of the fourth quarter and the predominately senior team finished out its collegiate careers as it so desperately wished on a winning note.

At the outset, the Frogs required three possessions to find the scoring combination. The play that put them under way was a 37-yard pass at the right side to O'Day Williams from Curtis. Then he threw to Swink for 16 yards and on the next play, Buddy Dike ripped through the middle for 17.

Dike again hit for one yard to the 6 and there Curtis picked Nikkel, one of three open receivers, for the touchdown pass.

At end of the first quarter the TCU seconds recovered a fumble and the regulars took over at the start of the second quarter and moved the 35 yards in six plays.

A 14-yard Curtis pass to Nikkel moved up to the 14, Dike punched out 2 and on second down from the 8, Curtis passed to Shofner in the end zone.

Syracuse's first score was a Brown show. The 220-pounder tore off 24 yards at the outset and added runs of 6, 5 and 18 yards. At the 2 he plunged over and made the first of his three conversions.

When the Orangemen recovered the fumble on the 24, Brown passed to Ridlon for 20 yards and scored from 4 yards out on a right side sweeper.

The 14-14 tie stood well into the third quarter, thanks to a TCU fumble recovery by Dan Cooper after Dike jolted Brown loose from the ball. The Frogs then went 60 yards to regain their lead. The outstanding plays were a 10-yard Curtis pass to O'Day

Williams, a 15-yard run by Curtis, a 6-yard screen pass play to Ken Wineburg and a 7-yard run to the goal line by Curtis.

Chuck appeared to roll out to the left for a pass but when he saw daylight he hot-footed to the corner for the TD.

Two runs by Swink for 19 yards helped launch the final scoring drive — the big play of which was the 30 yards gained on the Curtis-Swink pass. Dike then hammered 12 yards to the 3 and Swink lugged it over right tackle.

Brown made 28 of the 49 yards Syracuse advanced on a series of short gainers to its third touchdown, carried over by Brown from the 1. It was here that Mendoza contributed his all-important block of Brown's conversion.

Syracuse's final TD was made on the long Zimmerman to Ridlon pass.

TCU's backfield in the 1957 Cotton Bowl: (left to right) Chuck Curtis, Jim Swink, Buddy Dike and Ken Wineburg.

CHAPTER 31

Swink Ruled the Southwest

By Whit Canning
Fort Worth Star-Telegram

It was becoming a warm afternoon in Austin, and it occurred to TCU linemen Don Cooper and Vernon Uecker that a brief rest period would be beneficial.

So, instead of rising to follow the play in progress, they simply stayed put on the grass of Memorial Stadium and watched the show.

Unfolding for their viewing pleasure was the signature performance of one of the greatest running backs in college football history — Jim Swink.

It was Nov. 12, 1955 — and at that moment, Swink seemed to be leading about half of Travis County on a merry chase resulting in a touchdown run covering 62 yards and about eight city blocks.

It was a glittering moment in a glittering season in which Swink — a junior halfback at TCU — became renowned from coast-to-coast as an offensive weapon of seismic stature.

During the regular season, Swink scored 20 touchdowns, carried 157 times for 1,283 yards — an 8.2 average — and led the Frogs to a 9-1 record, a Southwest Conference championship, a No. 5 national ranking and a berth in the Cotton Bowl.

He also became a consensus all-American and finished second in the voting for the Heisman Trophy to Ohio State halfback Howard (Hopalong) Cassady.

A senior winding up a legendary career, Cassady had nowhere near the year Swink did, but was probably penciled in on most Heisman ballots at the beginning of the season after leading the Buckeyes to the national championship the previous year.

Suffice to say that when the Frogs arrived in Miami for a game at midseason, they were greeted by huge ads that read: "Come to the Orange Bowl Friday night and see All-American halfback Jim Swink, probable winner of the Heisman Trophy!"

An elusive, courageous runner with amazing balance and timing, Swink exasperated virtually every defense he faced in '55. Finally, TCU coach Abe Martin was pressured for an official scientific explanation.

"Aw, he's just a little ol' rubber-legged outfit nobody can tackle," said Abe.

Late in the season, Baylor coach George Sauer was asked to compare two teams that had defeated his Bears: TCU and Maryland — then the top-ranked team in the nation, en route to a 10-0 regular season finish (the Terps finally lost to eventual national champion Oklahoma in the Orange Bowl).

"Maryland," Sauer said simply, "does not have Jim Swink."

That TCU had him was the result of a rather odd circumstance: he was recruited on the advice of Allie White, who had never seen him play football.

"Well, we knew

An outstanding 1955 season made Jim Swink a cover boy in 1956.

Swink and TCU quarterback Chuck Curtis combined to score seven touchdowns against Texas in 1955.

about his high school football career at Rusk, but we just hadn't seen him play because he had been injured some," White says. "But I finally got down there to see him in a basketball game (Swink was the MVP in the high school all-star basketball game that summer), and on the basis of the way he moved on the court, I told Abe we ought to get him."

Swink first achieved notice in 1954, on a team laden with sophomore talent that finished 4-6 — with tremendous promise for the future. TCU had twin 20-7 victories over Southern Cal's Rose Bowl squad and a Penn State team led by Lenny Moore — and played an Oklahoma team then in the midst of a historic 47-game winning streak nearly off its feet before losing, 21-16. Swink finished with six TDs and 670 yards on 99 carries.

"I guess the first time we all realized just how good he really was," says Buddy Dike, TCU's star fullback during that era, "was when we were playing USC out there in the Coliseum. Jim made one run of about 30 or 40 yards where he broke six tackles, and it was just amazing."

Early in the '55 season opener against Kansas, Swink ripped off a record-tying 80-yard TD run, and the Frogs — with talented Chuck Curtis at the controls, two all-American linemen (Hugh Pitts, Norman Hamilton), a bevy of skilled runners and a superb end in Bryan Engram — were off on a run to glory.

By midseason, it was evident that TCU's left halfback had begun to amaze even his own companions, as evidenced by a comment from halfback Ken Wineburg: "We've all tried to imitate him, but none of us can throw a tackler off balance with that quick little side step the way he can. Where we stop and change direction, he makes one quick feint and goes on without changing speed."

By the time TCU played Baylor, the team's confidence in Swink bordered on cockiness.

"At one point," Uecker recalls, "we were on our 1-yard line, with about third-and-25, and Ray Taylor came in from the sideline and told Curtis, 'Abe says punt.'

"So Curtis asks him, 'Did he say when?' — and Taylor says no. So Curtis gives the ball to Swink, and he makes the first down. A couple of plays later he gives it to him again, and he goes 65 for a touchdown. In three plays, we moved 99 yards and scored."

Popular among TCU alums and students, Swink speaks at a pep rally 1957.

Acknowledging that Swink was equally devastating on the sweep (particularly with Engram clearing a path) or a simple quick hitter, Sauer said, "We didn't devise any special defense to contain him — because he's just as dangerous going up the middle as he is going around end. I don't think it's his speed so much as his balance — he's never off balance. And he's deceptively powerful."

"Every time his number was called," Uecker says, "we were told to block all across the line — because you never knew which way he would turn."

This fact became painfully evident to the Texas Longhorns two weeks later, when they entertained the Frogs in what was billed as the battle for the Cotton Bowl. In honor of the occasion, Texas supporters initiated their now famous "Hook 'em" sign and revived an ancient "hex" by burning thousands of red candles.

In response, the Frogs nearly burned the town. Curtis threw three long touchdown passes — and was completely overshadowed by Swink, who ran 15 times for 235 yards and had scoring runs of 1, 34, 57 and 62 yards. TCU scored four times in the fourth quarter and the Longhorns were demolished, 47-20.

The day's keynote event was the 62-yard sortie on which Swink swept left behind Engram's block, zigged back to the right, zagged back left, and eventually left his own blockers — Cooper and Uecker — lying on the turf.

"We decided to just stay there," Uecker says, laughing. "We couldn't keep up with him, anyway."

No matter. In the day's most amazing maneuver, Swink had picked up two new blockers — both wearing orange. Nearing the Texas 15, he had turned two defenders around to the point that, briefly, they were out in front, running interference for him.

One of them was all-American Herb Gray, who later said of Swink, "He's just the greatest I've ever played against."

Another convert emerged two weeks later, when TCU concluded the season with a victory over SMU.

"All year long, I never believed all that stuff I'd been hearing about Swink," said Mustang quarterback John Roach. "Now I know that every word of it's true."

In the Cotton Bowl game against Ole Miss, the Frogs' hopes crashed on the opening kickoff, when Curtis — ignoring Martin's instructions — tried to run the kick back and was carted off with a couple of broken ribs. With TCU's air attack gone, the Rebels stacked eight men on the line and eventually won, 14-13.

But they still could not completely contain Swink — who rushed for 107 yards and scored twice, once on a trademark zig-zag 39-yard run.

With every defense keying on Swink in '56, TCU and its star halfback enjoyed reduced success, as the Frogs finished second in the SWC and 7-3 overall.

Still, Swink led the conference in rushing (665 yards) and accumulated over 1,000 yards in tandem offense.

And with SWC champ Texas A&M on probation, the Frogs returned to the Cotton Bowl and defeated Syracuse's Jim Brown-led Eastern champions, 28-27.

Always an outstanding student, Swink successfully pursued a medical degree, and is now a prominent orthopedic surgeon in Fort Worth. He was inducted into the Texas Sports Hall of Fame in 1977 and the National Football Foundation Hall of Fame in 1980. In 1982, he was selected an NCAA Silver Anniversary honoree for his combined achievements in athletics and professional life, and was an inductee into GTE's Academic Hall of Fame in 1989.

Swink was given the Swede Nelson Award for sportsmanship by the Gridiron Club of Boston in 1957.

CHAPTER 32

HORNED FROGS SHOCK OHIO STATE, 18-14

BY FLEM HALL
Fort Worth Star-Telegram

COLUMBUS, OHIO, SEPT. 28, 1957 — Without the benefit of a completed pass, the Horned Frogs of TCU invaded this capital of power football and earned a startling 18-14 victory over the Buckeyes of Ohio State University this cool, clear Saturday afternoon before 81,734 unbelieving spectators.

TCU	6	6	6	0	18
Ohio State	7	7	0	0	14

The white-clad Christians scored a touchdown in each of the first three quarters.

The scarlet Buckeyes counted in the first and second quarters and led, 14-12, at the half.

TCU went ahead in the third minute of the third quarter and then valiantly fought off every fierce thrust of an opponent that expected to win by two or three touchdowns, a team that had been hailed as one of Coach Woody Hayes' most promising creations and one that is considered a good bet to win the championship of the Big Ten.

Lead Swaps Hands

The lead changed hands five times as the progressive score mounted in this manner (with TCU first) 6-0, 6-7, 12-7, 12-14 and 18-14.

Marvin Lasater, a sophomore who only moved into the starting lineup this week, dashed eight yards for the first Frog score.

Jimmy Shofner, the shining senior, returned a punt 90 yards for the second touchdown.

Jack Spikes, another sophomore who moved from halfback to fullback this week, ripped 16 yards through the middle for what proved to be the winning touchdown.

The Frogs used 15 plays on their 58-yard move after the opening kickoff to take the lead.

Shofner's dazzling sprint up the sideline for the second touchdown came on the first play of the second quarter.

The winner came relatively cheaply — on five plays from the 31 after Chico Mendoza recovered a fumble by OSU's fullback, Galen Cisco.

Ohio State had to move the ball 77 and 68 yards for its touchdowns and the actual scoring was done by 1- and 2-yard thrusts by Dick Lebeau and Don Clark.

The Bucks had their opportunities to win the game with modest moves, but could not cash them.

Fresh Team Comes In

Once in the third quarter they recovered a TCU fumble on the Frog 19, and made a first down on the 8. They pushed to the 5 before being thrown back to the 18, where the ball went to TCU on downs.

Again in the fourth period, Ohio State made a first down on the Frog 20 only to fall.

The latter situation was the most dramatic of the thrill-splashed afternoon. With two minutes and 40 seconds to play, the fiercely rallying Bucks had charged over the tiring TCU starters 50 yards to the Frog 33. There John Groom, the stalwart senior guard, was disabled and brought a delay that caused Coach Abe Martin to make a momentum decision.

He took out all of his first stringers and sent in the fresh second team that had done well briefly on two previous occasions.

It cost TCU 5 yards for delay of game to put reenforcement in the game and the Bucks whacked them for 5 more the first play.

But that was all.

With first and 10 from the 21, Clark took a lateral from the quarterback and tried to get off a pass but he was rushed backward by hard-charging TCU linemen and finally hit so hard by Don Floyd and Bill Roach that he was knocked loose from the ball.

Jim Shofner, an All-SWC halfback in 1957, returned a punt 90 yards for a touchdown against Ohio State.

TCU was the toast of the town after defeating the Buckeyes, who would be national champions in 1957.

Dale Walker recovered on the 28 and with only two minutes and nine seconds left to play, the game was practically over.

It was, for sure, when on third down Carlos Vacek squirted through the line and raced 14 yards for a first down. Only seconds remained on the clock and the Frogs kept moving, making 20 yards in the process.

Shofner made two great open field tackles that stopped the fast, brilliant running Clark when it looked as if he was gone for long runs.

Merlin Priddy, a sophomore fullback playing in his first game, made an equally fine tackle on the same runner, who is one of the better ball carriers in the Big Ten.

Mendoza and Cecil Carter, a third string guard, also made outstanding defensive plays that were highly important in containing the Buck attack.

From the first play, when Spikes lashed 5 yards off left tackle, until the last down, the Frogs challenged the Bucks on the ground and finally beat them by being more consistent in the second half.

There was nothing fancy or unusual about the TCU attack. It was the same split-T hitting at all the positions from end to end. But the flawless selection of quarterback Dick Finney and the excellence of the execution by Spikes, Lasater and Shofner behind the relentless blocking of Ken Miller, John Mitchell, Joe Robb, Jim Ozee and a dozen other linemen kept the Bucks rocked back on their heels.

Only three passes were thrown. The first one was open for a touchdown, but Finney's pitch was sour and wild. The second one, short and covered, was dropped by Lasater. The third one was intercepted by a brilliant piece of defensive work.

It was fourth down and 3 on the Buck 8, when Lasater took a handoff from Finney and behind good interference, hit inside left end for the first score.

Spikes' extra-point attempt was partly blocked, but appeared to have been too low anyway.

Ohio took the next kickoff and reversed the parade. The Bucks went further (77 yards) on fewer plays — 12. They killed the Frogs' defense with sweeps that got outside the cornerbacks, but from the 3-yard line they had to use three plays to score, with LeBeau making the last yard at left end. Don Sutherin converted the point-after kick.

The Frogs couldn't move the second time they had the ball and had to punt.

Carter made his fine play to halt the Bucks on their move.

Then, with fourth and 5 coming up, the quarter ended.

The Frogs deployed into their special punt return formation on the sure kicking down. Sutherin punted short and low. The ball hit between Spikes and Lasater and bounded into the waiting hands of Shofner.

Lasater blocked out the first Buck. Shofner ran inside another one and then cut sharply to the west sideline. The rolling wall of Frog blockers held off all except one Buck, Aurelius Thomas, but Shofner avoided all except a hand on the leg. It staggered him on the Frog 40, but he kept his balance and sprinted on across the goal line where he collapsed momentarily from exhaustion and elation.

Again the try for point with Finney holding and Spikes kicking was no good.

Ohio State raged back to the attack, continuing to rip the Frogs' five- and six-man line defenses at the wings. It looked as if the drive was stopped on the 19, but with third and 7 Frank Kemblas tossed a come-

back, or a button hook, pass to Leo Brown for a first on the 5 and from there LeBeau and Clark made it in on two plays. Sutherin kicked the extra point.

The half closed, 14-12.

During the intermission, Coach Martin changed his defense by putting the ends on the line and so wide that the sweeps were ineffective.

Thereafter the Bucks made more yards inside, but practically none outside.

There were three swift turns at the beginning of the third quarter.

Ohio State was penalized back to the 1-yard line for clipping after receiving the kickoff. The Bucks broke out of the hole with a 14-yard gainer and TCU was penalized another 15.

Then on the next play, Cisco fumbled and Mendoza made the recovery that set up the winning score.

Shofner made one yard. Lasater 4, Spikes two, and Shofner eight to a first on the 16.

From there on first down, Spikes went all the way on his own. He started at right guard, saw daylight to his left, cut sharply and drove hard. He was hit two or three times in the first eight yards, but shook off the blows and rumbled on across the goal.

It made no difference that his third place kick was also low.

Jack Spikes (20) stretches for extra yardage after being tripped up by an Air Force defender.

FROGS, AIR FORCE PLAY TO 0-0 DEADLOCK

BY JIM TRINKLE
Fort Worth Star-Telegram

DALLAS, JAN. 1, 1959 — Texas and Colorado cemented interstate relations but little was done to captivate 75,504 spectators as their two Cotton Bowl antagonists — TCU and Air Force Academy — struggled to a scoreless stalemate Thursday.

Air Force	0	0	0	0	0
TCU	0	0	0	0	0

The gentleman operating the scoreboard had the easiest occupation in all the land as the Southwest Conference champions and the future generals from Colorado Springs played the second 0-0 deadlock in the 23-year history of the New Year's Day classic.

Texas Governor Price Daniel wasn't among those in attendance but there is a notion that he and Colorado's chief executive, Steve McNichols, would have been but faintly aroused at the proceedings. There was no reason for fans from either state to feel any enmity.

It was the fourth tie game ever unreeled before a Cotton Bowl assemblage. Besides the scoreless conflict played by Arkansas and Louisiana State in 1947, there were ties between the University of Texas and Randolph Field, 7-7 in 1944, and the 13-13 tie between SMU and Penn State in 1948.

Statistically, there was but a hair breadth between the two clubs. The Horned Frogs amassed 227 yards in total offense while the Air Force Academy passed and ran for 231.

It was a disappointing final for both schools. The Frogs took the field bearing an 8-2 record. The Falcons were unbeaten in 10 games, including a tie with Iowa.

The Frogs fumbled the ball on eight occasions and lost three of these wasted possessions. One of these came early in the final period and sorely tried the composure of Coach Abe Martin as he saw the Falcons reclaim a bobble just eight steps from the Air Academy's end zone.

Another time, with the ball resting on Air Force's 15, quarterback Hunter Enis lost the ball. Teammate Bubba Meyer embraced it for a 6-yard loss and Jack Spikes' field goal attempt was far short.

The field, covered by a tarpaulin during the snowfall earlier in the week, was damp and contributed to the uneasy handling of the ball. The visiting Falcons also had difficulty retaining the ball and lost control on three of their five fumbles.

The defensive performances were outstanding. So fiercely did the men up front stand their ground in the shadow of their goal, five field goals were attempted. Veteran press box observers could not recall another game where the kicking tee received so much attention.

For the Frog defenders, strong exhibitions were given by all-America tackle Don Floyd, Sherrill Headrick, David McSpadden, Ramon Armstrong and Dale Walker.

The Air Academy's angriest lineman was not all-American Brock Strom. That honor went to tackle Dave Phillips, who beat out Headrick as the game's best lineman.

Jack Spikes, TCU's all-conference fullback, ran away with backfield laurels, cornering 42 of the 48 votes cast, with Rich Mayo, the Air Force quarterback, placing his name on three ballots.

Spikes attempted both of TCU's field goals, the first ear-

ly in the opening period when Armstrong recovered a fumble on the Falcon 23. After three plays lost to the 27, Spikes swung his foot into the ball as it was placed on the 35. The attempt was low.

The Airmen offered their severest threat midway through the second quarter when fullback Steve Galios, Mayo, Mike Quinlan and Phil Lane moved the ball 52 yards. Finally, it rested on the 8-yard line.

It was here that the Frog line gave its best performance, restraining the Silver and Blue on the 6, from where George Pupich missed a field goal to the left. It was a 13-yard effort.

Pupich Misses Kick

TCU chose to kick to start the second half and at first the decision seemed a bad one. The Falcons worked the ball to TCU's 12, when an offsides penalty came to the Frogs' assistance. Mayo missed on a third-down jump pass so Coach Ben Martin again sent Pupich into the fray for a field goal. This one missed to the other side.

Later in the same period, he tried one from the 35 and Marvin Lasater fielded it in the end zone. Lasater returned it to the 21 but a clipping penalty set TCU back on its 6-yard line.

It was on this series that the Frogs came close to besmirching the Falcon record. With Spikes and Marshall Harris

Don Floyd, an all-America tackle in 1958 and 1959.

151

doing their best running of the day, the Purple punched 86 yards to the Air Force 8.

After Spikes had ripped over guard for 17 yards and Harris added five more steps, the Frogs worked a double reverse from their 28. Harris came around to take the ball from Enis then handed off to Lasater. The San Angelo junior fled toward the east sidelines, stopped and threw deep to Meyer.

Meyer Misses Opportunity

Meyer, standing all alone, took the ball on the 40. The Sweetwater end might have won a foot race had he gone straight for the goal but he elected to cut back to his left, retreating a few paces. Meyer fumbled and end Jimmy Gilmore recovered on the 35 for a 37-yard gain.

Two carries by Harris put the ball on the 28, and again Spikes knifed through tackle for a 14-yard gainer to the 14. Enis gave the next assignment to Spikes and the 195-pound Snyder athlete pounded to the 8-yard line.

A Frog fumble on the next play, however, halted TCU's drive and gave Air Force possession deep in its territory.

But the Falcons couldn't move and punted to the 50, where the Frogs launched their last charge. Behind Joe Robb and Meyer, who were laying down vicious blocks, Spikes carried five straight times to the 16. Enis, fading to pass, slipped to the turf for a 6-yard deficit on the next play. Spikes recovered the loss with 2 yards to spare. Another fumble, recovered by Meyer, put the ball back on the 21 with fourth down. Spikes' field goal missed.

Spikes Gains 108

Spikes gained 108 yards on 17 carries, more than twice as much as his nearest challenger, Galios, who got 52 yards. Harry Moreland, carrying only three times, got 35 yards, one a 32-yard dash in the first quarter. Moreland might have gone all the way, too, except for a fumble as he bolted down the east sidelines.

He recovered but three plays later another fumble gave the Flyers possession.

TCU Nets $76,500

Texas Christian and Air Force Academy each will get a check for approximately $175,000 for playing in the Cotton Bowl.

Air Force will be able to keep all of its take except that it will pay some $80,000 of the amount as expenses. Coach Ben Martin said it cost $40,000 to bring the Cadet Corp here and another $40,000 to bring the remainder of the Air Force contingent. Thus, Air Force will end up with about $95,000 clear money.

Texas Christian will get about $76,500 out of the game. Under rules of the Southwest Conference, which sponsors the Cotton Bowl game, TCU will be permitted to keep $60,000 and share in the remainder along with the other conference schools. Each school will get about $16,500 except that Texas Tech, the eighth member of the conference, does not participate in bowl receipts because it has not started playing for a football championship.

Abe Martin (left) and Air Force coach Ben Martin posed with the Cotton Bowl trophy.

CHAPTER 34

High Cotton

BY WHIT CANNING
Fort Worth Star-Telegram

Sometimes, Hunter Enis sees Bubba Meyer in his dreams.

Or actually, dream. It's always the same one. It is New Year's Day 1959, and TCU is playing Air Force in the Cotton Bowl.

There is Meyer, wide open in the end zone. Here is Enis, the TCU quarterback, preparing to throw the touchdown pass. Then he slips and falls.

"It happened twice," said Enis, an oil company executive in Fort Worth. "Periodically, down through the years, I have dreamed about it.

"The night before the game, we had one of those freak snowfalls. The sun melted the snow the next day, although it was still cold. But there were still some slick patches on the field, and I had trouble all day getting my footing.

"If I could have just thrown that pass."

If Enis could have hit Meyer in the end zone, TCU's last adventure in the Cotton Bowl would have ended in victory, instead of a scoreless tie. Of course, no one at the time would have dreamed that the Horned Frogs would never return to Dallas as Southwest Conference champions.

It was a program riding high — a juggernaut in an era of one-platoon football where everybody played both ways and a small private school could be a big-

time power. During a five-year span from 1955-59, TCU had three SWC champions, three top-10 finishes and four bowl teams.

And in 1957, a 5-4-1 TCU team rolled into Columbus and knocked off Ohio State — which subsequently flattened the rest of its schedule, winning the Rose Bowl and a split national title (one poll picked the Buckeyes, the other picked unbeaten Auburn).

"Those people up there were the greatest football fans I ever saw," said Enis, then a junior and the alternate quarterback. "They had a 90,000-seat stadium, and when we got there about 10:30 in the morning, it was already half full.

"Jimmy Shofner had a 90-yard punt return, and when we went in leading at halftime, those people stood up and cheered us. They cheered us again at the end of the game, after we'd beaten their team (18-14)."

Sent in to run out the clock late in the game, Enis trotted into the huddle and announced that he was going to throw the ball.

"Shofner almost fainted," Enis said. "He said, 'You're gonna take the snap and pitch back to me, and that's all the throwing you're going to do, understand?'"

Enis got his chance the next year, when the Frogs (8-2) rolled to the Cotton Bowl, scarcely breaking a sweat. They lost early to Iowa's Rose Bowl champions and dropped the season finale to SMU after they had clinched the SWC title.

Everyone else was ground underfoot by

a team boasting five All-SWC selections: center Dale Walker, guard Sherrill Headrick, backs Marvin Lasater and Jack Spikes, and tackle Don Floyd (a two-time all-American). This did not include a spirited sopho-more named Bob Lilly, who as a senior would become the school's sixth all-American in six years.

As part of its success, the team always followed certain set rituals.

Before each game, Walker always threw up the green medicine he had been given to keep him from throwing up. Trusting defense, the Frogs always kicked off after winning the toss. After the opening kickoff, Headrick always called time out to rest.

Once, while pursuing an opposing running back, several Frogs players suddenly thought they detected the strains of the William Tell Overture.

They turned to discover Headrick, cheerfully hum-ming a little Lone Ranger music to himself while duti-fully chasing down the ball carrier.

"That's what I remember about that team," Enis said. "We had so much talent, and we had come up through such a successful program, that we simply never considered defeat. There was no one we didn't think we could beat."

"But mainly, we just had so much fun playing."

"Before every game, Sherrill would come over and give me a pep talk, to bolster my confidence. He'd say, 'Relax, we got this game won — unless you mess it up. And when you're looking for a receiver, remember — we're wearing purple.' "

During the '58 season, Enis directed TCU's

last Cotton Bowl team (the '59 tri-champions went to the Bluebonnet), the last victory against Arkansas for 22 years and the last victory against Texas in Amon Carter Stadium until 1992.

"I never would have believed it," Enis said. "The next time we beat Texas at home, I was sitting in the stands with my granddaughter."

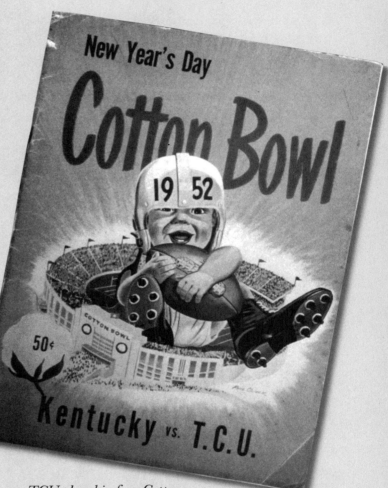

TCU played in four Cotton Bowls during the 1950's.

CHAPTER 35

Members of '59 TCU Team Recall Their Trip to 1st Bluebonnet Bowl

BY WHIT CANNING
Fort Worth Star-Telegram

FT. WORTH, DEC. 30, 1984—As the TCU Horned Frogs prepare to trot smartly into the Astrodome on New Year's Eve for their first major bowl appearance in a quarter of a century, memories appear. ...

Clemson	0	3	0	20	23
TCU	0	7	0	0	7

It was 25 years ago this month that another Purple band made the journey to Houston to inaugurate the bowl that has since moved from Rice Stadium into the Astrodome and survived a brief, ill-conceived name change to emerge, eventually, as a popular, growing concern.

But when it all began back in 1959, no one envisioned the ultimate appearance of a domed stadium in Houston (or anywhere else), or schizoid monikers like "Astro-Bluebonnet." No one then, in fact, deduced that in a few years the upstart University of Houston would supplant venerable Rice as the city's premier football power.

And no one, certainly, realized TCU, which in that era was one of college football's most consistent winners — a school that glittered with all-Americans — was about to fall dormant for 2½ decades.

No, when the founders of the fledgling Bluebonnet Bowl invited the Frogs down to play Clemson as a wrap-up to the '59 campaign, they were essentially trying to establish another major Texas bowl to complement and rival the Cotton.

There were also other differences. Today, TCU teams jet through the air to road games in gleaming silver birds, but for some members of that '59 team, the major memory is of a nearly interminable train ride.

"God, I'll never forget going down there on that goofy train," says Arve Martin, the team's starting center. "I think coach (Abe) Martin arranged that because he thought it would be fun, but it seemed like we were

Buddy Iles, an All-SWC end in 1960 and 1961, was one of the finest receivers in TCU history.

Harry Moreland sparked TCU's win over Texas in 1959.

on that thing for 20 hours."

Martin's view is shared by Paul Peebles, a starting end on the '59 team.

"I would guess," says Peebles, "that that train ride dominates our memories of the trip."

Another dominant memory is of the game itself, in which the Frogs played badly and lost, 23-7, when the Tigers exploded for three fourth-quarter touchdowns.

TCU lost two of its first three games in 1959 before winning seven straight heading into the Bluebonnet Bowl.

"We had a helluva team, but we were sputtering offensively," Peebles said of the early part of the season. "But there was just a special feeling with that man at quarterback. We felt no one could stop us."

"I remember Coach Martin called a meeting and said we were sputtering and asked us if we had any suggestions," says Martin. "Most of us were seniors and we loved Jackie. He was an individualist and a bit of a cut-up, but he was also the smartest quarterback we ever had out there, except maybe Hunter Enis.

"So we told Coach Martin, 'Why don't you start Jackie Sledge?' "

He did, and the team rolled through the rest of the year unbeaten, the climax coming in Austin when second-string halfback Harry Moreland raced 56 yards to cap a 14-9 win over previously unbeaten Texas.

"Moreland's speed gave us an extra weapon," says Peebles. "I remember when we ran sweeps my job was to block down on my man and clear a path, but nobody else on that squad was very fast. The first time Harry came around my end, though, I said, 'Well, well, what have we got here?' "

It was a talented team, and tracing the 25 years that have passed since, two dominant characteristics emerge — the amazingly high percentage of personal success most of them have enjoyed ... and how closely in touch they have remained through all the years. Martin and Peebles see most of their old teammates regularly.

"We were just such a close group of guys," says Martin. "We had a lot of love for each other."

The major tragedy concerns Floyd, who went on to play several years for the Oilers and earn All-Pro honors. Several years ago, still in his early forties, he collapsed and died of a heart attack.

The rest, however, are alive and definitely doing well.

Lilly, of course, became a Dallas Cowboy immortal. He now lives in Las Cruces, N.M., and is mainly doing television commercials at the moment.

Spikes, who also starred for several years in the pros, lives in Dallas and is in commercial real estate. Martin also lives in Dallas and owns his own insurance firm. Peebles is a Fort Worth attorney.

Sledge is with Texas Instruments and, rounding out the starting backfield, Marshall Harris runs a local mortgage company and Marvin Lasater, after several years as a Frog assistant coach, is in the insurance business locally, as is Moreland.

Jimmy Gilmore, the other end, is in the plumbing business in Enis and guard Ramon Armstrong is also in Enis, managing the large family farm.

"Ramon was the guy we all wanted to run with at TCU," laughs Martin. "He always had a new car."

Roy Lee Rambo, the other guard, is in business in Fort Worth and George has a Miller Lite distributorship in Amarillo.

Horned Frog coach Abe Martin poses with his all-America tackle Bob Lilly.

In the one-platoon era, the distinction between first and second teams was minimal, since both played quite a bit, and several non-starters who played prominent roles have wound up with highly visible careers.

Merlin Priddy, who played behind Spikes, has been the head coach at Arlington Heights for several years. Max Pierce, who played behind Priddy, is the base commander at Carswell Air Force Base. Substitute tackle Bobby Prince is a Texas Ranger.

"We were all close," says Martin, "and next to my daddy, I loved Coach Martin more than any man I ever knew."

"He gave me some idea of what a man of character was supposed to be," says Peebles.

"We had a great team, and I think if we'd gone with Jackie Sledge from the beginning, we could've really been something. If we had played Arkansas later in the year we would have certainly beaten them, and we might have been able to beat LSU, too. When we went down and played that one, they sent their famous Chinese Bandits out there and we ran 'em off the field."

That game hinged, among other things, on a fourth-down play at the Tiger goal in which Priddy, for the only time in his career, was stopped cold.

"It wasn't Merlin's fault, it was ours," says Peebles. "We didn't block the way we should have. He was a helluva football player."

Most, also, have continued to support the Frogs through the long lean years and are elated with the team's current success. For 10 years, Martin has been dragging a purple-and-white golf bag across Dallas fairways.

"Now," he laughs, "I've got a purple blazer too. It says, 'Unbeleeevable!' on it."

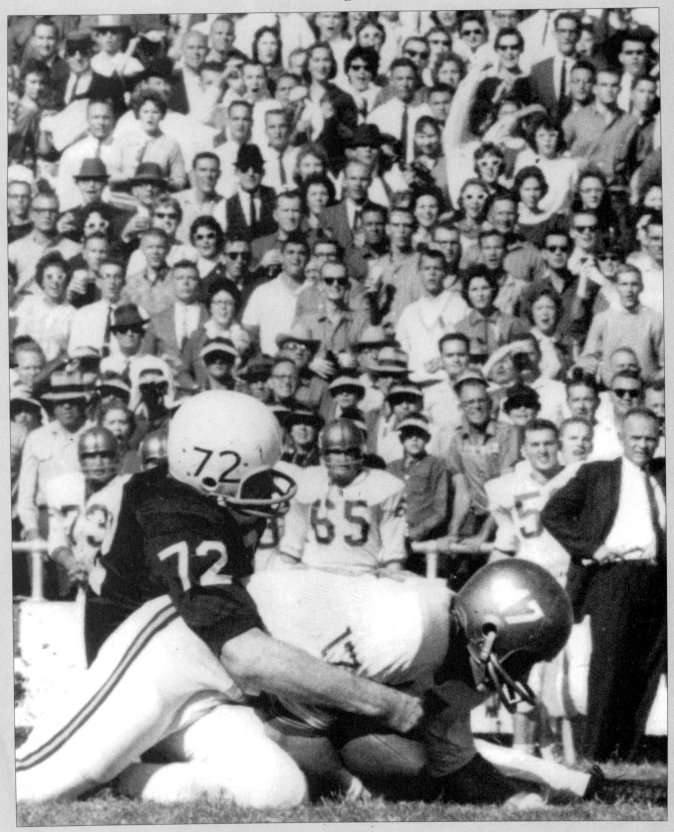

CHAPTER 36

Bob Lilly — college football's greatest defensive tackle — sacks a Baylor quarterback.

Bob Lilly: Nobody Got Past This Frog

BY WHIT CANNING
Fort Worth Star-Telegram

In early September, 1958, the *Fort Worth Star-Telegram* ran a photo of a TCU tackle, dressed in his workout uniform and smiling brightly at the camera.

Cradled aloft in his right arm, legs dangling a few feet above the ground, was 170-pound halfback Harry Moreland. Gripped in similar fashion on the left side was 165-pounder Carlos Vacek.

The young man grinning at the camera was Bob Lilly – a 225-pound sophomore from Throckmorton who became a topic of much conversation before he ever played a down of varsity football for the Horned Frogs.

A few days later, an article in the paper suggested that "he may be the finest sophomore lineman TCU has ever had."

As time would prove, Lilly was much more than that.

In his sophomore year, he became a starter on the last TCU team to reach the Cotton Bowl.

As a junior, he was an All-Southwest Conference selection on an 8-2 team that finished the season ranked seventh in the nation.

As a 6-foot-5, 255-pound senior, he became a consensus all-American and the first player ever drafted by the Dallas Cowboys.

For the next 14 years, he was a superstar in the National Football League, playing in 11 Pro Bowl games and two Super Bowls. As the signature member of the famed "Doomsday Defense," he helped lead the Cowboys to the NFL title in 1971.

He became the first player selected for the Cow-

Lilly played in the College All-Star Game prior to joining the Dallas Cowboys.

boys' "Ring of Honor" and, in 1980, was inducted into the Pro Football Hall of Fame.

"Well," he says, laughing, "I have to admit, it's a whole lot more than I ever figured on, back there when I was growing up in Throckmorton."

It was a saga that nearly ended before it began: by the time Lilly was a senior in high school, he was in Pendleton, Oregon.

"We moved up there because of the drought," he says. "It started in 1951 and lasted seven years, and by the time it was over a whole lot of farmers and ranchers were broke. There were about 1,200 people left in Throckmorton, and we just couldn't make it."

But he had been spotted a year earlier by TCU assistant Allie White, who managed to track him down. Lilly still has the two letters he received from White, offering a scholarship that included "room and board, free use of books and $10 a month laundry money to come and play football and keep good conduct and fair grades."

There was never a doubt in Lilly's mind about accepting.

"A few years earlier, Sam Baugh had come to speak at the high school (Throckmorton), and my dad took me up there to see him," Lilly says. "Ol' Sam turned a wastebasket upside down and put it on a desk and then sat on it, chewing on a cigar he never lit, and talked to us for hours.

"I had already known about TCU because of Pete Stout, who was from Throckmorton, but Sam kind of clinched me being a Frog fan. Besides, TCU went to the Cotton Bowl my last two years in high school, and it just seemed like a great place to go."

Among the major highlights of the following 18

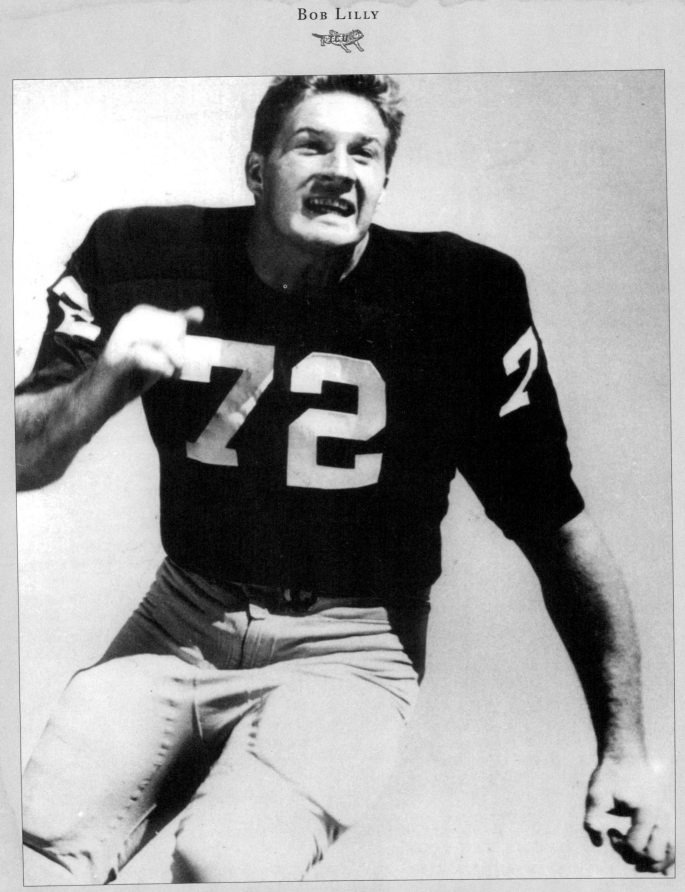

Lilly was a consensus all-America tackle in 1960.

years, he says, were his relationships with Abe Martin and Tom Landry.

"When I was a freshman at TCU, I was 1,700 miles away from my parents and my dad had a heart attack," Lilly says. "He eventually recovered – and moved back to Texas – but for awhile, he was incapacitated. It was pretty rough on everyone.

"Abe just took me under his wing – like I was one of his own kids – and became like a second father to me. I was treated that way throughout my college career, and I am very, very thankful that I chose TCU – because all the coaches were nice people.

"It was also just a treat playing for Tom Landry. He's a fine man, and he and Abe Martin were a lot alike – two gentlemen, good for their word, who had tremendous character and integrity. I learned a lot from both of them about how to live my life."

Martin was also equipped with an endless supply of pithy descriptions of people and events, such as the one he once used to describe Lilly: "Just a big ol' green pea, but he'll stand in there for you like a picket fence."

More like a concrete bridge abutment. With All-American Don Floyd at the other tackle, TCU's '59 team finished the year ranked 4th nationally in scoring defense, 5th in rushing defense and 9th in total defense.

By that time Lilly – known for a time as the "Purple Cloud" after landing on an unfortunate quarterback in an end zone that had been dusted with purple chalk – was becoming renowned for his size and strength, prompting the memorable line from More-

land: "If I was that big, I'd charge people $10 a day just to live."

In addition to halfbacks, he occasionally lifted automobiles up by the rear end. Fortified by a childhood spent baling hay, he first performed this feat – to help a motorist without a jack fix a flat – when he was a freshman in high school.

"But," he says, "it was just a little ol' Renault."

On a field of ice in Green Bay on Dec. 31, 1967, this legendary strength helped turn one of the most famous plays in NFL history in the opposite direction.

"We talked about it in the huddle," says Jerry Kramer, who became a Green Bay immortal with his block on Jethro Pugh, allowing Bart Starr to score the winning touchdown in the "Ice Bowl" NFL championship game. "We felt that with a double team, we could move Jethro out of there – but nothing was going to move Lilly. So we ran right."

A little over four years later (Jan. 16, 1972), Lilly won a Super Bowl ring when the Cowboys beat Miami, 24-3. His induction into the Hall of Fame eight years later, he says, "is probably the ultimate honor – to be enshrined with all those legends."

Now, he and his wife, Ann, live in Graham – where he pursues a variety of business interests and maintains a fairly hectic schedule.

"Looking back over everything that's happened in my life," he says, "its all just way beyond anything I could have comprehended years ago.

"But at the same time, I really still tend to think of myself as just a kid from Throckmorton."

CHAPTER 37

Texas coach Darrell Royal watches from the sidelines as the TCU defense stops the Longhorns.

FROGS SHOCK LONGHORNS, 6-0

BY BILL VAN FLEET
Fort Worth Star-Telegram

AUSTIN, NOV. 18, 1961 — Those surprising Horned Frogs have done it again!

Saturday they pulled the football season's greatest upset by winning a game in which no one gave them a chance. They struck the No. 1 Texas Longhorns with a 50-yard scoring pass six minutes into the second quarter, and then threw up a raging defense that protected a 6-0 lead until the end.

TCU	0	6	0	0	6
Texas	0	0	0	0	0

Guy (Sonny) Gibbs, the giant Frog quarterback, threw the long deep pass. Buddy Iles, the senior end, was behind the Longhorns' Jerry Cook and he made the catch at the 8. He barely made it into the end zone.

Texas end Tommy Lucas blocked the extra-point attempt. No more points were to go on the scoreboard on this cloudy, cool day.

The result stunned the 50,000 fans — Longhorns and Frogs alike — for this Texas team had been averaging five touchdowns all season and was firmly entrenched as the top team in the nation.

Now Texas faces a comeback battle Thursday in the traditional game with the Aggies at College Station if it is to share a title tie with Arkansas and gain the host role in the Cotton Bowl.

Arkansas and the Longhorns are tied with 5-1 records. The Razorbacks have one game left, too, but will be heavily favored over Texas Tech at Little Rock next Saturday.

Texas had its chances. The Longhorns moved all the way to the TCU 1-yard line on their first possession, where fullback Tom Crutcher tackled Jack Collins as the Longhorn senior sought to drive into the end zone.

Texas' Missed Opportunities

The Frogs forced Texas to kick from the TCU 29 later in the period, and once more before the period ended they were at the TCU 7, from where a field goal try was muffed.

Once more just before the half, Eldon Moritz tried a field goal from the 31 but this one was short.

Twice more in the second half the Longhorns were stopped. Once on a fourth down try at the TCU 27, Jerry Cook was stopped for no gain and in the fourth period the charging Frogs snuffed out the final Texas threat at the TCU 10.

The Frogs crashed and hooked their ends all day, and it played havoc with Texas' ball handing and attempted passing.

The Longhorn offense, which had been averaging more than 400 yards through the first eight victorious games was held to 198 yards Saturday, with only 138 steps on the ground.

Buddy Iles, Tom Magoffin, Bobby Plummer, Bill Phillips, Ray Pinion, Don Jackson, Robert Mangum, Don Smith, Bernard Bartek and others along that relentless front wall gave Texas quarterback Mike Cotten a bad time.

They didn't stop James Saxton, the skinny halfback who sped for 85 yards on 17 carries, but Saxton alone was not enough to overcome the Frog defensive efforts. No one else was effective.

Knocked Out

The 165-pounder was twice knocked unconscious and forced from the game, once after making a 45-yard run with a short pass in the first period, but he was in the game at the finish trying in vain for the one big play that would pull things out.

Texas' depth was supposed to be a decisive factor, but the Longhorns were pressed so relentlessly that Abe Martin and Darrell Royal wound up using the same number of men — 29 each.

Martin kept his top men in the game most of the time. He would rest them occasionally, but when Texas would move into TCU territory, he would call the regulars from the bench and send them into the game.

At the finish, these same starters were able to control the ball for nearly all of the fourth period.

With the clock grinding away, the Frogs ran plays in the final quarter with Texas having possession for only eight. On one time consuming possession, TCU used up over six minutes while moving from its own

But Abe Already Had UT's Number

WBAP newsman Jim Thomas called from Fort Worth to the TCU dressing room to interview Frog coach Abe Martin after TCU's victory over Texas Saturday afternoon.

A tired voice answered the telephone.

"I'd like to speak to Abe Martin," Thomas said.

There was a 30-second pause.

"This is the Texas dressing room," the unidentified Longhorn answered. "I don't think any of the boys feel like going next door to get him."

"Oh," Thomas said, and hung up.

10 to the Texas 45.

This upset must go down with the great ones scored by the Frogs against the Orange and White.

Just two years ago TCU broke an eight-game Texas winning streak, 14-9, and cost the Longhorns an outright SWC title.

The Other Upsets

Twenty years ago the Frogs on this same gridiron were the first to beat the great 1941 Longhorns, 14-7. In 1946, a Bobby Layne Texas team was upset by 14-0.

But none of those could be sweeter than this one for Frog partisans.

The Longhorns were practically untested. They had scored at least four touchdowns in every other game, and they were so firmly entrenched as the nation's No. 1 team after beating Baylor that they drew 41 of the 47 votes for the top position.

The Frogs were not supposed to have a chance. But they played as they did earlier this season against Kansas and Ohio State — and things went right for them.

Guessed Right

They did not lose a fumble, apparently did not break a signal, and the two interceptions against them, both by Duke Carlisle, did not prove costly.

On defense, they guessed right — and pressed through for the big play — all day.

When the Frogs scored their touchdown, Texas was

left trailing in a game for the first time this season. The Longhorns never caught up.

The game's initial minutes followed form, and it appeared the Longhorns would sweep to a quick score. But in those same beginning minutes, the Frogs may have won their battle.

The Frogs received the opening kickoff and on the first play from scrimmage, Gibbs threw a long pass from his own 24. Two Longhorns and Iles were there, and Carlisle came up with the ball at the Texas 35.

Saxton broke for 16 yards to the TCU 49, and then got another yard to the Frog 48.

Here the TCU defensive strategy became clear as Iles crashed in, and threw Cotten for a 7-yard loss back to the Texas 45 on an attempted pass.

Cotten, however, flipped a quick pass to Saxton, who went slashing down the sidelines for 45 yards to the TCU 10. There Donnie Smith hit him and almost knocked him down. As the squirming halfback tried to regain his balance and keep going, Plummer hit him heavily and the Longhorn was out cold.

Hit by Crutcher

He was revived and started to leave the field and collapsed again. He finally came out under his own power, and was to prove dangerous the rest of the way, although he later said he could remember little about the game.

From the 10, Saxton's substitute, Jerry Cook, rammed for 2 yards and Cotten then kept for 4 more. Cotten kept again and reached the TCU 3.

The Longhorns then tried the run-pass option by Collins. Although Bob Moses was open, Collins chose to run when he saw daylight. The daylight wasn't there long, for Crutcher met him at the 1.

This stand was like a bucket of gasoline on the Frog fire.

They came right back to stop the Longhorns on the big play of the next possession. Texas was at the TCU 31 and it was third down with 3 to go. Cook was stopped by Ben Nix as he tried a sweep, and it was fourth down, still with 3 to go.

Texas chose to kick at this young stage of the game, and Collins' punt rolled in the end zone.

Before the quarter was over Texas started another move from the TCU 36. Cotten set up a first down at the 8 with a 12-yard pass to Moses, and two smashes, by Tommy Ford and Cook, reached the 3.

Cotten rolled out to his right on an option play and here came Magoffin and Jim Fox charging through to toss him down at the 7 for a 4-yard loss.

Eldon Moritz came in to try a field goal, with the ball spotted at the 4, but Magoffin came charging in and Carlisle never got it set up for the kick try. Moritz booted it anyway, and the Frogs recovered at the 12.

In one of the greatest plays ever in TCU history, Sonny Gibbs hands off to Larry Thomas, then gets it back and ...

The wind, which was blowing from the south at the start of the game, changed to the north just before Gibbs threw his tremendous strike — which meant he was throwing into what must have been about a 7 mph breeze.

Great Catch

The Frogs had started from their own 20, and a pass and six running plays and a 10-yard pass had put the ball on the 50.

Gibbs handed the ball to Larry Thomas, then took it back and retreated. Iles meantime was speeding downfield, and had gained a step on Cook. He leaped at the 8, made a great catch, and fell across the goal in Cook's grasp.

Tommy Lucas blocked Jimmy McAteer's point try.

Texas started a long move from its 28 just before the intermission and set up a first down at the TCU 21.

The Frog first stringers had returned as the drive reached the 32, and on the first play from the 21, Iles rushed in and threw Cotten for a 9-yard loss. A 5-yard dash by Saxton and a dropped pass by Moses left the ball on the 25 with 51 seconds left.

Moritz' field goal try was far short.

The next Texas chance came midway in the third but with fourth and 1 at the TCU 27, Bill Phillips stopped Cook for no gain and the ball went over on downs.

The Frogs started a move from there, but Carlisle intercepted a pass at the Texas 38, and the Longhorns made their final move of the day.

Saxton once more made the big-play, a 22-yard burst on a trap that carried to the TCU 36 before Roy Dent got him.

At the TCU 28, Saxton had to ask quarterback Cotten for a repeat on the signals, then jumped back into his tailback spot, where he sped to a 13-yard gain to the 15.

Collins ran for no gain as the quarter ended, but on the first play of the last period, dashed for seven to the TCU 8.

Fortune Frowns

Here both good and bad fortune came to Texas. Saxton started to this left and had reached the 5, where it would have been a first down, when he dropped the ball. It rolled back and Don Talbert beat a pair of scurrying Frogs to it.

But on fourth down, Cotten tried to roll to his left once more and Crutcher and Donny Smith swarmed him back on the 10 — and the last Longhorn hope died.

The Frogs had one more great performance coming, however.

They started a steady, clock-using drive from that point, making three first downs — two of them on big third down plays.

Gibbs flings it downfield to Buddy Iles, who catches it at the 6 and carries it in for a TD.

Chapter 38

Cool Coach of the Horned Frogs

By Gene Gregston
The Saturday Evening Post
October 6, 1962

Among the high-geared young smoothies in big-time college football, 53-year-old Abe Martin, the homespun coach of Texas Christian University, seems like a country hick trying to beat a carnival man and his shell game. Just when you're feeling sorry for the hick, though, you find that he's outslickered the con man.

Abe Martin has developed some championship teams at TCU, but he is most notable as a giant killer. Last year, in his first losing season since 1954, his Horned Frogs won only three and tied two of their 10 games. One of the ties, however, came at Ohio State, the No. 1 team at the end of the 1961 season, and one of the victories — also on the road — was over the No. 1 team at the time, Texas.

This unpredictability is disconcerting, even to TCU fans. Polly Riley, Fort Worth's well-known amateur golfer, spoke for many after last year's Texas upset when she complained, "What I can't understand is how we can beat teams like Texas and lose to teams like Texas Tech. TCU seems to get ready for certain games and ignores the others."

Neutral Texans — perhaps a mere figure of speech where football is concerned — were disappointed that TCU had cost the Texas Longhorns their chance to give the state its first national championship team since 1939. And Longhorn rooters bitterly charged that TCU guard Bobby Plummer had deliberately smashed his knee into the head of Jimmy Saxton, Texas' all-America halfback, after a play had ended, thus forcing Saxton to the sidelines for most of the day. Game movies subsequently failed to establish conclusively whether this action was either illegal or intentional.

Abe Martin, who is sometimes called "the Jacksboro Philosopher" — after the West Texas town near which he grew up — sighs and says, "It was the greatest victory of my career, but I guess people would have been happier if we'd lost. I've never won a game that made so many people mad."

Honest Abe — another of his nicknames — always has a few minutes to spare for any visitor to his office. Martin sits back, a down-to-earth guy in a rumpled suit, the stub of a cigar in his mouth, his hat pulled over his forehead, his eyes peering over spectacles pushed down on his nose and his feet propped unceremoniously upon the desk.

From that relaxed conversational posture he dispenses commentary and dry humor in a soft, slow voice. "Shucks," he'll say, "this game of football ain't worth it if you don't have fun doing it. And it's hard to have fun if you're losing. That's why I'm glad to see us win once in a while."

He'll disclaim credit for a victory — "There ain't any geniuses in coaching." Or he'll observe about a losing streak, "We're just like the man who is having an oil well drilled. Everything is going fine, except that he isn't getting any oil yet."

Abe Martin is one of the lowest-salaried coaches in the Southwest Conference (about $14,500 a year). He has the smallest staff of assistants. His school has never been called on the carpet by the infractions committee of the National Collegiate Athletic Association for violations of the player-recruiting regulations. Whereas many coaches today frankly declare that their job is to win games, Martin still preaches, "You bet I'm building character, I don't see how you can find any grounds for having football if that isn't its purpose."

Victory Over the Strongest

Yet this coach with the old-fashioned ways has kept

Abe Martin played for TCU in 1928-30.

right up with the competition. In the past nine years he has led TCU to three conference titles and four bowl games, with an overall record for the period of 52 wins, 36 losses and 6 ties. These figures are the more impressive because, in addition to its tough league schedule, TCU makes a practice of booking for nonconference dates the strongest opponents it can find in other parts of the country. In 34 intersectional games through 1961, Martin's boys won 22, lost 9 and tied 3.

To cynical outsiders the Abe Martin story sometimes sounds too good to be true, but men who see him a lot insist that he's the real thing. "Some writers think Martin will con you," says Flem Hall, the veteran sports editor for The Fort Worth Star-Telegram. "But I've spent days with him in business and recreation, and he's always the same. If he's conning us, he's the greatest actor we've ever had."

Martin's solid coaching record over the years is no mystery to some of his colleagues. "Abe knows football and he's a fine handler of kids," says respected Jess Neely of Rice, senior coach in the conference. "He gets fine scouting and makes the best use of scouting material. He recruits big, strong boys, and he gets most of those he goes after."

Alabama's Bear Bryant, who coached for a while at Texas A&M testifies, "If there's any doubt about what a great coach Abe is, just play him a couple of times and you'll find out."

Martin depreciates his reputation as an upset artist. He contends that TCU played to normal expectations in most of last year's games, including the five losing ones. He admits that his boys outdid themselves against Texas, Ohio State and also Kansas, a highly regarded team the Horned Frogs squeezed past in their opener, 17-16.

He explains, "To begin with, our 1961 football team was real young and inexperienced. Only six seniors played much. These kids would get real high for people who looked like they'd eat us alive. They'd run scared.

"It's not all easy. Gosh dang, this football is tough. Texas didn't look at us as a real formidable opponent last year. But it can go the other way too. In 1955 (when TCU seemed headed for an unbeaten season) Texas A&M didn't have as good a football team as we

Abe visits with Bear Bryant (right) of Texas A&M.

Schmidt, then regained it as a senior. It was Schmidt who began calling him "Abe"; the coach got the idea from the syndicated newspaper feature, Abe Martin says.

The Influence of Tragedy

After finishing up his football at TCU, it took Martin another couple of years, sandwiched around odd jobs, to get his degree. He went into coaching as an assistant to his friend Mike Brumbelow at El Paso High School, succeeding him as head coach in 1934.

Soon afterward Abe Martin experienced the first of two tragedies that were to influence his lifelong attitude toward boys and football. In a game between El Paso and Phoenix, one of the Arizona players got a broken neck and died. Three years later, when Martin was head coach at Lufkin High in East Texas, he watched one of his own players bleed to death from a ruptured spleen.

"I seriously thought about quitting coaching," Martin says now. "But, there are so many other activities where a boy can get killed that aren't as worthwhile as football, I decided to stay with it.

"I guess when I started coaching I believed in playing football to punish. But since these accidents I've always been against what people now refer to as hardnose football, or piling-on and gang pursuit. Kids should be aggressive, but you should never play football to hurt."

In 1943 Martin's wife, Sally, persuaded him to try other work. He joined an oil firm in West Texas, but quit after a year and returned to high-school coaching. He says, "I learned that I'm not as interested in oil, oil companies or money as I am in people, particularly kids."

Through 1945 Martin's record as a high-school coach was 95 victories, 14 defeats and 1 tie. His teams took 9 district championships. In 1946 he switched to college football as assistant to Dutch Meyer, who had become head coach at TCU When Meyer quit after 1952 to work full time as athletic director, Abe Martin replaced him.

Meyer's last team had broken even. The Horned Frogs didn't do that well in Martin's first two years. They lost 13 of 20 games while he was in the process of junking his predecessor's famous spread and double-wing formations and converting to the T. But his

did. But they played up, and we didn't, and we lost."

This mellow master of football learned about hard effort early on the family farm outside Jacksboro, about 65 miles northwest of Ft. Worth. Born on Oct. 18, 1908, the third of five children of Mr. and Mrs. R.T. Martin, he was christened Othol Herschel. The elder Martins, who will have been married 60 years this November, can remember no special reason for the name.

The boy attended the one-teacher Stradley School. The teacher stimulated his interest in athletics by encouraging him and the only other good-sized boy in school to box.

At high school in Jacksboro he became friendly with an older athlete, Mike Brumbelow, who went on to TCU to play football. He urged Martin to follow. "Well, I don't know about this game of football," Martin's father said. "There's a lot Othol hasn't learned yet about this farming."

But the son went to TCU anyhow, even though he had to pay his own way until he was awarded an athletic scholarship on the basis of his play with the freshmen, who were coached by L.R. (Dutch) Meyer — today Martin's boss as TCU athletic director.

The varsity coach was Matty Bell, now athletic director of Southern Methodist. As a sophomore under Bell in 1928 Martin won a regular job at end. He lost his starting post as a junior under a new coach, Francis

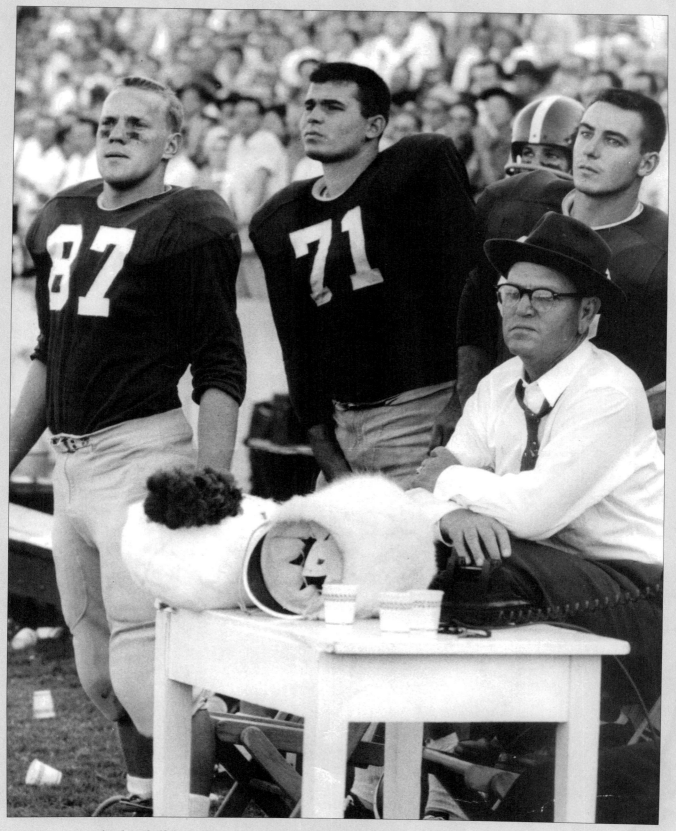

A relaxed Abe watches contently as his Horned Frogs dismantle Texas, 46-0, in 1956.

boys only once lost by more than two touchdowns, and from the beginning they showed a penchant for upsets.

In Abe's maiden season of 1953, for instance, TCU was a 32-point underdog to Michigan State, which had won 26 consecutive games. The Frogs led, 19-7, going into the fourth quarter, finally yielding to superior firepower, 26-19. The 1954 team had a similar near-miss against unbeaten Oklahoma, and then made an upset stick against a Southern California team that had been favored by 23 points.

By 1955, TCU itself was a team to beat. This has been the case in several recent seasons. When Martin's boys aren't on top themselves, though, they remain capable of beating the teams that are — as in 1957, when they hung an 18-14 defeat at Columbus on an Ohio State team that went on to finish first in the United Press national rankings.

After Martin's third year as head coach, the university's chancellor, Dr. M.E. Sadler, recommended the be given faculty tenure. TCU's trustees approved.

Doctor Sadler says, "I think athletic personnel should be treated the same insofar as security is concerned as members of the English department. And I don't think we should expect any better job from our coaches than our English teachers. Any school trying to carry on a clean, sensible athletic program cannot expect to win every year."

Few big-time football schools have such a history of coaching stability as Texas Christian University, a privately endowed, church-related (Disciples of Christ) institution with 8,400 students. Since TCU began playing competitive football in 1896 only one coach has been fired — a man who in 1912 was found using an ineligible player — and Abe Martin is only the fourth head coach the Horned Frogs have had since joining the Southwest Conference in 1923.

Even though TCU coaches have not been under pressure to win or else, the Frogs are second only to the University of Texas in percentage of conference games won during their 39 years in the league. And they are second — again to Texas — in the number of conference titles won or shared.

Obviously TCU has been recruiting players who could do the job, but the recruiting has been remarkably scandal-free. "I know people look at our record

A cagey Abe in the mid-1950's, mulling things over, in his "lucky brown hat" at a jaunty angle.

Abe presents a plaque to President Lyndon B. Johnson during his visit to TCU in 1968.

and say we must be hypocrites," says ex-sportswriter Amos Melton, who is an assistant to the TCU chancellor. "But if the time comes when we have to cheat, steal and lie, we won't have athletics."

Boost From the Frog Club

TCU operates its athletic department on the relatively small annual budget of $750,000 including payments on the bonded debt on 46,000-seat Amon G. Carter Stadium, which the Frogs rarely fill to capacity. Athletic funds are augmented by contributions from a booster organization, the Frog Club, which raised $20,000 in 1961 for miscellaneous recruiting expenses — chiefly travel by the coaches. There is a ceiling of $200 on donations, so that no individual can acquire undue influence, and the funds are not given directly to the athletic department but are administered by TCU's business office.

Until this year, when an assistant backfield coach was hired, Martin had only three varsity aides and a freshman coach. "TCU came to Little Rock last season," recalls Orville Henry of The Arkansas Gazette, "and the contrast was amazing. On one side of the field were Frank Broyles and seven assistants, all dressed in matching blue blazers and charcoal-gray slacks. On the other side was Abe Martin in a rumpled suit with a couple of assistants."

Martin insists that he doesn't want a big staff. "I like to coach kids," he says, "but I'd hate to have to coach a bunch of coaches."

His methods seem to work, although in the past two seasons — after previously drawing four bowl bids in five years — the Horned Frogs have had little to rejoice about except their occasional surprise wins. At the time of the Texas upset last year, line coach Allie White was away scouting the next opponent, Rice. He closed his report with the dry comment, "Rice doesn't look strong enough for us to beat." It wasn't just a gag: the following weekend Rice trounced TCU, 35-16.

Great Expectations for 1962

This season, with 27 lettermen returning, better things were expected. Heading the veterans was Sonny Gibbs, a huge quarterback the fans hoped would be TCU's eighth all-American selection since 1955.

Martin's only son, Don, never played college football. Abe advised the boy to forgo athletics and concentrate on his interest in medicine. Even though Don was in the upper 10 percent of the 1962 graduating class at Baylor's College of Medicine, the father says, "I think maybe he resented my telling him that. I'm not sure I was right, and I never will be sure."

Don once said of his father's job, "Winning's not a pleasure at home anymore. It's just a relief." As for Mrs. Martin, the strain of being a coach's wife has forced her to stop attending games. She doesn't even listen to them on the radio but waits at home for her husband's report.

Says Martin soberly, "I guess Sally sometimes thinks I could be doing something a little more important than this."

Most TCU football followers would disagree. They think that Abe Martin is in his proper niche, although they occasionally criticize him for not passing enough, for not being tough enough with the boys and for not getting the team "up" every single Saturday.

The consensus is probably expressed by Paul Ridings, a lifelong fan who serves as executive secretary of the Frog Club. Ridings wishes that TCU and Abe Martin were a little less conservative about football.

"But I think the school has the most sensible approach to athletics of any in the major-college field," he says.

CHAPTER 39

MINER RALLY FLOORS TCU, 13-12

By Galyn Wilkins
Fort Worth Star-Telegram

El Paso, Dec. 31, 1965 — Texas Western's Miners fired themselves up like a packet of New Year's Eve firecrackers at halftime Friday afternoon and blew apart TCU in a convincing Sun Bowl victory.

TCU	0	10	0	2	12
Texas W.	0	0	10	3	13

The Miners sulked off the field with a 10-point deficit at the intermission, but then pumped up Billy Stevens' arm and Joe Cook's foot and eventually deflated the Frogs, 13-12.

Stevens, who gained second rank among the nation's passers this season, proved his stardom to TCU by racking up 208 yards on 21 pass completions, most ever against an Abe Martin team.

The skinny sophomore had only seven strikes in the first quarter as the ball-controlling Frogs rammed to a 10-0 lead. Stevens made the 31st annual postseason game a vastly different story in the second half, however.

On the Miners' second play of the third period, Stevens shot a 34-yard touchdown pass to 165-pound flanker Chuck Hughes. A startling comeback had begun.

Minutes later, the Miners drove 70 yards for a tying 21-yard field goal by Cook. With two minutes left in the third, Texas Western, a raging defensive team by this time, hopped on a TCU fumble at the Frog 29.

TCU held at the 1-yard line. But Cook kicked an 18-yard three-pointer four plays deep in the final period to boot the Miners into a 13-10 cushion.

Time Runs Out

TCU's final two points were no gift. With 43 seconds left in the game and Stevens facing fourth down from his 7, the Miner quarterback raced back in his end zone for a safety. By surrendering two points he gave his punter a free kick from the 20.

Don Davis booted to Frank Horak at the TCU 28 and he ran it out of bounds at his 31. With 36 seconds left the Frogs got their last chance.

They could get only 8 yards before the clock ran out signaling Texas Western's eighth victory in 11 games this season. The triumph over the team that tied for second place in the Southwest Conference was, of course, steeped in prestige for the independent Miners who didn't win a game last season.

The Frogs, who held the upper hand in the first half with a touchdown and a field goal and 48 rushing plays to Texas Western's 20, bogged down in the second half with a total offense of 86 yards. They made 162 yards in the first half.

Open Targets

A large measure of credit for Stevens' great afternoon must be given to his receivers, who worked themselves into wide open targets in the midst of TCU's four-deep defense.

Although Stevens won the great air race in the end, TCU's senior quarterback Kent Nix, got a head start. He connected on 10 of 13 passes for 104 yards in the first half and hit on 5 of 5 on the Frogs' 43-yard touchdown drive that ended with six seconds left and wingback David Smith hauling in Nix's 11-yard pass for the score. Earlier in the second period Bruce Alford gave the Frogs a 3-0 lead with a 35-yard field goal.

The Frogs had another scoring opportunity in the first period, driving from their 32 to the Miner 21, but Alford missed a kick from the 28 in the second period, ending a frustrating TCU drive. The Frogs had a first down at the Miner 4, but wound up summoning Alford to kick from the 25.

Gresham Intercepts

The drive began on the Miner 44 after Dan Jones made one of TCU's interceptions on Stevens in the first half. On third down at the 16, Nix went back to pass, was trapped but escaped all the way to the 5. There he fumbled but end Charles Campbell recovered.

On the next two plays, Nix was downed for losses totaling 15 yards and Alford had to salvage three points.

E.A. Gresham picked off another Stevens pass with 1:02 left and the Frogs barged to a score on Nix's arm. He completed passes to Smith, Joe Ball and Campbell for a first down at the 11. Then he faded back and pitched to Smith, who had the safety beaten at the three. Smith sped across and Alford added the extra-point kick for a 10-0 lead. The Miners were not about to be convinced, however.

The tide changed abruptly on the third play of the second half as defensive halfback Curt Parsons intercepted Nix's pass, setting up the scoreless Miners at the TCU 44.

Stevens hit end Bob Wallace at the 34 and then sent Hughes deep on the next play. Hughes made a leaping grab at the 3-yard line with Jones draped on his

back and back-pedaled into the end zone, bringing the partisan crowd of 27,450 to its feet for the first time.

Tying Field Goal

Cook kicked the extra point to reduce the TCU lead to 10-7, and didn't have long to wait for another chance. The Frogs had to kick without making a first down after the kickoff and the Miners drove 70 yards for Cook's tying kick.

It took Texas Western 14 plays to get there and Stevens completed 6 of 9 passes. The Miners had a first down at the 7 but the Frogs stiffened with tackle Ronny Nixon leading the charge, holding at the 3. Cook's point-after kick at the 11 was perfect. This tied the score at 10-all.

Before the period was over — six and half more minutes — the Frogs suffered an interception and a fumble and made only one first down, their only fresh start of the quarter.

Tailback Steve Landon's bobble at the TCU 29 set up the Miners' winning field goal drive. Five plays later, the Miners started the fourth quarter with a first down on the Frogs' 5-yard line.

Middle Tough

The Miners couldn't fight the middle of TCU's line again and Stevens threw away a pass before Cook entered the game on fourth down with the ball on the 1. He kicked the Miners into their first lead of the game from the 8-yard line with 12:36 left.

The Frogs started a threat with 7:11 to play, but after a 20-yard trip to the Miner 44, Nix, undergoing a fierce rush, fumbled at his 49.

On his next possession, Nix and Campbell took the Frogs to a first down at the Miner 41. After a 9-yard pass to Joe ball, Nix's long pass was intercepted by Parsons at the 1 with 1:17 left.

Stevens' gift of the safety came with 40 seconds left. By that time the Frogs were beyond even Texas Western's help.

Stevens, whose touchdown pass was his 22nd of the year, was voted the game's outstanding player on the press box ballot. Ronnie Nixon, TCU's 212-pound junior defensive tackle, who also played end against the Miners, was named the best lineman.

CHAPTER 40

Punt Return By Thornton Ignites TCU

BY DICK MOORE
Fort Worth Star-Telegram

AUSTIN, NOV. 18, 1967— Ralph Boston never broad jumped farther than Marty Whelan when the little wingback came running off the field, hit and flew 30 feet into a swarm of his TCU teammates on the sidelines.

TCU	0	0	6	18	24
Texas	0	3	14	0	17

Kenny Post had just plowed through Texas' left defensive side for a touchdown that settled the issue — TCU's 24-17 win over Texas — although 61 seconds remained.

And 76 trombones in the "Music Man" never created as much noise as vibrated through the small confines of the Frog's dressing room as everybody and his dog wormed in to get on the band wagon that had been so empty four games ago.

Charles (Bubba) Thornton was bubbling tears as one teammate after another slapped him on the shoulder pads, rubbed his head, hugged his neck and even poured a soft drink over him.

★ ★ ★

"That gave us the momentum," shouted the usually calm E.A. Gresham, in reference to Thornton's 78-yard punt return that shaved Texas' lead from 11 points to just three when the Frogs went for two points and made it.

"You could feel something on the sideline. It was like an electric current sweeping through everyone," the elated senior added.

No one at all argued over Thornton's return being the key to TCU's astounding 18-point fourth quarter splurge.

And Thornton may have set some sort of precedent that other Southwest Conference players will follow. He threw the football into the stands as he ran

Ross Montgomery, an All-SWC halfback in 1967.

into the end zone.

★ ★ ★

"No, sir, I didn't think I was in the pro league," said the happy youngster, who didn't play a down until the Baylor game three weekends ago.

"I was just the happiest person in the world. Don't give me credit, though. Give it to the blockers. All I did was grab the ball and run."

"Whenever it's a high one like that, Mike Hall (the other safetyman) comes over and keeps that first man off of me," explained Thornton, a junior college transfer.

"The wall was set up perfect," said Hall. "I kept yelling at Bubba to take it. Then I started yelling: 'Follow me, follow me, follow me.' No one got through the wall.

"When we got to Bradley ... he was the last one ... two others already had him blocked out. I just went into him for good measure."

"When I cut back on those blockers, I knew I was gone," said Thornton. "I had three blockers for escort."

★ ★ ★

Less than two minutes later came the second back-breaking punt return that did the Longhorns.

Bradley, in what amounts to a quick kick, booted one from his own 28.

Cubby Hudler, running like the wind, scooped up the ball on TCU's 4-yard line, headed to the right sideline, then cut upfield.

"I'm still kicking myself," the senior said in the dressing room. "I could have gone all the way, I set up the block on Bradley, then cut the wrong way. I stumbled over my own man ... Donnie Terveen. He had Bradley down."

★ ★ ★

Hudler paused for a moment to catch his breath.

"I'm so tired, I'm about to pass out," he apologized. "I really got pooped on that one."

He explained that he had chased Marcus Gilbert on his record touchdown run of 96 yards, just missing the flying feet of the Longhorn. He chased him again on his 61-yard flight to the TCU 1-yard line that set up Texas' second touchdown.

"This had to be the greatest game I've ever played in. We came through when the chips were down. And they have a good football team," added the TCU co-captain.

"You know, we never got fired until Gilbert's first touchdown run. We weren't fired in the first half. We talked it over in the dressing room. Gilbert's run gave us the spark."

★ ★ ★

Some players, like defensive end James Vanderslice, confessed he had doubts when TCU dropped 11 points behind.

"Nah, I didn't think we could come back like we did. But it proves the character this team does have."

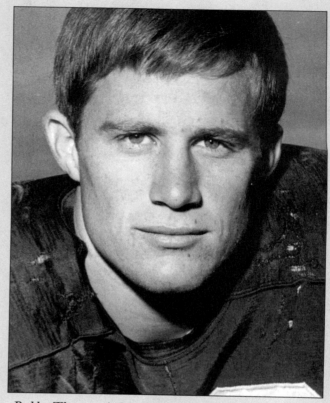

Bubba Thornton's 78-yard punt return gave life to the faltering Frogs.

Ross Montgomery disagreed.

"No, sir, I wasn't surprised the way we rallied. That was Texas we were playing."

Post, who scored the first and last TCU touchdowns, could hardly contain himself. Harassed by injuries in recent games, he produced in this one.

He described his first touchdown run from Texas' 4-yard line on a fourth-and-one situation.

"It was funny, I stumbled over someone right after P.D. Shabay handed me the ball. I was falling when someone bumped me and I regained my balance. I kept bumping people. Suddenly I had the momentum. I knew I was going to score. It felt great."

★ ★ ★

Shabay revealed that Post scored both touchdowns on the identical play.

"I think the play surprised them," said Shaby, talking about Post's initial touchdown. "I think they were looking for the pitch to Ross and the power sweep.

"It was the first time we had used this play from the wing-T to the right. James Ray and Fred Barber threw the key blocks both times."

CHAPTER 41

FROGS NIPPED AT WIRE, 42-35

By Jim Trinkle
Fort Worth Star-Telegram

FT. WORTH, SEPT. 21, 1969 — Mike Phipps flung himself into Purdue's record books on two pages Saturday. The Boilermakers needed every chapter to stave off TCU, 42-35, in the intersectional football debut for both teams.

Purdue	7	14	14	7	42
TCU	0	7	14	14	35

As Linzy Cole whipped the meager, sweating crowd into a frenzy with three touchdowns, Phipps kept Purdue out of reach with his dazzling passes.

Steve Judy passed for 4 touchdowns against Purdue.

His four touchdown passes equaled one school mark and his 390 yards in total offense rewrote the book in another department. But in the end, the Big Ten giants were hanging on, trying to catch their breath in the 86-degree heat, hoping they could keep Cole's mitts off the ball.

Sophomore quarterback Steve Judy matched Phipps' throwing with four scoring passes of his own. Two went to Cole from 5 and 3 yards and another found Sammy Rabb on a 35-yarder. John Beilue made his first visit to TCU's varsity scoring, catching a 3-yarder from Judy in the game's waning moments.

An estimated crowd of 25,000 — and a rather generous estimate it was — sweltered in the soggy humidity, but was stirred to occasions of rare excitement as the Frogs rallied from a 21-7 halftime burden and later from a 42-21 disadvantage.

Purdue scored from the opening kickoff but the Boilermakers had to travel 120 yards for their six points. The sum included 24 yards in penalties with Phipps going the last five yards for the touchdown. Jeff Jones kicked the first of six extra points.

For the afternoon, Phipps completed 11 of 24 passes for 286 yards, then stepped another 104 for the 390 total. The Boilermakers' 583 total production was another school high.

Ashley Bell caught scoring passes of 23 and 8 yards for the well-ranked invaders. Another went to Stan Brown for 67 yards and Greg Fenner picked off a hitch-hike aerial that skipped into his palms from eight yards.

Purdue's other touchdown was a 1-yard run from fullback John Bullock.

The heat and the score conspired to keep a bunch of people from witnessing TCU's tardy heroics.

Phipps' passes to Bell and Fenner and his early TD outgunned the Frogs at intermission. At that time all they could show was Judy's 5-yard bullseye to Cole, some poor tackling and a secondary that let Bullock take a swing pass 30 yards farther than any pass had ever traveled for the enemy in Amon Carter Stadium.

Luckily, the TCU defense and Purdue's over-eager

Linzy Cole's darting 70-yard punt return narrowed the score to 42-35.

offense kept the Boilermakers from scoring. The Indianans repeatedly were fined for being in motion in the line. Illegal procedure the officials called it, though Purdue had another word for it.

If it looked bad at recess, the situation was deplorable when Phipps staked Purdue to a 35-7 cushion midway through third period. He had lobbed a pass to Bell, who merely loped in from 23 yards out, then flung a home run pass to Brown that spanned 67 yards. Defender Ted Fay did a pratfall as the ball settled into Brown's clutch and he didn't have to extend himself.

Judy, who handled the ball on every TCU play, quickly took the Purple 66 yards on five plays. He nailed Rabb with a short pass to the right side and

Sammy tightroped the east sidelines for the score

Wayne Merritt had to kick twice because of a penalty, but he got the extra point.

On TCU's next possession Judy guided them 56 yards, passing to Cole for the final 3 yards.

He was called upon on a fourth-and-1 situation late in the fourth quarter and delivered a first down.

So then it was 35-21 and TCU seemed to be gaining momentum. Hopes were dashed when Rabb fumbled and Purdue's Bill Yanchar picked it up on the Boilermakers 31.

Along came Phipps. He flipped a pitchout to Randy Cooper, who outran Billy Fondren and rambled 34 yards to the TCU 1 where Gregg Webb bounced him out of bounds. Bullock got across for the touchdown on the third try.

The lure of six-packs and air-conditioning was too strong for some of the crowd to resist. Only 10 minutes remained in the last quarter and they headed home.

In a turbulent segment of time that saw the ball swap hands four times inside 90 seconds, Fondren gave the Frogs another chance by recovering Sam Carter's bobble on Purdue's 18.

Norm Bulaich got 11 yards on the first crack and a personal foul put the ball on the Boilermaker 3. Beilue, playing his first varsity game, raced clear in the end zone to take Judy's pass on the next play. Merritt's kick made it 42-28 — still a comfortable margin for Purdue.

The game took a new color when Scott Lougheed's punt settled into Cole's belly on TCU's 30-yard line. Cole went this-away and that-away into his waterbug fashion, then blared clear as he picked up blocking and went 70 yards for the touchdown, raising his arms like he had just KO'd Muhammad Ali at the goal line. This reduced Purdue's lead to 42-35.

Purdue didn't take any chances with the four minutes left on the clock. Phipps once raced 18 yards to keep the drive going. Bullock, on a fourth-and-1, lunged for first down yardage. On the last play, Phipps curled himself around the ball and clung to the seven-point victory.

Marty Whelan, running better than ever before, gained 44 yards in six carries to be TCU's top carrier. Judy, whose four TD passes matched a TCU mark held by Kent Nix, hit 19 of 35 for 213 yards.

CHAPTER 42

PITTMAN'S DEATH MARS WIN

BY CLIFFORD KING AND PAT TRULY
Fort Worth Star-Telegram

WACO, OCT. 20, 1971 — "We wanted to win it for him and in his memory," said TCU assistant coach Russell Coffee.

"Coach Pittman instilled something in these play-

TCU	7	13	7	7	34
Baylor	7	13	7	0	27

ers," said Baylor coach Bill Beall, "They weren't quitters."

Coffee, and TCU, had won a game. Beall, and Baylor, had lost one. But coaches, players and spectators at Baylor Stadium Saturday were together in sorrow and shock at the death of Horned Frog coach Jim Pittman.

An apparent heart attack struck Pittman early in the first quarter and he was taken to a hospital where he was pronounced dead.

The TCU players were told at halftime that Pittman had died, though some had heard it from a policeman on the sideline before the half ended.

The Frogs had only 10 months under Pittman. Few of them will ever forget those months.

"This game," said Frog quarterback Steve Judy later, "isn't important except that we won it for him. He always taught us to give 100 percent and I'm glad to say that we did that for him. He was just a great leader and a great man."

Bill Tohill, Pittman's chief aide at TCU and a member of Pittman's staff since 1966 at Tulane, said, "We made a promise to win this game for him. There are no words that can express my feeling about Pitt. He was a great person and I don't know any person with as many friends — real friends — as Pitt had."

TCU was on its way to its first touchdown when Pittman collapsed on the sideline. Behind the running

Jim Pittman's death on the sidelines of the 1971 Baylor contest was a difficult setback for TCU.

of Larry Harris and Kenneth Davis, Judy moved the Frogs from their own 46 to a score.

Davis, on a quick trap, ripped to the 13. Three plays later, Harris circled right end to give TCU a 7-0 lead.

The Bears came right back, getting a boost from a TCU interference call for a first down at their 34. Then, White broke for 20 yards and Cavender earned a first down with a fourth-down run to the TCU 33. Cavender got the touchdown two plays later, evading three Frogs on a trip at left end from the 23. Mike Conradt tied it at 7-7.

The pace was sustained as the Frogs moved 53 yards to go ahead. Davis, Harris and Patterson all contributed good gains before Judy threw to Ronnie Peoples in the end zone for the TD. This time Berl Simmons' kick was blocked by Roger Goree.

And Baylor was still charged-up from its previous taste of paydirt. Cavender got them moving with a 35-yard strike to Mike Chandler to the Frog 47. Then White and Williams began gouging big yardage out of the TCU defense before Cavender went 15 yards to the 3 and a penalty moved Baylor to the 1. Williams got the score and Conradt made it 14-13 with 11 minutes left in the half.

When Ken Balfanz fumbled the ensuing kickoff to Baylor at the Frog 41, the Bears hopped on their good fortune. A holding penalty slowed them, but was overcome by Cavender's pass to Ken Townsend and Chandler, moving Baylor to the TCU 24.

Three plays later, White burst through the middle for 18 yards and a TD. The extra point try by Conradt was wide, leaving Baylor in front 20-13.

TCU tied it two minutes before halftime, going 84 yards. Harris made key yardage, Lane Bowen chipped in two good runs, and Judy kept outside right tackle for the touchdown from the 3. This time Simmons was good with his kick for the 20-20 halftime tie.

Early in the third quarter a long punt by Harlan Deem — it left TCU at its own 7 — and an interception by Phil Beall at the Frog 34 led Baylor to a go-ahead score. On the Bears' first play, Matthew Williams went around right end and down the sideline for the touchdown, and a 27-20 lead.

The Frogs kept it even by marching 75 yards. Bowen, operating from both halfback positions, got 31 yards and Patterson helped, as did a Baylor foul call which

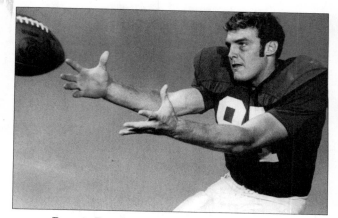

Ronnie Peoples, an All-SWC end in 1971.

moved TCU to the Bear 34. Patterson got a first at the 11, Bowen bullied to the 5, and Judy scored from there, stiff-arming Baylor's Gary Sutton on his way to the end zone. Simmons again tied it at 27-27.

They settled down then to a punting duel, relieved once by an interference penalty that got the Frogs a first down at their 42 when they seemed stopped. Judy then got 12 yards at left end and 17 more at right end to reach the Baylor 22. He kept it again, cutting neatly inside the contain man at right end, to the 10. Still at the 10 on third down, Judy again hit Peoples, who carried two defenders over the goal. Simmons' kick gave TCU a 34-27 lead with 10 minutes left to play.

The Bears came back with a first down at their 49, but on fourth down from the Frog 44, White could get only two steps to the 42 in the grasp of Craig Fife and Gary Whitman and the ball went over with less than seven minutes on the clock.

With just three minutes left, the Bears put the Purples in dubious field position again with a 67-yard Deem punt to the Frog 27. They got a break when Bowen fumbled to Baylor's Dan Mosley at the Frog 34, but Lyle Blackwood saved the situation with the diving interception two plays later at the TCU 19.

Faced with fourth down at their 25, the Frogs let the clock run as much as they could, even drawing a delay penalty. Finally Kent Marshall punted out of bounds at the Baylor 47 with eight seconds left and the Frogs came away both sad and victorious.

CHAPTER 43

TCU'S WASHINGTON FINDS THE MAGIC

By David Moore
Fort Worth Star-Telegram

Ft. Worth, Oct. 3, 1981 — TCU had the ball on its own 1-yard line, 99 yards and 5:20 away from another defeat to the Arkansas Razorbacks.

TCU	7	3	0	18	28
Arkansas	0	14	7	3	24

Stanley Washington stood on the sidelines. The man who had not done so much for the Frogs in the past two years had done nothing. No spectacular, leaping catches that defy gravity and make opponents shake their heads. No diving catches over the middle into the crunch of defenders.

Stanley Washington, the man the Frogs count on the most, had no receptions at all.

Then, just before Washington ran onto the field, reserve placekicker John Denton grabbed him by the arm.

"We need those magic hands of yours," Denton said, expressing the thought most of Washington's teammates have come to share. "If you got anything left in those hands of yours, let us have it."

Washington didn't have a reception, but he knew. He knew the magic was still there. That supreme confidence lifted Washington into the air for three receptions, two for touchdowns. And those receptions lifted the Frogs to a 28-24 victory over the Razorbacks — the Frogs' first in 22 years.

"As soon as I went out on the field when we had 99 yards to go, I started to get that feeling," said Washington. "I got the feeling that if I touched the ball, I was going to get it into the end zone."

"He's a clutch player," said quarterback Steve Stamp. "You know he wants the ball in that situation, and he's proved he can produce."

The catch that won the game came with just over two minutes remaining. The Frogs, trailing 24-21, had a third-and-10 on the Arkansas 15-yard line. The previous play, Stamp had tried to hit Washington in the end zone but the pass fell incomplete when the receiver tripped over two Razorback defenders.

"If we hadn't have scored, I would say that Wash-

Steve Stamp's touchdown pass to Stanley Washington ended 22 years of Arkansas dominance.

ington was interfered with on that play," said TCU coach F.A. Dry.

But Dry wouldn't have to worry about excuses. Washington lined up as a tight end on the left side of the Frog line. As the ball was snapped Washington took a slight delay, then cut across the field.

Stamp rolled to his right. Washington slanted behind the linebackers and in front of the cornerbacks.

"He was wide open," said Stamp. "It was just a matter of hitting him."

Stamp did hit him, right on those magic hands. Washington took the ball in stride and went into the end zone for the touchdown.

Washington, who had made several clutch catches against Texas Tech last year to give the Frogs their only victory of 1980, had just made the big catch in the biggest game for TCU in many years.

"It's really hard to describe how I felt," Washington said of breaking the nation's longest consecutive winning streak and upsetting the No. 19-ranked Hogs. "I just know this one far outweighs the one I made against Texas Tech last year."

Early, it appeared Washington didn't have the magic. Until the final five minutes of the game, the nation's leading receiver had only seen the ball come his direction for four plays, none of which were completed.

The Hogs were able to shut Washington down with a double-teaming zone coverage. On the right side, two men took Phillip Epps. On the left, only the cornerback came up to take Washington, but the safety came in after the play developed to protect deep, thus forming double-teams on both sides of the field.

"Even though I didn't catch a pass, the coverage wasn't that good," Washington said. "We were just playing conservative because we had our running game going and we didn't need to go long.

"But we still knew we could hit the passes outside. A couple of times out there, I could have caught a cold from being so wide open."

Washington, however, didn't catch a cold and he didn't catch any passes. The Frogs resorted to hitting their backs underneath the coverage and going to receiver Greg Arterberry, who constantly found himself open in the middle of the field.

Stanley Washington scored 2 touchdowns in the Frogs' win.

But then came the 99-yard drive and the Washington receptions.

After playing well early, the Frogs faded, as has been their habit in recent years. The slow fizzle found TCU down, 24-13, when it took over on the 1.

A couple of Stamp passes and an Arkansas penalty gave the Frogs a first-and-5 on the Razorback 42-yard line. Stamp dropped back in the pocket and looked down the left sidelines for Washington. Washington had gotten by the Arkansas defender and took the throw for 20 yards and a first down.

On the next play, Washington again beat the right side of the Arkansas secondary, this time in the left corner of the end zone. The Frogs went for the 2-point conversion, and tight end Bob Fields made the catch to pull TCU to within 24-21.

"I talked to Bob earlier, and I told him we would go to him in that situation," Dry said. "The reason I had to call a time out before we ran the conversion was because the kid we sent in to call the play didn't know it."

Freshman Byron Linwood recovered an Arkansas fumble on the next series, which set up Washington's game-winning catch just seconds later.

The Razorbacks got the ball again, but when Bill Pierce's pass on fourth down — with less than a minute to go — went fluttering to Amon Carter turf. All the Frogs had to do was run out the clock and watch the clock reach zero.

"I just couldn't believe it," said Stamp. "I looked up there and knew what we have wanted for so long finally happened. I just couldn't believe it."

The first thing that crossed Washington's mind when he saw time had run out was the slogan that was seen around the TCU campus this week — 22 is enough.

"That slogan was actually the first thing that ran through my mind," Washington said. "Then, I said to myself, 'Yeah, 22 was enough.'"

"I sat there the whole time, praying this wouldn't wind up like two years ago when we let the Arkansas game get away from us," linebacker Mike Dry said, remembering the 16-13 loss. "We got a chance to put a string together now, and we're going to do it."

Victorious Frogs 'Did What They Had to Do'

By Pat Truly
Fort Worth Star-Telegram

When Arkansas' Bruce Lahay kicked a 31-yard field goal with nine minutes to play Saturday night at Amon Carter Stadium, fans started to leave. You could see from the Pike's Peak of a press box, the taillights heading away from the parking lots while the scoreboard read Arkansas 24, TCU 13.

Oh, ye of little faith.

But then it did look like just another in a series, and in this TCU-Arkansas series, that would have meant No. 23. Twenty-three wins a row for the Razorbacks.

This series had become one of the obscenities of college football — the longest one-team domination of a rivalry in Southwest Conference history.

Year after year the Frogs spoke bravely. Generation after generation of TCU football players had to point out that they weren't part of the whole string of losses to the Hogs. And year after year they lost.

Every other year the TCU parking lots filled up with mobile homes and campers with "Land of Opportunity" license tags. The echoes of *Sooey, Pig* filled the Texas ozone. And year after year Arkansas won.

Heck, they may do it again. But this once they did not.

Nothing, not anything at all, that F.A. Dry could have done would have meant as much to his TCU constituency as beating Arkansas, 28-24, Saturday night.

Unless it was beating the Razorbacks by a bigger score.

It's a turning point, perhaps, in the Frog fortunes, which have been down so long.

A fellow was telling me just the other day that he wondered about Dry and his Frogs because there didn't seem to be much emotion on the sidelines.

Dry is just not a man who exudes emotion. He's a laboratory scientist at heart.

"The defense played its best game of the season tonight," he said in the locker room.

But what about this victory? After all, it's been 22 years.

"It feels really good," said the coach. "I imagine for those who've suffered through those 22 defeats, they feel good about it, too. It hasn't been 22 years for me."

Dry could afford to yawn. He beat the Razorbacks once or twice when he coached at Tulsa.

One thing he said rings extremely true, when you wash away the emotion that really does cling to a victory like this one.

"They did what they had to do," he said of his team.

Right there you have the difference, in other years, which had the same opportunity and didn't do what they had to do. There were years they perhaps should have beaten Arkansas. They led late in the game in 1972, 13-0, before Joe Ferguson threw four TD passes in the last 17 or so minutes. Two years ago TCU almost won, but lost, 16-13.

Almost is no longer good enough. It wasn't good enough Saturday night for Steve Stamp and Stanley Washington and a host of distinguished defensive players and blockers and runners (TCU, supposedly unable to make a dime on the ground, ran 171 yards against a stiff Hog defense).

Emotionless? Hardly.

"This has got to be the greatest victory for TCU in quite a while. We waited so long," Steve Stamp said.

It has yet to fully sink in, too, for these youngsters.

But one person at the game, and not even a veteran of those eternal years of losses to Arkansas, knew very well what it could mean, and the personal importance of the victory.

As Dry emerged, a big shambling man, from the dressing room, he was assaulted by a woman. She covered him with kisses while the Frog fans stood around and applauded.

Her name is Jan Dry, and apparently she just felt her husband deserved some personal congratulations.

CHAPTER 44

TCU GETS KICK OUT OF TYING TECH

BY DAVID MOORE
Fort Worth Star-Telegram

LUBBOCK, Nov. 7, 1981 — It was an afternoon when the kicking game kicked Texas Tech in the teeth.

TCU scored on a 70-yard punt return and had another touchdown set up by a 61-yard return. The Frogs recovered two consecutive squib kicks in the fourth quarter to score 10 more points. Greg Porter hit two field goals.

TCU	6	0	9	24	39
Texas Tech	7	10	15	7	39

Tech, meanwhile, had a punt blocked out of the end zone for a safety. And with two seconds remaining in the game, the Red Raiders had a chance to win, but John Greve's 28-yard field goal attempt fluttered left.

"That's the latest I've ever dodged the bullet," TCU coach F.A. Dry said.

In all, TCU collected 33 points from the specialty teams' play. Since the game ended in a 39-39 tie, it is not difficult to figure out how important the kicking game was to the Frogs (2-5-2) and how deflating it was to Texas Tech (1-7-1).

"Our offense played well enough to win, and our defense played well enough to win," Tech coach Jerry Moore said. "But our kicking game went sour and the whole game hinged on that."

When Tech's kicking game went sour, TCU quarterback Reuben Jones was there to take advantage of it.

Eddie Clark started the game, but ineffectiveness and a bad ankle sent him to the sidelines for the second half. That's when Jones came in. In his three years at TCU, Jones has been maligned more than he's been used. But the junior saw his first extensive action of the season, and performed well enough to bring the

Frogs coach F.A. Dry (above) and his son, Mike (right), both savor the moment after Mike blocked a Tech punt.

Reuben Jones had a career day against Tech, hitting on 19 of 34 attempts for 297 yards and 1 touchdown.

Frogs back from a 23-point third-quarter deficit.

"I thought Reuben came in and did a superior job today after having been spotty throughout his career," Dry said. "He seemed to turn things around in practice this week and he came to play. You could see the determination in his face."

Jones finished his two quarters of play with 19 of 34 completions for 297 yards and one touchdown.

"I've been waiting on an opportunity to play, so when it finally came today I just tried to go in and play to the best of my ability," Jones said.

It was a game that appeared lost of the Frogs. TCU managed only 37 yards after two quarters and went into the locker room trailing, 17-6.

Tech opened the third quarter by scoring a touchdown on its first possession. The Raiders scored again with 7:06 left in the quarter to boost their lead to 32-9.

"When we went ahead there I really thought we were in great shape," Moore said.

But the fourth-quarter jinx that hit Tech in last year's

game against TCU hit the Raiders again. Just like last year, the Frogs came up with a 24-point fourth quarter to salvage another game from the loss pile.

The game was as incredible as it was three hours and 41 minutes long. Early, it appeared there was no way Tech could lose. Late, it appeared there was no way Texas Tech would allow itself to win. But even then, the Raiders came up with a key interception that put them in position for a game-winning field goal.

"That was one of the wildest games I've ever seen," Dry said.

■ Kickoffs: TCU trailed, 32-32, early in the fourth quarter. Porter went with a squib kick, which he does on a majority of his kickoffs. "We really worked hard on that squib kick all week because we knew he was going to do that," Moore said.

The Raiders didn't work hard enough. The first kick ricocheted off Rufus Johnson and was recovered by Mike Flynn on the Tech 34-yard line. The Frogs got a field goal out of the series to trail, 32-24.

Next, Porter planned an onsides kick. "I hit it really hard, the way it's supposed to be done," Porter said.

The ball hopped and jumped by several Tech players and went rolling down to the 6-yard line, where it was recovered by Marvin Foster. Three plays later, Jones hit fullback Kevin Haney with a 3-yard TD pass to make the score, 32-30.

■ Punt returns: John Thomas fielded a punt in the first quarter and went to his right, but five Raiders were waiting for him. Thomas reversed field, got a clearing block to his left and ran at least 100 yards to end up with a 61-yard punt return.

Three plays and 11 yards later, Marcus Gilbert caught a 3-yard TD pass for TCU's score in the game.

TCU was down and seemingly out by a 32-15 score to open the fourth quarter. But at 13:23, flanker Phillip Epps took a Marty Buford punt on TCU's 30-yard line. He returned the ball 70 yards, making it the longest punt return for a touchdown TCU has had since a 65-yarder was accomplished in 1969.

■ The point after touchdowns follies: TCU's first four touchdowns failed to produce the point after. The first Frog attempt was blocked by Tech's Gabe Rivera.

On the next three touchdowns, TCU went for the 2-point conversion and failed every time.

CHAPTER 45

TCU's storming defense halts Arkansas quarterback Danny Nutt.

TCU STUNS ARKANSAS, 32-31

BY MIKE JONES
Fort Worth Star-Telegram

FAYETTEVILLE, ARK., OCT. 6, 1984 — TCU football Coach Jim Wacker is going to have to retire one of his favorite adjectives. Nothing could be more

TCU	7	3	7	15	32
Arkansas	3	14	0	14	31

unbeleeeevable than the scene that unfolded here Saturday afternoon.

In one of the all-time great comebacks in TCU and Southwest Conference history, Wacker's never-say-die Horned Frogs stunned the Arkansas Razorbacks, 32-31, scoring two touchdowns and a 2-point conversion in the final 10 minutes battling against the wind.

Down, 31-17, with 10:19 to play and operating with two gimpy quarterbacks, the Frogs mounted two unbe-

lievable drives and capped it with an improbable conversion that came with only 15 seconds left in the game.

"It all comes down to believing in yourself," Wacker said afterwards amidst a boisterous and tearfully joyous scene. "We could have laid down and died, but we didn't. What a great bunch of kids. What a great victory.

"This team," he said, "is finding out what it's made of."

The monumental win, the first in Fayetteville for TCU in 29 years and only the second win over the Razorbacks in a quarter century, upped the Horned Frogs' record to a 3-1 overall and 1-1 in SWC play.

"This may be the most important game of the season for us," said wide receiver James Maness, who caught the winning two-point conversion from quarterback Anthony Gulley. "We've got some tough games coming up the rest of the season, but at least now we know we're going to win our share of them.

"I'll admit it looked awfully grim," said Maness. "We just finally hooked it up, got it together and did it.

"What a great feeling."

Down, 17-10, at the half on a gift touchdown from an officiating staff that never seemed to have its act together, the Horned Frogs knotted the score at 17-17 on a 67-yard interception return by redshirt freshman cornerback Garland Littles three minutes deep into the second half.

But TCU was soon obviously in trouble. The once-explosive Veer offense was now spewing smoke. Entering the final period, the defense was worn out. Arkansas had the ball 11 minutes of the third quarter.

When Arkansas backs Bobby Joe Edmonds and Marshall Foreman broke for touchdown runs of 37 and 59 yards early in the fourth quarter, it looked like another long plane ride home from The Hills.

What this team needed was a miracle. It got several, but they were of the self-made variety.

After Gulley, the starting quarterback, injured his left shoulder on a hit midway through the third quarter, he could not run the Veer option to the left, because he could not pitch out. Anthony Sciaraffa, coming off a layoff because of an injured right ankle, could not throw very well going to the right because of having to plant and throw off his right foot.

So Wacker simply alternated them according to situation.

After Sciaraffa got the drive started with a 15-yard pass to flex end Dan Sharp, Gulley came in and took the Horned Frogs the remaining 65 yards to a touchdown with 7:58 to play to cut into the Razorbacks' 14-point lead. The score came on an 18-yard play-action pass from Gulley to running back Kenneth Davis — who snuck through the line and behind the

defense to take the perfect pass in the end zone.

Ken Ozee's extra-point kick made it 31-24.

Arkansas then threatened to wrap it up, but the gassed TCU defense held just enough as safety Byron Linwood stopped Razorbacks quarterback Danny Nutt for a 1-yard gain on third-and-4 at the TCU 12.

As if according to script, Arkansas kicker Greg Horne — who had kicked a 24-yard field goal in the first quarter — missed a chip shot 27-yard attempt from the left hash mark right.

Then came The Drive.

There was 3:45 left on the clock and 80 yards to cover. It would be a cinch.

The first big play was fourth-and-6 at the TCU 24. Sciaraffa rolled left and under pressure somehow found Sharp, who had lined up tight left.

"Their end came on a smoke and I drifted out in the flat," said Sharp "I had to go up for the ball and luckily, I came down right on the first down marker."

Sciaraffa then hit Maness over the middle for 24 and went back to Sharp on the next play for 19 to the Arkansas 26, putting Sharp over the 100-yard receiving mark.

Following a 5-yard procedure penalty and an incompletion, the Horned Frogs came up with another oh-so biggie.

This time it was Maness making a great catch over the middle, leaping high and a winning a tug-of-war for the ball with Arkansas cornerback Greg Gatson.

"I never saw (Gatson)," said Maness. "He probably should have intercepted it, but I guess I just wanted it more. Once I had it in my hands, there was no way anyone was going to take it away from me."

His catch set up first-and-goal at the Arkansas 4-yard line, with 1:19 to play. Gulley gained nothing on

Garland Littles (20) intercepted an Arkansas pass and returned it 67 yards for a TCU touchdown.

a keeper, then followed with two incompletions. But Arkansas' Gatson was flagged for interfering with Sharp on third down, giving TCU first-and-goal at the 2.

TCU used its last time out with 47 seconds left. Davis took a handoff from Gulley and leaped, but was thrown back. Then Sciaraffa entered, thinking he was going to pass on a pre-called play. But when he raced in, the players were in a formation wrong for the play he thought he was to run.

Sciaraffa could do but one thing. He scored, taking the snap and jumping over the line.

Then, the two-point conversion.

Gulley was the man under center. He retreated under tremendous pressure from Arkansas end Raven Caldwell. Shaking loose, he saw Maness in the end zone, pointed to a spot and drilled him near the end line.

"(Caldwell) grabbed me by my face mask," Gulley said. "But he must not have wanted to get a penalty, because he immediately let go. I think that was the only thing he could grab at the time.

"The play was supposed to go to Kenneth (Davis) in the flat, but he wasn't open. Then, I saw Maness."

"Boy am I glad he did it," said Maness. "I saw that Gulley was in trouble and I thought, 'Oh, no, they're gonna get him.'

"But then," Maness said, "I saw him come back up and I worked my way to an open spot. I didn't think the ball was ever going to get there. When it did, I caught it with my whole body."

The TCU bench and its small but enthusiastic following in the stands went utterly wild. So did some Arkansas fans, who threw pint whiskey bottles at the bench.

It was a wild finish to an entertaining game.

CHAPTER 46

TCU coach Jim Wacker consoles center Jim Cook after the Horned Frogs' 31-14 loss to West Virginia.

WEST VIRGINIA RIPS TCU, 31-14

BY MIKE JONES
Fort Worth Star-Telegram

HOUSTON, DEC. 31, 1984 — The weather was good, the hotel nice, the seafood fresh and plentiful.

Yeah, TCU had a fine time during the week leading up to their first bowl appearance in 19 years. The same can hardly be said of the appearance itself.

| W. Va. | 14 | 17 | 0 | 0 | 31 |
| TCU | 7 | 0 | 7 | 0 | 14 |

Playing possibly their worst game of the season and without injured all-American halfback Kenneth Davis,

the Horned Frogs dropped a 31-14 decision to West Virginia Monday night in the 26th annual Bluebonnet Bowl.

The Frogs finished the season 8-4, their most successful season in 25 years. But in three straight losses to end the season, their performance amply illustrated that the rebuilding job of Coach Jim Wacker can still use more bricks and plenty of mortar.

"We didn't play well and probably coached worse than we played," Wacker said. "They whipped us every way you can whip us.

"Losing Kenneth Davis took the wind out of a lot of sails," he said. "We probably relied on him too much during the season. But losing an all-American ... yeah, it hurts."

Davis was lost for the night after only six carries, suffering a severe upper calf bruise to his left leg on the final play of the first quarter. Davis spent the second half in the dressing room and without him, TCU had no rushing threat. The Frogs finished the night with a season-low 279 yards total offense and only 150 yards rushing — three yards more than Davis' season average.

And the defense? What defense? Though the Frogs somehow managed to shut out the Mountaineers in the second half, what they gave up in the first half alone was more than enough.

"Fortunately, we played a little better in the second half," Wacker said.

West Virginia, which had averaged 303 yards total offense through 11 games, blitzed and outmuscled the Frogs for a season-high 496 yards. That's more than the Mountaineers managed against the likes of Ohio University.

West Virginia quarterback Kevin White, twice pulled during a three-game losing skid at the end of the regular season, looked like an all-American against the Frog defense. Voted the Most Valuable Player, White bombed TCU for 280 yards and two touchdowns on 16 completions.

Elusive wide receiver Willie Drewrey caught six passes for 152 yards.

Offensively for TCU, quarterback Anthony Gulley was the leading rusher with a net of 38 yards. Gulley generated almost all of TCU's offense. He completed 9 of 14 passes for 150 yards and touchdowns of 20 yards to Keith Burnett and 5 to Dan Sharp.

By halftime the Frogs had to be wondering if it was still too late to turn down a bowl invitation. TCU had found itself in its deepest halftime hole of the season after 30 minutes of bowl experience.

The Mountaineers came out slinging and by the end of the first quarter had 155 yards passing, 2 more than their season average for an entire game.

White threw to Drewrey for gains of 33 and 28 yards on the game's first two plays and it only took seven more plays for West Virginia to take a 7-0 lead.

It looked so easy that on fourth-and-goal from the TCU 2, the Mountaineers spurned a field goal try and

The Frogs were dealt a big blow when Heisman candidate Kenneth Davis was injured.

went for the touchdown. White dropped back, then hit tailback John Gay with a little flip pass at the goal line for the touchdown.

The Frogs came back to tie it with Gulley at the controls. Davis carried four times for 19 yards, but the big plays were a 21-yard scramble by Gulley and a 13-yard pass to James Maness to the West Virginia 11. On third down at the 4, the Frogs showed flow left. But Gulley rolled right and found Sharp for the score.

With 6:40 to play in the quarter, it looked like a ball game. But not for long.

The teams traded punts after Maness dropped what should have been a touchdown catch at the 1 and then the Mountaineers struck long again. White hit Drewrey for 20 yards to get West Virginia out of a deep hole at the 7. Then two plays later he found flanker Gary Mullin behind cornerback Garland Littles for a 62-yard scoring pass with 14 seconds left in the quarter.

Frogs Singing Bluebonnet Blues

By Galyn Wilkins
Fort Worth Star-Telegram

Maybe it was an omen when Texas A&M jumped from its mysterious hiding place five weeks ago and scored 35 points on Texas Christian University. Maybe it was an ever darker symbol when the TCU chancellor's house was blitzed by burglars while he was here celebrating the Frogs' renaissance.

Maybe it was an uncomfortable sign when West Virginia hit a 33-yard pass on the first snap of Monday night's Bluebonnet Bowl, the place where TCU's renaissance was supposed to take another unbelievable step.

Nothing, in other words, was going to go right for the Horned Frogs. And nothing did. They were already behind, 14-7, when star running back Kenneth Davis was KO'd for the night with a leg injury. They were behind, 31-7, at the half. Listen, the chancellor had insurance but there isn't any insurance against a 31-7 deficit or a 31-14 final score.

So the bubbles in TCU's New Year Eve's champagne went flat early and, omens aside, there are several substantial reasons why.

One could reason, for example, that TCU's offensive dependency on precise handoffs and split-second timing had collected more rust than West Virginia's basic plowshare attack.

Linebacker Gearld Taylor watches the final seconds.

One could think that West Virginia had more recent experience in preparing for and playing bowl games. This was a new toy for the Frogs, who floated to Houston on a euphoric magic carpet of eight wins, their first bowl excursion in 19 seasons. The other guys had been to bowls the last four years. All week the Frogs had talked about trying to keep the game "in perspective" despite the party atmosphere. For West Virginia, it was just another hard night's work.

By halftime there was new meaning to the Frogs' battle cry of "UNBELEEEEVABLE!"

This was unbeleeeevable: Kenneth Davis leaving on a stretcher at the end of the first quarter and the Frogs facing a 31-7 deficit at the half.

There were some evil signs heading into this one and maybe everyone but the bookies, who made the Frogs 3½-point favorites, saw it coming.

Davis went out on the first play following the kickoff. Barry Riddick came in for Davis and freshman Roscoe Tatum lined up in a new formation at wingback right. Reversing his field, he attempted to take a pitch from Gulley — but bobbled it. West Virginia linebacker Van Richardson, who put the initial hit on Davis, recovered at the 2.

On third down, tailback John Holifield jumped over from the 1 less than two minutes into the second quarter.

West Virginia again struck quickly two series later, after an interception by TCU cornerback Billy

Oliver thwarted one march at the Frogs 10.

This time White hit Drewrey for 36 yards, then connected with a wide open Ron Wolfley coming out of the backfield for 22 more down to the TCU 5. White and Wolfley teamed up again on the next play for the score on a simple rollout.

At 28-7, the game began to look bad for the Frogs. But it got three points worse as West Virginia moved 74 yards to a Paul Woodside field goal with four seconds left in the half.

The Mountaineers had 355 yards total offense at halftime, 55 more than their season average.

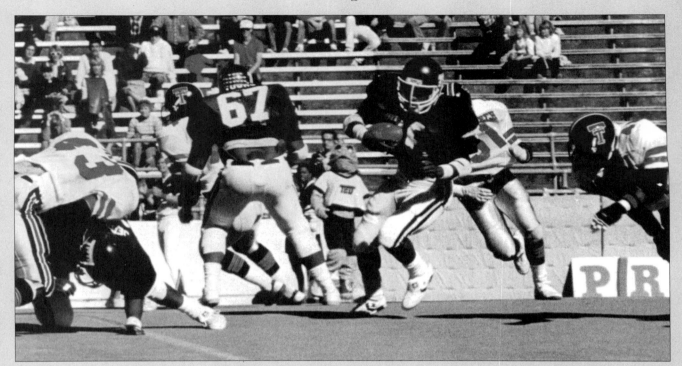

CHAPTER 47

Kenneth Davis exploded for runs of 82, 89 and 50 yards in a 219-yard performance against Texas Tech in 1984.

Kenneth Davis' Purple Glory

BY MIKE JONES
Fort Worth Star-Telegram

One of the most memorable gains of Kenneth Davis' time at TCU came 11 years after he no longer played football for the Horned Frogs. On May 11, 1996 — some 15 years after he first set foot on the university as a blue chip recruit out of Temple, Texas, and to little fanfare — the former TCU all-American and veteran of nine NFL seasons as a running back with the Green Bay Packers and the Buffalo Bills walked across a stage and received his college diploma.

"It was a very special moment in my life, a very emotional time for me and my family," Davis said. "My mom and dad were there with bells on and so were all my brothers and sisters. I was just so glad that my family could be there for that moment, because of all the things that had gone down."

When Davis finally completed a decade-old pledge to his mother that he would one day be part of graduation ceremonies, the memories of years gone by swirled through his mind.

The driving force in the Horned Frogs' unforgettable 1984 season, Davis also was the central figure in the exposure in September 1985 of numerous NCAA recruiting violations that in May 1986 resulted in crippling sanctions that included loss of scholarships, television money and three years of probation.

But as much as he harbors a private pain over the events that shattered a not-so-impossible dream of a Heisman Trophy and playing on a Southwest Conference championship football team, he is at peace with his past.

"When I was dismissed (from the football team and withdrew from school) in 1985, it never took away my love for TCU," said Davis, a five-figure contributor to the recent fund drive for the Walsh Complex that houses facilities for athletic training, rehabilitation and weight conditioning.

Nor should the events of 1985 detract from the significance of 1984's accomplishment and the moments of joy Davis gave a university and its long-suffering fans during a season when Frogs became princes once

Against Baylor in 1984, Davis had touchdown runs of 20 and 60 yards in TCU's second-half comeback victory.

more.

"Kenneth Davis did more for TCU football in one season than almost anyone else did in a whole career," said John Denton, the former Frog punter and teammate. "And certainly more than anyone in a long, long time."

Davis was TCU's first consensus all-American since Bob Lilly in 1959. Pumped by thrilling long-distance runs out of the Veer offense, his 1,611 yards gained in '84 erased the 29-year-old rushing record of Jim Swink, yet another Horned Frog immortal.

Davis led the nation that season with an incredible 7.64 yards-per-carry average, was third nationally in both per-game rushing total (146.5 yards) and touchdowns (17). The unanimous Southwest Conference player of the year also became the first back in SWC history to rush for more than 200 yards three times in a single season, was voted the SWC player of the week a record four times, authored seven runs from scrimmage of more than 50 yards and finished fifth in the Heisman balloting.

"For me, the 1984 season ranks above going to four Super Bowls," Davis said. "I loved playing for Buffalo and I loved my profession. But 1984 was something special."

Indeed. With his initial carry of the season — a 32-yard scoring run in an unexpected 62-18 victory over Utah State — Davis broke from the shadow of an undistinguished collegiate career and past a startled secondary.

Before his injury took the heart out of TCU's offense in the Bluebonnet Bowl loss to West Virginia, Davis sparked the Frogs to a then-SWC record 5,109 yards total offense. Most of it aground.

Highlights included a 239-yard effort in game No. 2, a 42-10 romp over Kansas State. A rare 18-yard touchdown reception in TCU's unforgettable rally to a 32-31 victory in Arkansas. Touchdown runs of 20 and 60 yards in a second-half comeback victory over Baylor. Runs of 82, 59 and 50 yards in a 219-yard afternoon against North Texas State. And second-half scoring runs of 39 and 75 yards during a 203-yard performance against Texas Tech, the season's eighth victory that propelled TCU into the Top 10 for the first time in 25 years and prefaced a sold-out Amon Carter Stadium showdown for the SWC lead against Texas

Davis was a consensus all-America halfback as a junior in 1984.

on national television.

"It's hard to explain the satisfaction you would get off Kenneth's runs," said Tommy Sheehan, a guard and a key figure in the Frogs' iron-man offensive line of 1984. "You work so hard as an offensive lineman and then to see the fruits of your labor come out in a Kenneth Davis touchdown was probably the most fulfilling time I ever had a football player. And in many ways, it was the most satisfying time of my life because we had never seen some of the things that happened to us.

"That 1984 season was more fulfilling because Kenneth Davis gave presence to us all in the shape and form of satisfaction in the jobs that we did."

At a stubby 5-foot-11 and 212 pounds, Davis presented a combination of exceptional leg power, balance, and a surprising stiff-legged kick that resulted in a burst of acceleration.

"He wasn't Thurman Thomas or Barry Sanders, with real-quick lateral movement, but Kenneth had real explosive straight-ahead speed," recalled Anthony Sciaraffa, along with Anthony Gulley, one of two quarterbacks who were the primary field generals of Coach Jim Wacker's Veer offense.

"He didn't have a real big juke fake, it was more a slip-of-the-hip thing. But he could be standing still and hit full speed really quickly."

Davis could break for the long gainer from inside or out. But the prevalent memories are of his long-distance sprints down the sideline after taking the pitch on the Veer's third option, cradling the ball in the outside arm and swooping out of the backfield into the secondary to duel one-on-one with a defensive back caught in the quandry of trying to stop a runaway freight running on undefined track.

For Davis, it was life itself, the sustenance of his being.

"To be out there turning that corner with either Gulley or Sciaraffa pitching that ball was like breathing," Davis recalled. "It was like second nature, like an artist working something on canvas. There were few thrills like that.

"You just don't know the feeling when someone pitches that ball and it's floating out there to you. It seems like it takes forever to get there, because you're ready to go. And then again, when it's there and you touch it, the moment is gone and you're gone. And then it seems like everything has happened simultaneously, all of a sudden."

Certainly all of a sudden is what it must have felt like to defenders who knew what was coming yet nevertheless were sometimes powerless to stop it, fighting in a dream, throwing punches that never land.

"In college you don't really have the time to change your schemes, so you know people are going to be prepared for you week in and week out," Davis mentioned. "But it didn't stop us. It was incredible."

Though that near-championship season ended with three consecutive losses to Texas, Texas A&M and West Virginia, the best lives on in memory.

"We learned so much more than the game of football," Sheehan remembers. "Things I practice in the work I do today (as an Irving policeman). The mental toughness, the integrity. That was the most important part of it for me.

"As life has gone on, I've found that you draw from your most intense experiences. And I draw from those days, from the satisfaction and togetherness of that season."

So it was, and is, with Kenneth Davis, comfortably retired from the NFL and looking for new opportunities.

"I played with four guys and probably three coaches at Buffalo who are going to be in the NFL Hall of

Davis looks for open yardage in the Rice defensive secondary.

Fame," Davis noted. "I was surrounded with tremendous talent.

"At TCU in '84 we didn't have a whole lot of tremendous talent. We just had a lot of guys who were willing to give it all for whatever it was worth, working together in a collective way. Those are the kinds of things in life that you can never put a pricetag on.

"I don't know if what happened that season was unexpected," he considered. "Most of all — for us — it was unknown. We started climbing that hill and we never wanted to step back. We saw a new horizon each time we took a step. And that was the part that was so challenging, so emotional.

"What made us so successful was that we kept reaching for those goals. We kept on climbing."

Some hills just take longer to climb than others.

CHAPTER 48

JEFFERY FINDS CURE FOR TCU

BY MIKE JONES
Fort Worth Star-Telegram

NEW ORLEANS, SEPT. 13, 1986 — Ironically, in the land of the famous Bourbon Street hangover, TCU found a cure for a 10-month losing headache. Meet Tony (Plop-Plop, Fizz-Fizz) Jeffery. Oh, what relief he was.

TCU	0	10	24	14	48
Tulane	3	14	0	14	31

Breaking loose from both the Veer and the Wishbone, the Gladewater junior burst upon the 1986 scene with 343 yards rushing on only 16 carries, scoring five touchdowns as the Horned Frogs buried Tulane, 48-31, in a wild-and-wooly season opener before 34,187 in the Superdome.

"The best performance I've ever seen by a running back," gushed Frog coach Jim Wacker, who saw the end to a five-game losing streak dating to November. "Was this ever what the doctor ordered."

Jeffery's afternoon was by a single yard the best performance by a running back in the 71-year history of the Southwest Conference and the sixth-best ever in NCAA Division I-A competition.

Former University of Texas all-American fullback Roosevelt Leaks in 1972 gained 342 yards — on 37 carries — against SMU in the Cotton Bowl for the previous SWC high.

Jeffery set TCU records for rushing, touchdowns in one game — equalling his total number of scores in 1985 — and highest average gain per carry.

Jeffery, who did not gain a yard on two first quarter carries, averaged 21.4 yards each time he touched the ball.

Jeffery scored on runs of 11, 38, 32, 81 and 67 yards. The 32- and 38-yarders came out of the Wishbone, as did a non-scoring 34-yard jaunt. In addition to the 67- and 81-yard TD's out of the Veer, Jeffery also popped for 25 and 67 yards out of the two-back tandem.

His first question to Wacker after the game was, "Coach, can we spend the night?"

Bourbon Street was off-limits to the team Friday night, but certainly this bunch is due for some cajun-

Tony Jeffery's 343 yards on 16 carries broke the SWC rushing record.

style celebration.

"Oh, what a difference a year makes," observed junior offensive tackle Brian Brazil. "It's like night and day. This was the most fun we've had in a long time."

The Frogs were 3-8 last season.

"It isn't that hard when you're getting the kind of blocking that I was from the offensive line and downfield," said Jeffery. "They were opening big holes. And the quarterback (mostly David Rascoe) was doing a great job of reading the tackle and then making the pitch. I would just read my blocks and take off."

Truthfully, Jeffery did some brilliant open-field running, zig-zagging around sprawling defenders.

"He made some moves that were just flat unbelievable," said Wacker. "Most of what he got was on his own. He juked some of 'em and he ran over some others."

Along the way, the Frogs rushed for a school-record 508 yards, breaking the mark of 494 set two years ago in that smashing 62-18 victory over Utah State that sent the Frogs off to an 8-4 season.

The total offense of 557 yards is third-highest in TCU history, behind that 677-yard day against Utah State and a 667-yard effort late in 1984 against Rice.

Jeffery's performance overshadowed a brilliant afternoon by the Tulane tandem of quarterback Terrance Jones and receiver Mark Zeno.

Jones, only a sophomore, set Green Wave offensive records for passing yardage (388), total offense (484) and plays of record (62) out of Coach Mack Brown's high-octane option attack.

Zeno, who caught three passes for 116 yards against the Frogs last year, burned them for 191 yards on 10 receptions, including an 8-yard scoring catch.

"Those two are about as good a 1-2 combination

Jeffery on the Run

Tony Jeffery's 343 yards on 16 carries against the Green Wave is the most by a TCU back. Here's a look at the Top 10 TCU one-man rushing days:

Name	Year	Att.	Yds.
Tony Jeffery	1986	16	343
Bobby Davis	1970	18	247
Kenneth Davis	1984	29	239
Jim Swink	1955	15	235
Kenneth Davis	1984	16	219
Ross Montgomery	1967	36	213
Kenneth Davis	1984	29	203
Tony Jeffery	1984	13	182
Mike Lutrell	1973	32	180
Kevin Haney	1979	22	178

as you'll ever see," said Wacker. "Did they ever give us fits. Our defense isn't that bad. They made us look bad."

Tulane led TCU, 17-10, at the half. But the Frogs had done some sputtering to contribute to the deficit. Back Bobby Davis (12 carries for 70 yards) lost a pass in the open field that led to a 41-yard Tulane scoring drive, and wide receiver Keith Burnett couldn't pull down what would have been a high jump-catch inside the Tulane 5-yard line that was intercepted just before the half.

"If we'd been catching the ball, we'd have been ahead at the half," said Wacker.

But the Frogs did a number in the third quarter. The defense, which had been riddled for 288 yards total offense in the first half, finally asserted itself.

In the third quarter, Tulane netted only 14 yards total offense without a first down.

In the meantime, TCU put up 24 points on a 39-yard Lee Newman field goal (set up by a 34-yard Jeffery gain) and six-point romps of 38, 32 and 81 yards.

The teams traded a pair of touchdowns in the fourth quarter, Jeffery adding his final score from 67 yards out and Rascoe from 15 yards out with 57 seconds left in the game. Jeffery eclipsed the SWC rushing record on an 8-yard sweep to set up Rascoe's score.

Jeffery finished 14 yards shy of the all-time NCAA mark set by halfback Rueben Mayes of Washington State against Oregon in 1984.

"Was he that close?" asked Wacker. "We knew in the fourth quarter he was close to the conference mark, but even if we had known he was only 14 yards away we wouldn't have had him in the game as late as we did if Tulane hadn't kept scoring. Jeffrey wasn't in there to set records. He was there to win the ball game."

Dream Comes True for Jeffery

BY GALYN WILKINS
Fort Worth Star-Telegram

Tony Jeffery – remember him? Remember the future he promised TCU as a sleek streak of a freshman two years ago? Jeffery saw him again in the turbulent wee hours Saturday morning. He saw the young freewheeling Jeffery in his dreams as he tossed and turned in his hotel room.

"I'm not sure I saw this coming," he said in the late afternoon, "but I dreamed I had a good day."

It was better than a good day, of course. Better than a great day. Better than any Southwest Conference running back ever had. His 343 yards was the gaudiest parade seen in New Orleans since Mardi Gras.

He crashed Tulane's season opening party with a dramatic 186-yard, three touchdown explosion in the third quarter. It was as if he had suddenly awakened from a nightmare.

And in fact he had.

Last year, when he woke up on a late September morning to find his roommate and team godfather, Kenneth Davis, gone from his side, Jeffery felt the offensive weight of the team fall on his young shoulders. From an 840-yard season as a freshman, he tailed off to 695.

Would he survive that terrible march, in which he and the Frogs were merely trying to survive so they could go somewhere and hide?

He knew he would. The coaching staff knew he would. "We're waiting for him to explode," Coach Jim Wacker said in the spring. "We have to have a good year for him."

It didn't hurt Saturday that Davis, now with the Green Bay Packers and conveniently in town to run against the Saints Sunday, was on the TCU sideline.

When the Frogs took a 34-17 lead into the fourth quarter and the conquest of Tulane appeared certain, they took on another objective.

"We knew he was closing in on the record," said right guard W.C. Nix. "Someone on the sideline was keeping track. We were determined to get it for him."

Late in the fourth quarter, on TCU's next-to-last possession, Jeffery passed the 14-year-old record of Texas' Roosevelt Leaks. Only the sideline accountants lost sight of him in the pile of yards. The Frogs thought he had tied the record and didn't know he broke it by a yard until the official audit reached them.

As you might expect, given the excitable buoyancy of the man, Wacker was dazzled by Jeffery's extravagance and said, "It was the best effort by a running back I've ever seen."

The third period had to be one of the toughest one-way quarters ever played by a TCU team. The Frogs scored three touchdowns and a field goal on five possessions and Tulane didn't make a first down.

"It was a matter off getting everything back together," Jeffery would say later. "We made a lot of mistakes in the first half."

On the second series, Jeffery broke three tackles on his way to the end zone. It was a sparkling display of power and balance, by far the best play of a game that would eventually end with 1,121 yards of offense.

But then, as 34,187 lucky witnesses in the Superdome would soon discover, Jeffery was just then getting warmed up.

He had three more touchdown streaks, each seemingly more dazzling than the last. Tacklers ricocheted off him, harmless bullets off a guy who had just stepped out of a phone booth. He ran over tacklers on the goal line twice. He made more wicked moves Saturday than a Bourbon Street exotic dancer in a career.

"Oh, man, did he come to play today!" a hoarse Wacker shouted as he barged into the winners' locker room.

Said Kenneth Davis: "Oh, man, did he make people forget me in a hurry."

CHAPTER 49

TCU wide receiver Stephen Shipley (87) races toward the end zone on an 86-yard pass from Leon Clay.

FROGS SHOCK AIR FORCE

BY MIKE JONES
Fort Worth Star-Telegram

FORT WORTH, OCT. 21, 1989 — TCU coach Jim Wacker could be excused if he was at a loss for a new and imaginative adjective to describe the Horned Frogs' shocking 27-9 upset of 19th-ranked Air Force yesterday afternoon at Amon Carter Stadium.

Air Force	3	0	0	6	9
TCU	6	7	7	7	27

So Wacker unabashedly reached back into the archives and brought forth a bauble tarnished from little recent use.

"This is just an unbelievable win for us, and it's been a long, long time since I've been able to use that word,"

Wacker said.

True enough. Yesterday's stunning intersectional upset of the Falcons (6-2) has to rank as the most monumental TCU victory in the Wacker era since the original unbelievable – that 32-31 victory against the University of Arkansas in 1984.

"This is one of the greatest victories we've had since I've been here," Wacker said.

And one that should gag the Wacker critics for the time being.

Winning for the fourth time in the last five games, TCU raised its season record to 4-3.

"TCU brought the fight to us, and I salute their staff and their team," Air Force coach Fisher DeBerry said.

With its second heroic effort in as many weeks,

TCU's defense grounded Falcons quarterback Dee Dowis, the Academy's Heisman Trophy candidate. And the job the Frogs did on Dowis may have inadvertently kept the Davey O'Brien Award from leaving the state of Texas. Houston quarterback Andre Ware — who appears at Amon Carter Stadium in two weeks — in less than three hours became the odds-on Davey O'Brien Award favorite.

Time and again, the Frogs cut Dowis off from getting to the corners. When he did, he didn't get far. And when he pitched, TCU's run support from the secondary was there.

"We had a sea of purple around the ball all day," TCU defensive coordinator Marc Dove said.

Despite the absence of three defensive starters out with injuries, TCU permitted Dowis — the nation's 10th ranked rusher with a 120-yard average — only 28 yards on eight carries, a career low in 28 games as a starter. Almost half of that total came on a 13-yard run in the fourth quarter. Dowis went to the air 19 times, completing only five for 69 yards. Safety Levoil Crump, the defensive leader with 12 tackles, intercepted him on third-and-37 with 6:21 to play.

"I'll take the blame for this loss," Dowis said. "TCU is tough. They just came out and stopped us."

The Falcons entered the game with the nation's top-ranked rushing attack, averaging 408 yards a game. TCU held them to 229.

"I can't say enough for our players' heart and desire," Dove said. "We needed that kind of performance today. Although we played a great football game and shut 'em down Air Force is a great football team. Their record and their numbers both indicate that."

The Frogs not only overcame Dowis, they survived

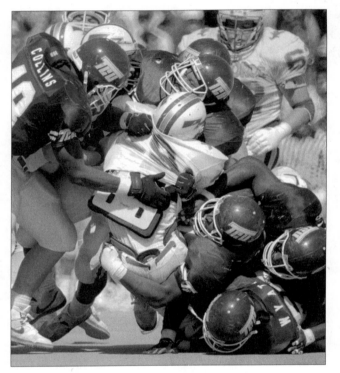

Air Force's Rodney Lewis is stacked up by a swarm of TCU defenders.

the loss of their total offense leader, Ron Jiles. The TCU quarterback went out with a sprained right wrist with 1:03 remaining in the first quarter and did not return, though X-rays proved negative.

Redshirt freshman Leon Clay entered the game with TCU ahead, 6-3. Clay not only successfully completed the touchdown drive in progress, but he also connected with freshman wide receiver Stephan Shipley for touchdown passes of 86 yards and 23 yards in the second half. The Frogs compiled 429 yards of total offense and 18 first downs.

Clay's totals for the day: Ten completions in 11 attempts for 165 yards and two touchdowns.

"The first time Leon has been in a game that's meant something, and look what he does," Wacker said. "What an incredible job."

Clay's performance was even more significant considering that Jiles, who carried a 243-yard total offense average into the game, was upstaging Dowis.

Jiles set up the Frogs' first touchdown on their opening drive of the game with a 27-yard scramble to the Air Force 5. On second-and-goal from the 3, he went left on the option. Running into a white-shirted wall, he reversed his field and sprinted to the right corner of the end zone to complete an 87-yard, 10-play drive.

When Jiles went out, the Frogs had a first-and-10 at the Falcon 25.

"In the huddle, we just told each other to keep our heads up," Palmer said. "The way our running game was going, we knew Leon could do just as a good a job handling the ball off as Ron could."

Clay did more than that. He passed to slotback Michael Jackson for gains of 4 and 14 yards and a first down at the Air Force 6. He then handed the ball off twice to Palmer, the last one going for a leaping yard and a 13-3 TCU lead at 13:52 of the second quarter.

Things looked shaky for the Frogs' offensive early in the second half, but the defense kept the Falcons from capitalizing on good field position early in the quarter before Clay and Shipley found daylight.

Air Force got nothing out of two series that began at the TCU 42 (after a 22-yard punt by Rex Roberts) and the 41 (after a Curtis Modkins fumble).

TCU took over at its 16 on a punt with 9:03 remaining in the quarter. Clay lost 2 yards on a scramble. He then rolled out right under pressure, looking for Shipley, an offensive hero in last week's victory against Rice.

"It was supposed to be a 5-yard stop route," Clay said. "Ship saw I was in trouble and kept going. I just lofted the ball and he went up and caught it. After that, it was all Shipley."

Shipley took the ball over his shoulder at the TCU 45. Air Force corner Robert Lietzke went up with Shipley, came down on his back side emptyhanded and Shipley was off to the races and an 86-yard touchdown. It was the longest TCU pass reception since an NCAA-record 99-yard pass from Scott Ankrom to James Maness against Rice in 1984.

Butterflies Aside, Freshman Frog Turns in Exceptional Game

By Galen Wilkins
Fort Worth Star-Telegram

Leon Clay usually has Saturday afternoons off. No linebackers beating on him in relentless workouts, no coaches yelling at him, no endless meetings. No hits, no long runs, no errors, no bruises.

In other words, a big upset to him on most weekends means having to take a shower after the game, sending his uniforms to the laundry and wearing a Band-Aid out of the locker room.

Clay's statistics for six games as the No. 2 TCU quarterback — one pass completion in three shots, 28 yards on six runs — picture a player whose feet were not even damp, much less wet. Clay's numbers would come up next year.

"Leon!" The way it came out of TCU coach Jim Wacker's throat early yesterday afternoon, it sounded like a frantic SOS.

Leon Clay, whose number suddenly came up with 1:03 remaining in the first period against 19th-ranked Air Force, jumped. A bunch of butterflies suddenly took flight in his stomach.

"Big butterflies," he would say. "The biggest I've felt since my first game in high school."

On Clay's freshman shoulders the Frogs placed a 6-3 lead. No telling how long he would have to carry it. No telling how long it would take to fix Ron Jiles' sprained right wrist.

"He had a big frown," Wacker said later. "I told him to show me a big smile and go out and have some fun. I had to tell him again, but then his face really lit up."

Wacker could have told Clay he was the luckiest No. 2 quarterback in the country at that given moment. In the first place he had a three-point lead. Second, he had running back Tommy Palmer, who had taken flight on a 180-yard afternoon. And third, he had a defense intent on suffocating Air Force's volatile offense.

Before Clay could start having fun and turning his day off into one of the biggest upsets in Wacker's TCU years, he had to make some kind of a play that would shake the jitters out of his fingers.

"On his second play, they blitzed him," Wacker said. "He saw it coming, checked off to a pass over the middle and hit it. Beautiful."

That took some of the jitters out of Wacker, too. He went into the game figuring he needed the experienced Jiles at his creative best to have a chance.

"I had no idea what Leon would do," he said. "I

"It was just a spur of the moment decision to go deep when I saw Leon in trouble," Shipley said. "Leon put the ball on the money."

He did it again early in the fourth quarter after another stand by the defense.

Linebacker Jason Cauble, who made a big fourth-down stop of Rice quarterback Donald Hollas a week ago, foiled the Falcons' "fumble-rooskie" play that had worked for a touchdown against Notre Dame last week.

On fourth-and-4 at the TCU 11, the 200-pound Cauble dropped 245-pound guard Steve Wilson for no gain.

TCU then moved 89 yards in 15 plays behind Palmer's running to the touchdown that slammed the door in Air Force's face.

On third-and-5 from the Falcon 23, Clay dropped back and lofted the ball toward the corner of the end zone on a timing pattern. Shipley was where he was supposed to be when the ball got there.

"There aren't many defensive backs who can go up and get the ball against a 6-foot-5 receiver," Clay said.

Shipley took the perfectly thrown pass over the top of 5-9 cornerback Eric Faison.

Air Force drove to a late touchdown with 1:31 to play. A run for two points failed.

don't think he had any idea, either. But he came through. He held onto the ball, he hit a couple of touchdown passes that put it on ice. He did the things he had to do."

Jiles would spend the rest of the afternoon on the bench, his wrist on ice, "his" team and Clay, his protege, becoming more confident by the moment.

The game became one shot of relief after another for Clay, who would up hitting 10 of 11 for 165 yards. On top of that he was fumble-proof.

"I'm the relief pitcher on this team," he said. "This is Ron's team. But I'll tell you, it was a relief to keep it going after he went out. It was a relief to get out of the hole in the third quarter."

If the Frogs were ever in danger of letting this game slip away, it was three minutes deep in the third when an out-of-bounds punt gave them the ball six inches in front of their goal.

"Anything could happen back there," Clay said. "I was thinking, 'Don't fumble — not here.'"

Anything could happen. But good things were happening to TCU, so naturally Palmer streaked

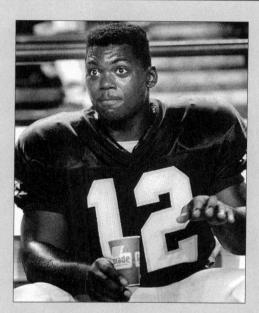

Freshman Leon Clay completed 10 of 11 attempts for 165 yards.

across right end for 26 yards with the first nervous snap.

What to make of this 27-9 upset? Did TCU, like Leon Clay, suddenly reach into the future and snatch it back to the present? Wacker himself would say, "I thought we'd be doing things like this next year because we're so young and so beaten up."

College football, one of its ancient philosophers once said, is a game in which ordinary teams often do extraordinary things.

Considering TCU's youth and injury-riddled roster, this was an extraordinary performance. But not necessarily a fluke.

"We're beginning to feel like a team getting it all together," Jiles said. "We're getting to know each other and know the offense. And today you see what our defense can do."

"Isn't this the dangdest game?" Wacker said. "You never know ... you never know."

Clay, of course, never knew he'd sweat out a uniform yesterday. He must know now, though, that it looked good on him.

CHAPTER 50

RAZORBACKS FROG-TIED

By Mike Jones
Fort Worth Star-Telegram

Tony Rand blocked a punt and recovered in the end zone for a touchdown.

LITTLE ROCK, OCT. 6, 1990 — They're baaaack.

On the sixth anniversary to the day of TCU's historic 32-31 football victory against Arkansas in Fayetteville, Ark., that launched the 1984 Bluebonnet Bowl season, the Horned Frogs pulled another unbelievable shocker on the Razorbacks.

TCU	14	20	6	14	54
Arkansas	10	0	8	8	26

Ripping up its comeback script of the past three games, TCU struck early and often to blindside the No. 21-ranked Razorbacks, 54-26, here at War Memorial Stadium before 51,612 stunned fans.

"Maybe this removes any question about whether our last three comeback wins were flukes," said tight end Kelly Blackwell, who caught eight passes for 120 yards and a touchdown.

Maybe so.

The Frogs are 4-1 for the first time since 1984 and off to a 2-0 start in the Southwest Conference for the first time since 1958. They had not won in Little Rock since 1951, and this is only their third victory against the Razorbacks in 31 years.

The 54 points were the most an Arkansas team has given up in an SWC game in 68 years and the most TCU has scored in the 70-year history of the series. Or in any other SWC game since the school joined the league in 1919.

"When you're hot, you're hot," an ecstatic Coach Jim Wacker said. "And tonight, were we ever hot."

In an effort to jump-start themseleves, TCU players said before the game that they were going to pretend the first quarter was the fourth, when they had authored those three consecutive heart-stopping victories against Missouri, Oklahoma State and SMU to which Blackwell referred.

The strategy worked. And how.

Saftey Tony Rand roared in to block an Arkansas punt and recovered the ball in the end zone for the Frogs' first touchdown less than two minutes into the game. That play launched an offensive explosion that accounted for a season-high 514 yards and changed the scoreboard on eight of TCU's first nine possessions, spilling over into the third quarter, which the Frogs entered with a 34-10 lead.

Jeff Wilkinson kicked two of his school record-tying four field goals in the third quarter to post TCU's biggest lead, 40-10, with 8:58 remaining in the period.

The offense operated almost flawlessly, averaging a gain of 7.4 yards a play without a turnover.

Quarterback Leon Clay turned in another superb performance, completing 19 of 28 passes for a career-high 332 yards and four touchdowns. Clay also added the period to the game's exclamation point, scoring the final touchdown on a 1-yard run with 3:39 to play.

"It's not like I was doing anything special," said Neon Leon, who has accounted for 10 TD's in the last two games. "They were the ones running for all those touchdowns."

Clay's scoring strikes included perfectly launched missiles of 88 yards to flanker Kyle McPherson and 57 yards to slotback Richard Woodley.

Blackwell caught an 18-yard touchdown pass, and split end Stephen Shipley was on the receiving end of a 7-yard touchdown catch.

Running back Curtis Modkins chipped in 124 yards on 23 carries.

"We kept telling the kids they'd been getting better each week, but we had not put it all together," Wacker said. "I'll guarantee you, tonight, we put it all together."

TCU's defense continued its trend of setting the table for the offense with two interceptions and a fumble recovery that led to 17 points. The Frogs also posted a late first-half goal-line stand that denied Arkansas points after the Razorbacks had first-and-goal at the TCU 2-yard line.

"That was a big letdown, not scoring right before the half (was over)," said Arkansas quarterback Quinn Grovey, who has lost only five times in 25 career starts for the Hogs.

"They dominated us. I always felt like we could come back ... but they kept scoring."

After Rand's blocked punt rocketed the Frogs to the start they were looking for, Arkansas came right back to drive to a field goal. TCU answered with a 79-yard, 10-play drive that culminated in Blackwell's 18-yard touchdown catch.

The Hogs came back to go 56 yards in only four plays, scoring on a 36-yard pass from Grovey to split end Derek Russell.

But then TCU's defense got a handle on the Arkansas attack and the Frogs ended the game of ping-pong in startling fashion with a 20-point second quarter.

Included were the 88-yard scoring catch by McPherson and the 57-yard TD strike from Clay to Woodley that came in bam-bam succession in less than 90 seconds.

"Leon blew the game wide open with those two long touchdown passes," Wacker said. "When you

Leon Clay completed 19 of 28 passes for 332 yards and 4 touchdowns and ran for 1 touchdown.

Offensive Notables

Clay's performance was the best by a TCU quarterback since Steve Stamp passed for 399 yards vs. Rice in 1981. His four touchdown passes were the most since David Rascoe hit four vs. Texas Tech in 1987 and the 88-yarder was the second longest in TCU history. ... Modkins posted the fourth 100-yard game of his career and his 121 yards were the most ever by a TCU running back against Arkansas.

can strike like that, the other team is in trouble."

Arkansas coach Jack Crowe, who is now 2-2, said the Frogs highlighted his team's deficiencies.

"Our team has been fragile in a number of areas since the beginning of the season. It showed up tonight," Crowe said. "Our offense moved the ball well (409 yards) but the three turnovers took away any opportunities we might have had."

Chapter 51

Pat Sullivan, the 1971 Heisman Trophy winner, was chosen to lead TCU back to its glory days of yesteryear.

Sullivan Era Begins at TCU

By Mike Jones
Fort Worth Star-Telegram

Fort Worth, Jan. 2, 1992 — One of the major criticisms leveled at Jim Wacker in the earlier years of his nine-year tenure was his tendency to make brash promises that he was not always able to keep.

Today, however, the man who succeeded Wacker as TCU's football coach and the man who hired him were eager to take Wacker's place on the end of the limb.

"Our ultimate goal is not to get to the Cotton Bowl," new Horned Frogs coach Pat Sullivan said at his introductory news conference. "Our goal is to win it."

Moments later, Chancellor William E. Tucker, who headed the six-man search committee that tapped Sul-

livan on New Year's Eve, also alluded to lofty intentions.

"A few years ago, we said we wanted our program to be competitive," recalled Tucker, who also hired Wacker in December 1982. "Now, we do not want to just be competitive. We want to win. We believe this coach is a winner."

So began what the principals obviously believe is a new era of football at TCU.

Sullivan accepted TCU's offer of a five-year contract, something the school was unwilling to give to Wacker. Terms were not disclosed. Based on Wacker's total package, allowing a variance and including such perks as a car, country club membership, etc., the total package is estimated at $750,000.

Athletic director Frank Windegger would not discuss contract specifics but replied, "This contract has stability not only for Pat Sullivan, but for TCU as well."

The 1971 Heisman Trophy winner at Auburn — who put aside a 10-year business to begin coaching in 1986 — Sullivan, 41, was announced after a search that began in earnest by telephone Saturday night. Auburn athletic director Pat Dye, contacted for permission to talk to Sullivan, was among the first dialed after the committee's initial meeting that afternoon.

"Pat was our unanimous choice," said Buddy Dike, a former letterman who is also a member of the board of trustees and the committee. "Once we talked to him, I didn't feel it was necessary to go any further.

"We could have spent all week talking to people, but timing is so important because of recruiting that we acted when we felt we had found the guy we were looking for."

Dike echoed Tucker's sentiments that Sullivan could take TCU football to a higher level and added that he felt Sullivan would unite Horned Frog lettermen and alumni who over the years became split on the Wacker issue, regardless of his won-loss record.

"Being the kind of player he was, I think Pat will relate to the ex-lettermen really well," Dike said. "I think Pat brings us an added dimension. He strikes me as the kind of guy who can bring everyone together."

Dike said he had no problems with the fact that Sullivan has in title never been a coordinator and his only coaching experience has been his six seasons at Auburn as quarterback coach.

"Almost all great head coaches were assistant coaches at one time or another," Dike reasoned.

Sullivan left later in the afternoon to return to Alabama to say his goodbyes, clean out his desk and talk to some of his now-former players whom he has not been able to contact previously.

Sullivan described himself as "a player's coach" and Auburn quarterback Stan White agreed.

"We had more than a coach-player relationship," White said. "He has a way of knowing how you feel, the things you're going through, especially during the rough times.

"I hate to see him leave Auburn, but I think he'll make a great head coach."

Sullivan promised his teams would excel in three areas.

"There may be more talented teams, but there is no reason we can't be the most prepared, the most disciplined and best-conditioned team in the Southwest Conference or in the country," he said.

He said he and his wife, Jean, were attracted to TCU by the people they met and the opportunity for him to become a head coach.

"The No. 1 thing that sold us was that everyone I talked to (in the process) was the kind of people I like to be around," Sullivan said. "Everyone was on the same page and wanted the same thing ... to have a winner in football while maintaining an outstanding academic program. It was an atmosphere I felt comfortable in."

Asked if he were familiar with the disadvantages he would face in recruiting against SWC giants Texas and Texas A&M, Sullivan replied, "What disadvantages?"

He admitted he had not yet completely toured TCU's athletic facilities.

Sullivan also fielded some questions concerning any involvement he might have with the problems emerging at Auburn in the Eric Ramsey controversy. He said he had no first-hand knowledge of the situation, a contention backed by Auburn officials and also, Windegger said, by NCAA enforcement executive David Berst.

"All I know is basically what I've heard and what I've read in the newspapers," Sullivan said.

Tucker said that if Sullivan was not considered "clean" by National Collegiate Athletic Association standards, "He would not be standing here today."

Windegger said he was first impressed with Sullivan less than a month ago, several weeks before Wacker resigned Dec. 26. Windegger was attending a National Football Foundation Hall of Fame banquet in New York. Sullivan was one of the inductees.

Sullivan was chosen to give the acceptance speech for all 15 inductees, including actors Ed Marinaro and Alex Karras. At the close of his speech, he received a standing ovation.

"I was so impressed (with Sullivan), I turned to a friend and said, 'That guy is something else. Why hasn't someone snapped him up as a head coach?' " Windegger recalled.

This week, someone did.

CHAPTER 52

SHOCKER: TCU 23, TEXAS 14

BY MIKE JONES
Fort Worth Star-Telegram

FORT WORTH, Nov. 7, 1992 — Longtime TCU sufferers with tears in their eyes hugged and savored the moment. Jubilant fans and several Horned Frogs players swung from the crossbar of the goal post in the south end zone at Amon Carter Stadium. Minutes later, team captains shaved secondary coach Paul Jette's head.

| Texas | 0 | 7 | 7 | 0 | 14 |
| TCU | 14 | 2 | 0 | 7 | 23 |

"Where's the party, man?" TCU safety Greg Evans said. "Just give me directions."

Roll back the rug and get out the 45's. Party with the ghosts at Carlson's Drive-Inn. TCU has beaten Texas again, shaking off the longest losing streak to a Southwest Conference opponent in 77 years of league membership.

The Horned Frogs yesterday parlayed a team effort into a monumental 23-14 victory against the 20th-ranked Longhorns. It was the first TCU victory against Texas since 1967, the first in Fort Worth since 1958.

More importantly for the present — and the future — the victory gave rookie coach Pat Sullivan something to hang his program's hat on after winning only one of his first eight games.

"The University of Texas has a program rich in tradition, and Coach (John) Mackovic has done a great job this year, but today was our day," said Sullivan, who was 8 the last time TCU defeated the Longhorns in Fort Worth. "The key to this victory was heart."

Mike Adams runs into TCU's (left to right) Shelby Carroll, Carter Coleman, Sadd Jackson and John Washington.

Everybody played a part.

TCU's offense put together the season's longest scoring drive and converted a defensive turnover for a 14-0 first-quarter lead. And for the second consecutive week, the Frogs' defense played with the heart of thieves.

The defense stifled Texas' running game, intercepted three passes, caused a fumble to set up a touchdown, forced a kicking-game mistake that amounted to a momentum-maintaining safety shortly before halftime and sacked UT quarterback Peter Gardere seven times.

Cornerback Tony Rand added the defensive exclamation point by returning an interception 58 yards for the clinching touchdown with 7:21 remaining.

"Texas can say they had an off day, that they weren't ready, that they were sick or whatever they want to say," linebacker Mike Moulton said. "But the fact remains, we kicked their butts."

Moulton was a key figure in funneling UT's trademark sweep inside to pursuit. TCU held Texas to a net rushing gain of 52 yards after the Longhorns had rolled up 600 yards in their past two games against Houston and Texas Tech.

Mackovic was generous with his compliments and made no excuses.

"Don't take away that TCU outplayed us," Mackovic said. "The mistakes by our team were only dramatically shown because of their play. They were well prepared."

The loss severely damaged Texas' national status and no doubt will drop the Longhorns (5-3, 3-1 in SWC) out of the Top 25. It also likely knocked them out of Cotton Bowl contention and erased them from the Blockbuster Bowl's list. TCU certainly kicked the pins out from under the momentum of UT's five-game winning streak in recording the first SWC victory under Sullivan.

"We've been on a hard grind for over a month," Mackovic said. "(But) if you're not ready to play on any given Saturday, you're going to get beat."

Clearly, TCU was ready to play.

Mixing plays well between the pass and run, the Frogs drove 83 yards to the game's first touchdown with 3:30 remaining in the quarter on a 1-yard dive by Curtis Modkins.

Leon Clay and Pat Sullivan at practice.

Little more than a minute later, TCU scored again. Freshman defensive end Chris Piland ripped the ball out of the hands of Longhorns running back Adrian Walker, and tackle Royal West recovered at the UT 20.

John Oglesby gained 12 on first down. Then quarterback Leon Clay threw perfectly to spilt end Stephen Shipley on a post pattern for the score and a 14-0 lead after Jeff Wilkinson's point-after-kick.

"Leon put it right over the head of the linebacker. If it had been any lower, he would have knocked it down," said Shipley, who caught his 13th career touchdown.

Texas' only scores came on drives of 36 and 15 yards — one after a shanked punt, the other after an interception.

Walker scored Texas' first touchdown on a 15-yard scamper after TCU was forced to punt twice because of a procedure penalty. Kevin Cordesman, who had kicked for 39 yards the first time, wobbled one only 21 yards on his second try. Walker scored with 5:38 remaining in the second quarter.

A heads-up play on punt coverage by redshirt freshman Rick LaFavers forced UT's Grady Cavness into a mistake — batting the ball out of the end zone to prevent LaFavers from jumping on it — resulted in a safety and a 16-7 lead with 20 seconds remaining in the half.

"The little extra momentum that safety gave us just before the half really helped," Sullivan said.

Texas closed to 16-14 on Curtis Jackson's 1-yard run with 10:16 remaining in the third quarter, a drive that was set up when Cavness intercepted Clay and returned 5 yards to the 15.

The key series took place midway through the final period.

Texas took over at its 35 on a punt. Gardere then scrambled for 14 yards and a first down, before TCU's defense slammed the door.

Moulton sacked Gardere for a 6-yard loss on a first down. Linebacker Sadd Jackson then dropped Phil Brown after a 4-yard screen pass.

Then came the game's deciding play.

Texas lined up with three receivers left. One went deep. One flared into the flat. Flanker Justin McLemore ran a curl 12 yards deep — the yardage needed for the first down.

"Our linebacker picked up the back in the flat, so I just hung back on the curl route," Rand explained. "Gardere had been telling us where he was going to throw all afternoon. He was

Texas' Joey Ellis breaks up a pass to TCU's Jimmy Oliver during the second quarter.

looking at the curl, and I just robbed it."

He then jumped into Curtis Modkins and cut down the right sideline. He juked Gardere at the 15, then spun around tackle Troy Riemer at the 5 and scored.

Sullivan was with Rand step for step down the sideline.

"I thought I was going to pass him on the way to the end zone," Sullivan said.

For TCU, almost anything was possible on this day.

Big 'D' at TCU

BY MIKE HEIKA
Fort Worth Star-Telegram

TCU defensive coordinator Reggie Herring drew a fist from his ankles and thrust it triumphantly into the air as the final seconds of the Horned Frogs' 23-14 upset of Texas ticked off the clock.

Defensive tackle Royal West danced and threw his 280-pound frame into the arms of his teammates. Tony Rand stayed on the field long after his teammates had headed to the locker room so he could field television interviews and savor the moment.

It was definitely a day for the Frogs' defense.

"You don't know how much this means to the kids," Herring barked, still shouting an hour after the game had ended yesterday. "I can't describe to you the pressure that these kids have been under because of the losing season and how physically outmanned they have been.

"We've got mostly 210- to 220-pound linemen, and we have one linebacker who's 185 pounds, and we're going against their 300-pounders on the offensive line. People have no idea just how tough it is.

"But they went out and showed guts and character, and they won decisively. There is nobody out there who can call this a fluke, and I want you to print that."

TCU's defense held Texas to 228 total yards — the same Texas offense that was averaging 428 yards of offense per game.

Despite an offensive line that averaged 280 pounds a man, Texas rushed for just 52 yards against TCU's defense.

"They played well and deserve all the credit," Texas center Turk McDonald said. "They flat out beat us."

That was sweet music for a defense that was play-

Long Time Coming

TCU's 23-14 victory was its first at home against Texas since 1958. A look at the Horned Frogs' Ft. Worth futility against the Longhorns through the years:

Year	Winner	Loser	Score
1958	TCU	Texas	22-8
1960	Texas	TCU	3-2
1962	Texas	TCU	14-0
1964	Texas	TCU	28-13
1966	Texas	TCU	13-3
1968	Texas	TCU	47-21
1970	Texas	TCU	58-0
1972	Texas	TCU	27-0
1974	Texas	TCU	81-16
1976	Texas	TCU	34-7
1978	Texas	TCU	41-0
1980	Texas	TCU	51-26
1982	Texas	TCU	38-21
1984	Texas	TCU	44-23
1986	Texas	TCU	45-16
1988	Texas	TCU	30-21
1990	Texas	TCU	38-10
1992	TCU	Texas	23-14

ing hurt. Defensive end Tunji Bolden wasn't expected to play because of a hip flexor and contributed a few plays. Defensive end Brad Wallace came back from a leg injury he suffered during the game and played down the stretch.

Defensive tackle Brian Brooks continues to play with a stress fracture in his leg. And linebacker Brad Smith continued to limp after every play, leading the defense as he does every week despite a list of injuries that would send most players to the sideline.

"Before, it seemed like we just gave up when we heard the word (Texas)," Smith said. "But our coaches convinced us we could win if we just play 'guts out' football."

CHAPTER 53

Chris Brasfield scored on a 62-yard screen play, which sealed TCU's victory.

Frogs quarterback Max Knake completed 13 of 24 passes for 236 yards and 3 touchdowns in TCU's 44-29 win.

DAVIS DASHES PAST NEW MEXICO

BY JOHNNY PAUL
Fort Worth Star-Telegram

ALBUQUERQUE, N.M., SEPT. 10, 1994 — A broad smile came across the face of Andre Davis.

TCU's talented junior tailback had no idea how many yards he shredded New Mexico's defense for in front of

| TCU | 10 | 14 | 7 | 13 | 44 |
| N. Mexico | 0 | 12 | 7 | 10 | 29 |

27,957 here at the Lobos' University Stadium.

"I know for quite a few," Davis said, "probably close to 200."

Talk about your low-ball estimates.

Davis rushed for 325 yards and two touchdowns on 31 carries, and the Horned Frogs recorded a much-

deserved 44-29 victory.

TCU (1-1) needed almost every yard in this better-than-point-a-minute contest.

"I know that neither Dennis (New Mexico coach Dennis Franchione) or I would want to admit it, but this game was critical to both teams," TCU coach Pat Sullivan said. "Whoever won would go away with something positive and some momentum for next week, while the loser would be in an early hole."

Davis found holes all evening.

His rushing total ranked as the 20th best in NCAA history. The TCU single-game rushing record is held by Tony Jeffery, who rushed for 343 yards against Tulane in 1986.

"Well, with those holes I was having to run through I had to have a lot," Davis said. "I certainly couldn't have done it without all the great blocks I had from everyone — the offensive line, the fullbacks, tight ends and wide receivers."

Although the Lobos (0-2) never led, they never allowed the Frogs to breathe easy.

Wide receiver Chris Brasfield, though, helped ease the Frogs' worst fears when he took a screen pass 62 yards for a touchdown on the first play from scrimmage after New Mexico scored its final touchdown with 6:36 remaining to play.

The touchdown gave TCU a 15-point lead, but the defense had to protect it as New Mexico threatened twice late in the final quarter.

"Our team showed some character," Sullivan said. "We jumped out early, then New Mexico came back and got right back into the game. But we responded well. That's something to be proud of."

TCU took a 17-0 lead as it dominated the first quarter and the opening minutes of the second.

TCU quarterback Max Knake — who completed 13 of 24 passes for 236 yards — threw the first two touchdown passes to tight end Brian Collins for a 7-0 lead, and fullback Koi Woods gave the Frogs a 17-point advantage when he scored with 13:27 remaining in the first half.

The Lobos, though, answered.

New Mexico tailback Eric Young's 2-yard touchdown run in the third quarter made the score 24-19, and his 15-yard touchdown reception with 12:22 remaining to play pulled the Lobos to 31-26.

However, only seven plays later, Davis went 44 yards for his second touchdown with 10:03 remaining in the final quarter.

"He's a good football player," Franchione said, "and we've made a career for him the past two years."

Davis ran through New Mexico's defense for 167 yards on 31 carries a year ago in Fort Worth, when the Frogs won, 35-34.

In all, the two offenses combined for:

- 73 points;
- 1,202 yards of offense;
- 563 yards of rushing;
- 58 first downs.

"If they didn't stop themselves, I don't think they got stopped," Franchione said. "You can't miss a turn when they're doing that."

Davis didn't, not with the likes of Barret Robbins, Boyd Milby, Kevin Brewer, Brandon Hickman, Ryan Tucker and Clifford Barnes.

"We just have some guys that have been playing together for three years now and running the same plays for three years," Sullivan said. "They carried out their assignments, played mistake-free for the most part and put points on the board. The credit has to go to Pete Hoener (TCU's offensive coordinator) and his kids for the job they did."

Davis Runs for 325 Yards to Accent Offensive Show

BY MIKE JONES
Fort Worth Star-Telegram

In the victorious visitors' locker room at New Mexico's University Stadium last night, TCU players joined arms and voice in a chorus of the old Bill Withers' classic, *Lean On Me.*

After 1,202 yards of total offense at an altitude of 5,120 feet in the Horned Frogs' 44-29 victory against UNM, everybody needed somebody to lean on.

"I don't think I've ever pass-rushed so many times in my life," TCU defensive tackle Royal West said, who was in on each of the 62 passes attempted by Lobos quarterback Stoney Case.

"Hey, I'm tired," Frogs coach Pat Sullivan said. And he didn't even play.

If anyone should have been gassed, it was Frogs running back Andre Davis, who carried 31 times for a career-high 325 yards. But if he was, he never mentioned it.

"My ankle is bothering me a little bit," Davis said with a shrug. "But I'll be OK.

"It was emotional night for us. We thought we went out last week and proved we were a good football team (in a 27-17 loss at No. 18 North Carolina). But there were a lot of people who doubted us and didn't think we could do it. But tonight was a whole team effort. The offensive line did a great job and the defense came through when they had to. It was an all-around team effort."

It certainly was a stellar effort from the offensive line, which consistently beat the Lobos off the ball.

"We were a lot quicker than they were up front," center Barret Robbins said. "But one of the big things is that we had our assignments down and that's one of the benefits of being with these coaches for two seasons and two spring trainings.

"New Mexico threw a lot of different looks at us up front we weren't expecting. But we adjusted."

The way Davis was running last night, it was not necessary to hold blocks for long, quick guard Boyd Milby said.

"This was the old Andre tonight," Milby said. "He was slashing and hitting those holes as soon as they opened up. That makes our job a lot easier."

Sullivan said his biggest fear was that Davis — or fullback Koi Woods — would get hurt.

"Midway through the second quarter, they had both run 36 plays," Sullivan said.

Indeed, when Davis went to the sidelines after his TCU record-setting 87-yard touchdown run gave the Horned Frogs a 24-6 lead with 8:27 left in the half, the Frogs did not make a first down after scoring on their first four possessions.

"What can I say about Andre tonight?" Sullivan questioned. "It was just a great performance, by Andre as well as the offensive line."

Davis has gained 456 yards in two games against the Lobos.

Andre Davis

"If he could play us every week, he'd win the Heisman Trophy," New Mexico coach Dennis Franchione said.

At midweek, West put this game in the "must" category for the Frogs.

"We had to have it," he reiterated last night. "This was a huge win for us. We had to get this thing going in the right direction for our confidence."

Davis set a record for most rushing yardage against New Mexico, surpassing the 316 yards that Emmitt Smith of Florida gained against the Lobos in 1989. Davis fell short of Tony Jeffery's TCU record of 343 yards gained against Tulane in 1986. His 347 all-purpose yards tied Jeffery's afternoon in the Superdome in New Orleans.

CHAPTER 54

TCU CLAIMS A SHARE OF TITLE

By Johnny Paul
Fort Worth Star-Telegram

FT. WORTH, NOV. 25, 1994 — Success often comes with a price, and TCU coach Pat Sullivan yesterday stuck one of the university's suit-and-tie guys — Chancellor William Tucker — with the bill.

| Texas Tech | 0 | 7 | 7 | 3 | 17 |
| TCU | 0 | 10 | 6 | 8 | 24 |

"I spent some of your money today," Sullivan informed Tucker in a jubilant locker room. "I told the kids that if they won, they would get rings."

The Horned Frogs' 24-17 victory against Texas Tech, witnessed by 43,219 at Amon Carter Stadium and a national television audience, gave TCU a share of its first Southwest Conference championship since 1959. It also all but ensured that the Frogs (7-4) will receive an invitation to a bowl game — probably the Independence — for the first time since 1984.

"They displayed the things that championship teams do during that fourth quarter," said Sullivan, who guided the Frogs to their co-title in three seasons. "They needed something they could take with them for the rest of their lives, and now they've got it."

The Cotton Bowl-bound Red Raiders (6-5) forged ahead, 17-16, on Tony Rogers' 41-yard field goal with 6:23 remaining. After the kickoff, 69 yards separated the Frogs from the end zone when quarterback Max Knake addressed his offensive mates.

"I told the offensive line, 'Look, this is up to you guys,'" Knake said. "'If you open the holes, Andre will get us there.'"

Andre is tailback Andre Davis, who entered the contest as the nation's fourth-leading rusher but had only 36 yards in 17 carries to that point.

"I kind of knew it was going to fall on my shoulders," Davis said. "Coach (running backs coach Bud Casey) said we were going to find out what men are made of. That made me feel good, because I hadn't done much all day."

He almost single-handedly cost Texas Tech an outright championship.

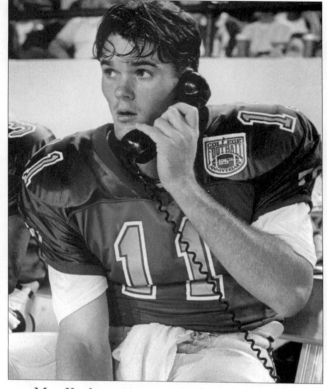

Max Knake gets instructions from the press box.

Davis' first carry during the game-winning march produced 12 yards. Then, he scooted 28 yards on the drive's second play, which gave the Frogs a first down at the Tech 29. He did not touch the ball for two consecutive plays, and TCU faced third-and-6 at the Tech 25. The coaching staff opted for one of the Frogs' bread-and-butter plays — Smoke Draw.

"It's a play," Davis said, "that's been very successful for us this year."

Success measured 14 yards and another first down, and the Frogs went to the well again two plays later — same play, same ball carrier. Tech defenders first hit Davis at the 6-yard line, but he kept his legs churning until he crossed the goal line for the game-winning touchdown with 3:59 remaining.

The ensuing two-point conversion featured the same play, same ball carrier and same result.

"He's something, isn't he?" Sullivan said of Davis, who finished with 107 yards on 23 carries. "He's a special football player."

TCU coach Pat Sullivan enjoys a victory ride following the 24-17 win over Texas Tech.

The Frogs, though, would not have been in position to win had it not been for Knake, who continually delivered the big play. He threw for 267 yards with 12 completions in 23 attempts.

"I can't say enough about the way Max played," Sullivan said. "He's come so far."

Texas Tech's defense, which bottled TCU's running and short-passing game, forced the Frogs to go up top.

"That's what they gave us," offensive coordinator Pete Hoener said. "We had to make it work."

Senior receiver Jimmy Oliver, TCU's fastest player, twice beat Tech cornerbacks deep for touchdowns. The first, an 89-yard reception on a fade pattern, gave the Frogs a 10-0, second-quarter lead. The second, a 62-yard reception on a deep post, gave TCU a 16-14

TCU Struts Big-Time Look Against Tech

By Galyn Wilkins
Fort Worth Star-Telegram

Texas Tech's football pilgrims brought a unique habit to Amon Carter Stadium yesterday — tortillas. Tortillas by the hundreds, enough edible Frisbees to feed a Spanish regiment, floated onto Amon Carter Stadium yesterday morning.

It could have been much worse for TCU's Horned Frogs, of course. Those pitched discs could have been bricks. Or boll weevils. They could have been loaded with hot peppers.

And the Red Raiders could have shown up for the Breakfast Bowl with one or two more double-barreled Zebbies and Byrons.

Far as anyone could tell, no one was hurt in the tortilla blizzard. And in the end, even though they threw a combined 360 yards at the Frogs, quarterback Zebbie Lethridge and running back Byron Hanspard caused no permanent damage, either.

Afterward, when TCU coach Pat Sullivan's blood pressure had slowed to a mere boiling point, he took another look back at a hard-earned 24-17 victory and those two impressive freshmen and said, "That's going to be a good team next year, too. Real good."

Yesterday, though, Tech came to town good enough to win a trip to the Cotton Bowl in a wildly convoluted Southwest Conference race that seemed almost like a lottery.

But in the end, the Raiders were asked to stop Andre Davis and create a touchdown against a no-choke purple defense.

If any of the 43,219 customers — has TCU football turned into a sport for morning persons? — wondered how far Sullivan has brought the Frogs since four victories last season and since a 42-18 midseason disaster at the hands of Baylor this year, they could review the last six munutes of yesterday's Brunch Battle.

In those half-dozen minutes, the Frogs drove 69 yards for the lead, ran across a two-point conversion and deflected two Red Raiders assaults. There

Andre Davis scored the game-winning touchdown.

lead with 11:22 remaining in the third quarter.

"We figured they were going to key on Andre, just for the simple fact that he's the best there is," Oliver said. "Somebody had to step up if they were going to take Andre out."

The defense also rose to the occasion, constantly harassing Tech quarterback Zebbie Lethridge, whom they sacked nine times for 49 yards in losses.

"I just wanted to win," said defensive end Vincent Pryor, who recorded $4\frac{1}{2}$ sacks.

Pryor's teammates surely will absolve him, as the Frogs did end a 35-year championship drought.

"For the most part, we played like a championship team week in and week out," said defensive guard Royal West, who contributed with two sacks. "In a way, it kind of makes you sick how we played against Texas and Baylor (34-18 and 44-18 losses). We could have been playing for something bigger today."

were more big plays in those last minutes than in six years of pre-Sullivan futility.

Sullivan spoke of "a lotta heart and composure." He also could speak of the emerging Max Knake, who speared the Raiders with two long TD passes to Jimmy Oliver, and of Andre Davis, who personally yanked the game out of the Raiders' grasp on the Frogs' winning TD drives.

"When I came here, we couldn't run the ball," said Sullivan, as an introduction to the new fact that the Frogs can run it as well as throw it and catch it. Davis stepped off 63 of the 69 yards during the winning drive.

"That was big-time football," cheered linebacker coach Charlie Rizzo. "You realize we had nine sacks? Big-time football."

Big-time crowd, big-time rallies, big-time finish. "Hopefully, we've started something here," said Sullivan, heading for his backyard grill to await a bowl summons.

"We worked hard at getting to a bowl. That's all we talked about."

At least some of his warriors were thinking Cotton, though.

"This was our Cotton Bowl," said

safety Rick LaFavers. "It's tough to see them (the Raiders) go after today, but we reached a goal. We worked toward winning seven games and getting into a bowl."

Their reward likely will be a invitation from the Independence Bowl today. A Wednesday night in Shreveport might not be on the social calendars of many college football players, but the Frogs would ask you to realize that their phone hasn't rung for 10 years and their Decembers have been cold and joyless.

Though they accepted the bottom line of yesterday's joy ride with quiet pride, they should be allowed to boast of how they arrived at 7-4.

Tortilla blitz, Red Raiders blitz, they survived everything thrown at them by the Lubbock residents. Then they showed off a new and unique habit of their own — dragging a game out of the fire in the last moments.

CHAPTER 55

TCU CAN'T OVERCOME ELEMENTS

Quarterback Max Knake was unable to rally his team.

BY JOHNNY PAUL
Fort Worth Star-Telegram

SHREVEPORT, LA., DEC. 28, 1994 — A decade slipped by before TCU's Horned Frogs resurfaced from oblivion into the postseason. The Frogs mostly slipped here, however, as they trudged and muddied themselves on the rain-drenched field of Independence Stadium.

Virginia	0	10	10	0	20
TCU	0	3	0	7	10

Some 27,242 fans — a majority of them TCU supporters — withstood the temptation to stay home, snuggle underneath a blanket and join their Frogs in spirit by watching ESPN's national broadcast of the 19th annual Independence Bowl.

The view, though, became painstakingly clear no matter the vantage point. Virginia proved too good for these upstart Frogs and captured its first bowl win in five attempts since 1987 with a 20-10 victory.

"We can't use the field as an excuse in any way," TCU coach Pat Sullivan said. "I couldn't be more proud of our football team, but we weren't quite good enough in a couple of ways."

The 18th-ranked Cavaliers (9-3) dominated the point of attack, where so many games are won or lost.

The Frogs and their Southwest Conference-leading offense, which averaged 411.6 yards per game this season, sustained nothing on this chilly, wet night. Virginia, which entered the contest with the nation's No. 1-ranked defensive unit against the run, surrendered only 191 yards and 11 first downs.

Meanwhile, the Cavaliers consistently pounded the Frogs (7-5) en route to 237 rushing and stunned them when quarterback Mike Groh completed a 37-yard touchdown pass to Tyrone Davis for an insurmountable 17-3 lead with 9:08 remaining in the third quarter.

Groh, selected the game's most valuable player on offense, completed 14 of 23 passes for 199 yards with one interception to complement the powerful running of tailback Kevin Brooks and fullback Charles Way.

Brooks, who rushed for a game-high 114 yards on

TCU Bowl Results

TCU's Horned Frogs have appeared in 15 bowl games in school history including the Independence Bowl against Virginia, posting a 4-10-1 record.

Year	Bowl	Outcome
1921	Dixie Classic	Centre 63, TCU 7
1936	Sugar	TCU 3, LSU 2
1937	Cotton	TCU 16, Marquette 6
1939	Sugar	TCU 15, Carnegie Tech 7
1942	Orange	Georgia 40, TCU 26
1945	Cotton	Okla. A&M 34, TCU 0
1948	Delta	Mississippi 13, TCU 9
1952	Cotton	Kentucky 20, TCU 7
1956	Cotton	Mississippi 14, TCU 13
1957	Cotton	TCU 28, Syracuse 27
1959	Cotton	TCU 0, Air Force 0
1959	Bluebonnet	Clemson 23, TCU 7
1965	Sun	Tex. Western 13, TCU 12
1984	Bluebonnet	W. Virginia 31, TCU 14
1994	Independence	Virginia 20, TCU 10

17 carries, and Way (90 yards on 24 attempts) led an assault that appeared to be threatened only once.

The Frogs managed their only touchdown early in the fourth quarter and even then they needed four downs to convert from a fresh set of downs that began at the Virginia 1-yard line.

TCU quarterback Max Knake, who suffered his worst game during his breakthrough season, threw a 1-yard touchdown pass to tight end Brian Collins to pull the Frogs within 10 points with 13:28 remaining.

Yet, the Frogs never scored again. The running of junior tailback Andre Davis, who rushed for 97 yards on 24 carries, failed to provide enough offense on a night when Knake struggled.

"I played terrible," said Knake, The Star-Telegram SWC Offensive Player of the Year. "If I would have played better, there may have been a different outcome."

Knake did not use the rain as an alibi for his performance, which included only eight completions and an interception in 24 attempts for 65 yards.

"It may have been raining but there were plays when the ball was dry in my hands and I didn't make the play," Knake said. "I owe that to my preparation."

Virginia defensive end Mike Frederick, though, woke up with a smile yesterday.

"As a defense, we were happy when we woke (yesterday) morning and saw the rain," said Frederick, the game's most valuable defensive player. "This was a challenge of our strength against theirs, which was a good offensive line. We took this as a challenge."

Virginia's defense appeared almost invincible during the first half, when the Frogs netted only 87 yards and four first downs.

Sullivan, who coached the Frogs to a share of their first SWC championship in 35 years and first bowl game since the 1984 team played in the Bluebonnet Bowl, agreed.

"The effort and fight they showed for 60 minutes was incredible," Sullivan said. "They played with the heart of a champion. You want to hang your head, but the love and emotion they showed just makes you sick to lose.

CHAPTER 56

Memorial Stadium: Once TCU's Home on the Road

By Whit Canning
Fort Worth Star-Telegram

When TCU invades Memorial Stadium Saturday, two old pals will clasp hands in warm and sincere greeting for the last time in the forseeable future.

With a cheery salute, the Horned Frogs and the Texas Longhorns will go their separate ways after this one, as the Southwest Conference sinks below the horizon.

This is therefore, the last opportunity Austin residents will have to see the "Cockroaches." That is the description Darrell Royal used to describe TCU after the Frogs had wrecked his 1961 team's dreams of a national title.

For TCU, it became an immediate rallying cry for future engagements; for Royal – who was 6-5 in his first 11 meetings with the Frogs – a remark he spent years trying to refute.

Even today, he says, "I never called those people cockroaches. I said they were like a bunch of cockroaches."

The full text was, "It's not so much what they eat and carry off, it's what they fall into and mess up."

Royal's attempts to maneuver around the statement draw a laugh from the man largely responsible for it.

That man is Buddy Iles, who caught a 50-yard pass from Sonny Gibbs for the only score in that 6-0 victory.

"Darrell and I have actually become pretty good friends since then," says Iles, now a Marshall businessman. "I've tried to tell him that his version is the

Red Oliver scores a touchdown in TCU's 14-0 win over Texas in 1932.

same as calling someone a cockroach, but he doesn't see it that way."

In any case, the top-ranked Longhorns fell with a thud that day. But it was hardly the only notable victory for the Frogs in Memorial Stadium – an alien battleground on which, for years, they seemed to feel strangely at home.

Highlights from TCU's biggest wins there:

1941: TCU 14, Texas 7

With a collection of stars including Jack Crain, Pete Layden, Noble Doss, Mal Kutner, Chal Daniel and Spec Sanders, the Longhorns were considered the greatest team in SWC history up to that time – ranked No. 1 in the nation and featured in *Life* magazine after flattening six foes by a combined 230-27 margin. Then they were tied, 7-7, by Baylor.

TCU was next, and while the Frogs (7-2-1) were a good team, they were not considered to be in the same class with Texas, a three-touchdown favorite.

But Dean Bagley ran 55 yards for a TCU touchdown and Derrell Palmer led a defense that shut the Longhorns down with five first downs and 148 yards.

Late in the fourth quarter, Emery Nix – who had thrown for 337 yards against Baylor two weeks earlier – led the Frogs on a 73-yard drive capped by a 19-yard pass to Van Hall with eight seconds left.

With Rose Bowl hopes dashed, Texas consoled itself by smashing Texas A&M, 23-0, and Oregon, 71-7, in its final two games, and the victory catapulted the Frogs into the Orange Bowl.

Henry Moreland (22) leaves behind a trail of Texas defenders as he sprints 56 yards for the winning TD in 1959.

1949: TCU 14, Texas 13

The Longhorns finished 6-4, which was misleading, since their losses – two of them to top-10 teams – were by a combined margin of 10 points. They were led by the passing combo of Paul Campbell (1,372 yards) and Ben Procter (43 catches, 724 yards).

TCU (6-3-1) had an even better passing attack, led by Lindy Berry (1,445 yards), but was not considered as strong a team overall. Dutch Meyer, however, had a plan.

Offensively, the Frogs kept the ball on the ground (Berry had a 33-yard scoring run); defensively, they smothered Campbell with a rush off a nine-man line.

"My job was to guard Procter (now a TCU professor)," Berry says, laughing. "I did a terrific job – I think he only caught eight or nine passes. But we won the game."

1955: TCU 47, Texas 20

This was the signature game in the illustrious career of Jim Swink, who ran through the Longhorns for 235 yards on 15 carries with scoring runs of 1, 62, 57 and 34 yards – thus negating Texas fans' attempts to "hex" the Frogs by burning red candles all week.

The Longhorns' new "Hook 'Em Horns" hand gesture was also of little help, as TCU quarterback Chuck Curtis complemented Swink's performance by throwing for 175 yards and three touchdowns, as the Frogs rolled up 523 yards.

"They just overwhelmed us," Texas coach Ed Price said of the Cotton Bowl-bound Frogs. "On one run there, Swink zig-zagged through us so often I kept waiting for him to stop and rest."

1959: TCU 14, Texas 9

Despite a Friday snowstorm, five chartered planes and 9,000 fans followed TCU's defending SWC champions to Austin for a showdown with Royal's second-ranked Longhorns, who came in at 8-0.

One headline during the week read, "Defending Champion Meets Heir Apparent" since the Frogs, at 5-2, seemed to be struggling. But when it was over, Royal said with his usual candor: "We just got a real good whippin'."

Trailing, 9-0, at the half, the Frogs limited Texas to one first down and 21 yards in the final 30 minutes behind a defense led by all-Americans Don Floyd, Bob Lilly and Jack Spikes. In the end, the Frogs won it on the lightning legs of Harry Moreland.

With the score 9-7 in the fourth quarter, Moreland slid through a hole in the right side of the line, juked defensive back Mike Cotton, veered left, and turned toward the goal line, outrunning Cotton and Rene Ramirez on a 56-yard sprint.

After a triumphant leap in the end zone, Moreland was enthusiastically pummeled by his teammates, prompting the former Arlington Heights High School star to observe, "I haven't been hit this hard all year."

TCU finished with a 17-6 edge in first downs and 233 yards to 97 for the Longhorns. At the end of the season, TCU (8-2), Texas (9-1) and Arkansas (8-2) were ranked in the top 10 and shared the SWC crown in a three-way tie.

1961: TCU 6, Texas 0

The Longhorns were 8-0, ranked No. 1, averaging 33 points per game, and no one had played them closer than 21 points. They had the nation's fourth-best offense (second in rushing), directed by Cotton and led by all-American James Saxton. They were favored by 22½ points against a TCU team en route to a 3-5-2 finish.

But the Frogs were a quirky bunch, having knocked off a Kansas team quarterbacked by John Hadl and tying an otherwise unblemished Ohio State team, costing the Buckeyes a national title. TCU was led by the towering, 6-foot-6 Sonny Gibbs, the SWC's total offense leader, and sophomore fullback Tommy Crutcher.

Also, it was turning into a bad week in Austin. A few days before the game, nine UT students admitted accidentally killing the Baylor mascot – a bear cub named Ginger – during an attempted kidnapping the previous week. Various Texas officials, including Royal, apologized and promised restitution.

On Texas' first possession, Saxton was knocked cold by Bobby Plummer and Crutcher stopped Jack Collins on fourth down at the TCU 1-yard line. A pattern had been established; Texas was halted five more times during the game inside the 30-yard line. And although the Longhorns maintained advantageous field position through most of the contest, they were held to 198 total yards.

In the second quarter, the Frogs were sitting at midfield when Gibbs called a flea-flicker. Gibbs pitched the ball to halfback Larry Thomas and then took it

The TCU bench celebrates Moreland's 56-yard run to beat Texas, 14-9, in 1959.

back from Thomas on a handoff on a play that was originally designed as a run. But when Gibbs saw the Texas halfbacks coming upfield, he said, he "threw the heck out of it."

The pass found Buddy Iles running free at the Longhorns' 8-yard line. Texas' Jerry Cook made a desperate, diving tackle near the goal line, and it is Gibbs' view that "Buddy actually landed on the 2 and bounced over the goal line, but they gave it to us."

It was the only time in the course of a 10-1 season that Texas trailed.

In the fourth quarter, a disoriented Saxton fumbled inside the TCU 10, and the Frogs knocked six minutes off the clock in a drive to the Texas 45, where they punted the Longhorns into a hole from which they never emerged.

★ ★ ★

In 1965 and 1967, the Frogs beat 6-4 Texas teams, but as TCU defensive back Cubby Hudler once said, "Beating Texas is the greatest feeling in the world."

In '65, Emery Nix's son, Kent, directed TCU's Sun Bowl team to a 25-10 victory featuring four Bruce Alford field goals. When it was over, guard Porter Williams proclaimed: "The cockroaches are back!"

In '67, Bubba Thornton's 78-yard punt return keyed an 18-point fourth-quarter outburst that felled the Longhorns, 24-17.

After he scored, Thornton (now the UT track coach) jubilantly tossed the ball into the stands. It was the last moment of jubilation in Memorial Stadium for the Frogs, who have lost 13 consecutive games there.

CHAPTER 57

TCU to Join WAC

By Johnny Paul
Fort Worth Star-Telegram

Ft. Worth, April 22, 1994 — The Western Athletic Conference's Council of Presidents formally announced yesterday its intentions to expand the 10-member league to 16 by 1996 and extend invitations to TCU and five other universities.

"I'm very pleased that TCU has been included to explore membership in the WAC," said TCU Chancellor William Tucker, whose university joined SMU, Rice, Nevada-Las Vegas, Tulsa and San Jose State as those expected to join the league. "I'm also very pleased that some of the other members of the Southwest Conference were invited to explore membership into the WAC."

Tucker is expected to recommend to the Board of Trustees during a meeting scheduled at 4 p.m. today that TCU enter further expansion discussions with the WAC. Then, the matter will be put to a vote.

"My advice to you all is this is a done deal," said Hawaii President Kenneth Mortimer, chairman of the WAC's Council of Presidents. "The consultation that needs to occur on the separate campuses is something that we all need to respect.

"I think the consultation process with faculty, students and with boards of trustees and regents will be completed later in the week or early next week."

Mortimer said logistical concerns remain unresolved.

"There is going to be substantial conversations among us about the issues I've mentioned — that is, financial arrangements, the divisional structure and eventual scheduling," Mortimer said. "All of that needs to be worked out."

The WAC did not issue a deadline for response from the six universities, Mortimer said, "But a natural time line would be the Council of Presidents meeting in June."

Mortimer also applauded TCU.

"TCU is a marvelous addition," he said. "They have made a commitment to maintain a presence in Division I-A, and we're just excited about competing with them."

Several details remain undecided:

■ Divisional alignment. A fax sent Tuesday by Brigham Young President Rex Lee outlined a divisional plan, but he later termed the release premature. It placed TCU in the Eastern Division with Air Force, Colorado State, Rice, SMU, Tulsa, UT-El Paso and Wyoming. Brigham Young, Fresno State, Hawaii, New Mexico, San Diego State, San Jose State, UNLV and Utah were in the Western Division. A North-South arrangement also has been discussed.

"There has been no decision on conference structure ... and it will need to be discussed in the coming months," Mortimer said. "Travel costs, of course, will be a major factor in the divisional structure."

University presidents will make the decision, most likely after consultation with their athletic directors. New members will be consulted, Mortimer said, but he stressed that the current WAC members probably will make the decision.

■ When to begin play. Expanded competition in football cannot began until the 1996 season because of the current College Football Association contract, which ends after the '95 season.

"It's quite likely that some of the other sports would get going before then," Mortimer said. "I would foresee some interesting discussions about scheduling, particularly in the non-football sports, in the next year or so."

Officials at Texas and Texas A&M have expressed an interest in beginning non-football competition in the Big Eight as soon as possible, provided the SWC schools not involved in the Big Eight merger found a new league. TCU athletic director Frank Windegger said he could not comment on that before SWC athletic directors meet May 24-28 at Beaver Creek, Colo.

"That will be a mutual decision when we have our conference meeting," Windegger said. "We will do what's mutually beneficial for all.

■ Football playoffs. One WAC athletic director said a playoff game would be worth at least $1 million, and WAC commissioner Joe Kearney said the league intends to schedule that playoff to conclude the 1996 regular season.

WAC commissioner-elect Karl Benson said Wednesday that Las Vegas is being considered as a

host site for the title game, provided city officials enlarge the 32,500 seat Silver Bowl or build a bigger stadium. Mortimer expressed interest in allowing sites to bid for the championship game on a yearly basis.

■ Television contracts. WAC officials soon will complete plans for a five-year, $24 million contract with ABC and ESPN for football rights from 1996 to 2000.

Expansion will not affect those negotations, Kearney said.

■ Manageability/scheduling of a 16-team conference. The size of the conference makes it not only difficult for scheduling purposes, but WAC officials remain concerned that drifts will develop between the two divisions. Mortimer said he believed that can be addressed.

TCU 8, Toby's Business College 6
Nov. 28, 1896, Waco
Season records at kickoff: TCU 0-0, Toby's 0-0
Head Coaches: None
Top Players: TCU's Addison Clark Jr., A.C. Easley
(First collegiate football game for Horned Frogs.)

TCU 19, Arkansas 2
Oct. 22, 1920, Fayetteville, Ark.
Season records at kickoff: TCU 2-0, Arkansas 2-2
Head Coaches: TCU's W.L. (Billy) Driver, Arkansas' G.W. McLaren
Top Players: TCU end Dutch Meyer, halfback Wylie Harris; Arkansas fullback Benny Winkleman
(Key victory in Frogs' first undefeated (9-0) regular season.)

Centre 63, TCU 7 (Dixie Classic)
Jan. 1, 1921, Fort Worth, Panther Park
Season records at kickoff: TCU 9-0, Centre 8-2
Head Coaches: TCU's W.L. (Billy) Driver, Centre's "Uncle Charley" Moran
Top Players: TCU tackle Billy Acker, Centre's all-America tailback Bo McMillin
(An obvious mistake, but first postseason bowl game for any Texas school.)

TCU 7, Oklahoma A&M 6
Oct. 20, 1923, Stillwater, Okla.
Season records at kickoff: TCU 0-0, Oklahoma A&M 2-2
Head Coaches: TCU's Matty Bell, Oklahoma A&M's John Maulbetsch
Top Players: TCU end Blair Cherry, tackle Judge Green
(TCU's first game as Southwest Conference member, a win.)

TCU 3, Texas A&M 0
Nov. 7, 1925, Fort Worth, Clark Field
Season records at kickoff: TCU 3-0-1, Texas A&M 4-0
Head Coaches: TCU's Matty Bell, Texas A&M's Dana X. Bible
Top Players: TCU quarterback Herman Clark, Texas A&M tailback Joel Hunt
(Center Johnny Washmon's field goal upsets the eventual conference champion.)

SMU 14, TCU 13
Nov. 25, 1926, Dallas
Season records at kickoff: TCU 6-0-2, SMU 7-0-1
Head Coaches: TCU's Matty Bell, SMU's Ray Morrison
Top Players: TCU fullback Blackie Williams, SMU tailback Gerald Mann, "the little Red Arrow"
(In long-awaited clash of unbeatens, Frogs' last-minute field goal is ruled wide.)

TCU 0, Texas A&M 0
Oct. 22, 1927, Fort Worth, Clark Field
Season records at kickoff: TCU 3-0-1, Texas A&M 4-0
Head Coaches: TCU's Matty Bell, Texas A&M's Dana X. Bible
Top Players: TCU end Rags Matthews, Texas A&M tailback Joel Hunt
(Rags stops Hunt in famous tie, the only blemish on '27 record of great Aggie team.)

Texas 6, TCU 0
Nov. 14, 1928, Fort Worth, Clark Field
Season records at kickoff: TCU 7-1, Texas 5-2
Head Coaches: TCU's Matty Bell, Texas' Clyde Littlefield
Top Players: TCU quarterback Howard Grubbs, Texas tailback Dexter Shelley
(Frogs lose to late score in first big game with conference title at stake.)

TCU 15, Texas 12
Nov. 15, 1929, Austin
Season records at kickoff: TCU 7-0, Texas 5-0-2
Head Coaches: TCU's Francis Schmidt, Texas' Clyde Littlefield
Top Players: TCU halfback Cy Leland, Texas tailback Dexter Shelley
(Leland's 90-yard kick return for touchdown sparks Frogs to first win over Longhorns.)

TCU 7, SMU 7
Nov. 30, 1929, Fort Worth, Clark Field
Season records at kickoff: TCU 9-0, SMU 6-0-3
Head Coaches: TCU's Francis Schmidt, SMU's Ray Morrison
Top Players: TCU's Howard Grubbs, Cy Leland, SMU tackle Marion (Scrap Iron) Hammon
(Grubbs engineers fourth quarter drive to tie game, wrap up first conference crown for TCU.)

TCU 40, Arkansas 0
Oct. 11, 1930, Fort Worth
Season records at kickoff: TCU 3-0-1, Arkansas 1-2
Head Coaches: TCU's Francis Schmidt, Arkansas' Fred Thomsen
Top Players: TCU backs Cy Leland, Grassy Hinton, Arkansas tailback Jack Dale
(Leland leads way as Frogs romp to win in first game played in new stadium.)

TCU 3, LSU 0
Sept. 22, 1931, Fort Worth
Season records at kickoff: TCU 2-0, LSU 0-0
Head Coaches: TCU's Francis Schmidt, LSU's Russ Cohen
Top Players: TCU tailback Grassy Hinton, LSU tackle Jack Torrance
(Tackle Ben Boswell's field goal gives Frogs first win over major intersectional opponent.)

TCU 7, Rice 6
Nov. 21, 1931, Fort Worth
Season records at kickoff: TCU 8-2, Rice 6-2
Head Coaches: TCU's Francis Schmidt, Rice's Jack Meagher
Top Players: TCU halfbacks Blanard Spearman, Red Oliver, Rice tailback Jack Frye
(Spearman's zig-zagging 61-yard punt return proves the difference in a tough, exciting battle.)

TCU 0, SMU 0
Nov. 28, 1931, Fort Worth
Season records at kickoff: TCU 9-2, SMU 9-0
Head Coaches: TCU's Francis Schmidt, SMU's Ray Morrison
Top Players: TCU tailback Grassy Hinton, guard Johnny Vaught, SMU tailback Speedy Mason
(Frogs fight champion SMU to tie, knock perfect-record Ponies out of Rose Bowl bid.)

TCU 14, Texas 0
Nov. 11, 1932, Fort Worth
Season records at kickoff: TCU 7-0-1, Texas 6-1
Head Coaches: TCU's Francis Schmidt, Texas' Clyde Littlefield
Top Players: TCU's all-America guard Johnny Vaught, Texas backs Ernie Koy, Harrison Stafford
(With seven All-SWC players, Frogs overwhelm Longhorns on Veterans Day to clinch title.)

TCU 0, Centenary 0
Nov. 7, 1933, Shreveport, La.
Season records at kickoff: TCU 5-1, Centenary 3-0-2
Head Coaches: TCU's Francis Schmidt, Centenary's Homer Norton
Top Players: TCU halfback Charlie Casper, Centenary's All-America end Paul Geisler
(Frogs hold nationally-ranked Centenary's "greatest team" to scoreless tie.)

TCU 30, Texas 0
Nov. 28, 1933, Austin
Season records at kickoff: TCU 6-2-1, Texas 4-3-1
Head Coaches: TCU's Francis Schmidt, Texas' Clyde Littlefield
Top Players: TCU halfback Charlie Casper, Texas halfback Bohn Hilliard
(Casper races 105 yards for TD as Frogs help send Steers to first losing season in 36 years.)

TCU 7, Rice 2
Nov. 24, 1934, Houston
Season records at kickoff: TCU 6-3, Rice 8-0-1
Head Coaches: TCU's Dutch Meyer, Rice's Jimmy Kitts
Top Players: TCU halfback Jimmy Lawrence, Rice's all-America halfback Bill Wallace
(Lawrence stars as Frogs pull off big upset over SWC champs, spoil Owls' Rose Bowl hopes.)

TCU 28, Baylor 0
Nov. 2, 1935, Waco
Season records at kickoff: TCU 6-0, Baylor 6-0
Head Coaches: TCU's Dutch Meyer, Baylor's Morley Jennings
Top Players: TCU quarterback Sam Baugh, center Darrell Lester, Baylor tailback Lloyd Russell
(Baugh crushes Bears with three TD passes in collision of undefeated teams.)

TCU 27, Rice 6
Nov. 23, 1935, Fort Worth
Season records at kickoff: TCU 9-0, Rice 8-1
Head Coaches: TCU's Dutch Meyer, Rice's Jimmy Kitts
Top Players: TCU quarterback Sam Baugh, Rice's "Touchdown Twins," Bill Wallace, John McCauley
(Baugh's passing stuns Owls on another Big Game Saturday for Frogs.)

SMU 20, TCU 14

Nov. 30, 1935, Fort Worth

Season records at kickoff: TCU 10-0, SMU 10-0

Head Coaches: TCU's Dutch Meyer, SMU's Matty Bell

Top Players: TCU's Sam Baugh, Jimmy Lawrence, SMU's All-America scatback Bobby Wilson

(SMU grabs Game of Century and Rose Bowl bid with long, daring pass to Wilson in fading moments.)

TCU 3, LSU 2 (Sugar Bowl)

Jan. 1, 1936, New Orleans

Season records at kickoff: TCU 11-1, LSU 9-1

Head Coaches: TCU's Dutch Meyer, LSU's Bernie Moore

Top Players: TCU's all-America quarterback Sam Baugh, LSU end Gaynell Tinsley

(Tillie Manton boots 26-yard field goal in mud, TCU rated nation's No. 1 team.)

TCU 18, Arkansas 14

Oct. 3, 1936, Fort Worth

Season records at kickoff: TCU 1-1, Arkansas 1-0

Head Coaches: TCU's Dutch Meyer, Arkansas' Fred Thomsen

Top Players: TCU's Sam Baugh, end Walter Roach, Arkansas quarterback Jack Robbins

(Baugh outduels Robbins, TCU again beats team that ends up as conference champion.)

TCU 0, Mississippi State 0

Oct. 21, 1936, Dallas, Cotton Bowl (State Fair attraction)

Season records at kickoff: TCU 3-2, Mississippi State 3-1

Head Coaches: TCU's Dutch Meyer, Mississippi State's Jack Sasse

Top Players: TCU quarterback Davey O'Brien, Mississippi State halfback Ike Pickle

(Sophomore O'Brien, subbing for injured Sam Baugh, punts a record 24 times to preserve tie in big intersectional game marred by rain and mud.)

TCU 9, Santa Clara 0

Dec. 12, 1936, San Francisco, Kezar Stadium

Season records at kickoff: TCU 7-2-2, Santa Clara 8-0

Head Coaches: TCU's Dutch Meyer, Santa Clara's Buck Shaw

Top Players: TCU's all-America Sam Baugh, Santa Clara's all-American tailback Nello Falaschi

(Baugh's passes upset nation's last unbeaten team, knock Broncos out of No. 1 ranking.)

TCU 16, Marquette 6 (Cotton Bowl)

Jan. 1, 1937, Dallas

Season records at kickoff: TCU 8-2-2, Marquette 7-1

Head Coaches: TCU's Dutch Meyer, Marquette's Frank Murray

Top Players: TCU's all-America Sammy Baugh, Marquette all-America tailback Buzz Buivid

(Baugh outclasses Buivid in inaugural Cotton Bowl as end L.D. Meyer scores all 16 points.)

Fordham 7, TCU 6

Oct. 23, 1937, New York City, Polo Grounds

Season records at kickoff: TCU 1-1-2, Fordham 2-0-1

Head Coaches: TCU's Dutch Meyer, Fordham's "Sleepy Jim" Crowley

Top Players: TCU quarterback Davey O'Brien, end Don Looney, Fordham's "Seven Blocks of Granite"

(As O'Brien dazzles Easterners, Frogs lead powerful Rams for 57 minutes but lose squeaker.)

TCU 7, Rice 2

Nov. 20, 1937, Fort Worth

Season records at kickoff: TCU 2-4-2, Rice 3-2-2

Head Coaches: TCU's Dutch Meyer, Rice's Jimmy Kitts

Top Players: TCU's Davey O'Brien, Rice's new "Touchdown Twins," Ernie Lain, Ollie Cordill

(Frogs shock SWC champion Owls again, ironically by same score as 1934 upset.)

TCU 28, Temple 6

Oct. 7, 1938, Philadelphia

Season records at kickoff: TCU 2-0, Temple 1-1

Head Coaches: TCU's Dutch Meyer, Temple's Pop Warner

Top Players: TCU's Davey O'Brien, Temple halfback Al Juralewicz, guard Chuck Drulis

(O'Brien dazzles the East again. Pop Warner call Davey "greatest passer I've ever seen.")

TCU 39, Baylor 7

Oct. 29, 1938, Fort Worth

Season records at kickoff: TCU 5-0, Baylor 4-0-1

Head Coaches: TCU's Dutch Meyer, Baylor's Morley Jennings

Top Players: TCU's Davey O'Brien, halfback Earl Clark, Baylor's "Bullet Bill" Patterson

(O'Brien turns TCU's biggest standing-room-only game since 1935 SMU clash into a Purple rout.)

TCU 20, SMU 7

Nov. 26, 1938, Dallas

Season records at kickoff: TCU 9-0, SMU 6-2

Head Coaches: TCU's Dutch Meyer, SMU's Matty Bell

Top Players: TCU's Davey O'Brien, center Ki Aldrich, SMU tailback Ray Mallouf

(O'Brien and seven other Frogs go 60 minutes to wrap up national title in all major polls.)

TCU 15, Carnegie Tech 7 (Sugar Bowl)

Jan. 2, 1939, New Orleans

Season records at kickoff: TCU 10-0, Carnegie Tech 7-1

Head Coaches: TCU's Dutch Meyer, Carnegie Tech's Bill Kern

Top Players: TCU's Davey O'Brien, Ki Aldrich, Carnegie Tech tailback George Muha

(Davey's second-half passes and field goal handle the "Beast of the East" in thrilling game.)

TCU 20, Indiana 14

Oct. 11, 1941, Bloomington, Ind.

Season records at kickoff: TCU 2-0, Indiana 0-2

Head Coaches: TCU's Dutch Meyer, Indiana's Bo McMillin

Top Players: TCU quarterback Kyle Gillespie, Indiana's all-America halfback Billy Hillenbrand

(Triple-threat Gillespie leads Frogs to first victory over opponent from Big Ten.)

TCU 14, Texas 7

Nov. 15, 1941, Austin

Season records at kickoff: TCU 5-2, Texas 6-0-1

Head Coaches: TCU's Dutch Meyer, Texas' Dana X. Bible

Top Players: TCU quarterbacks Emery Nix, Dean Bagley, Texas all-America backs Jack Crain, Pete Layden

(Last-minute TD pass, Nix to Van Hall, stuns nation's No. 1 team and *Life* magazine's cover boys.)

TCU 15, SMU 13

Nov. 29, 1941, Fort Worth

Season records at kickoff: TCU 6-2-1, SMU 5-3

Head Coaches: TCU's Dutch Meyer, SMU's Matty Bell

Top Players: TCU's Kyle Gillespie, halfback Frank Medanich, SMU fullback Presto Johnston

(Gillespie rallies Frogs in second half. Victory earns TCU the Orange Bowl invitation.)

Georgia 40, TCU 26 (Orange Bowl)

Jan. 1, 1942, Miami

Season records at kickoff: TCU 7-2-1, Georgia 8-1-1

Head Coaches: TCU's Dutch Meyer, Georgia's Wally Butts

Top Players: TCU quarterback Kyle Gillespie, end Bruce Alford, Georgia tailback Frank Sinkwich

(Sinkwich's finest game enables Georgia to outlast TCU's second-half comeback.)

TCU 7, UCLA 6

Sept. 25, 1942, Los Angeles, Memorial Coliseum

Season records at kickoff: TCU 0-0, UCLA 0-0

Head Coaches: TCU's Dutch Meyer, UCLA's Babe Horrell

Top Players: TCU quarterback Emery Nix, UCLA's all-American tailback Bob Waterfield

(Nix outshines Waterfield as Frogs defeat the eventual host team in Rose Bowl.)

Baylor 10, TCU 7

Oct. 10, 1942, Fort Worth

Season records at kickoff: TCU 5-0, Baylor 5-1

Head Coaches: TCU's Dutch Meyer, Baylor's Frank Kimbrough

Top Players: TCU's all-America tackle Derrell Palmer, Baylor tailback Kit Kittrell

(Frogs fall from unbeaten ranks as hair-splitting calls by officials deny TCU two touchdowns.)

TCU 13, Texas 7

Nov. 14, 1942, Fort Worth

Season records at kickoff: TCU 5-2, Texas 7-1

Head Coaches: TCU's Dutch Meyer, Texas' Dana X. Bible

Top Players: TCU tackle Derrell Palmer, end Bruce Alford, Texas backs Roy McKay, Jackie Field

(Sub tailback Beecher Montgomery directs Frogs to upset over conference champions.)

TCU 13, Texas A&M 7

Oct. 21, 1944, College Station

Season records at kickoff: TCU 2-0-1, Texas A&M 3-1

Head Coaches: TCU's Dutch Meyer, Texas A&M Homer Norton

Top Players: TCU quarterback Joe Kucera, Texas A&M fullback Paul Yates

(Kucera's runs and passes put TCU's "Fightin' Fifteen" on surprising path to SWC title.)

TCU 7, Texas 6
Nov. 18, 1944, Fort Worth
Season records at kickoff: TCU 5-1-1, Texas 4-3
Head Coaches: TCU's Dutch Meyer, Texas' Dana X. Bible
Top Players: TCU all-America tackle Clyde Flowers, center Jim Cooper, Texas tailback Bobby Layne
(End Harry Mullins kicks the vital extra point that all but sews up the championship.)

Okla. A&M 34, TCU 0 (Cotton Bowl)
Jan. 1, 1945, Dallas
Season records at kickoff: TCU 7-2-1, Oklahoma A&M 7-1
Head Coaches: TCU's Dutch Meyer, Oklahoma A&M's Jim Lookabaugh
Top Players: TCU fullback Norman Cox, Oklahoma A&M all-America halfback Bob Fenimore
(Frogs' thin war-depleted squad is no match for the powerful Aggies.)

TCU 14, Texas 0
Nov. 16, 1946, Fort Worth
Season records at kickoff: TCU 1-6, Texas 7-1
Head Coaches: TCU's Dutch Meyer, Texas' Dana X. Bible
Top Players: TCU backs Lindy Berry, Carl Knox, Texas all-America quarterback Bobby Layne
(Spirited defense and Knox's punting score impossible upset over one of nation's powerhouses.)

TCU 20, Oklahoma 7
Oct. 28, 1947, Norman, Okla.
Season records at kickoff: TCU 2-3, Oklahoma 2-2-1
Head Coaches: TCU's Dutch Meyer, Oklahoma's Bud Wilkinson
Top Players: TCU backs Lindy Berry, Pete Stout, Oklahoma back Jack Mitchell, tackle Wade Walker
(Hot and cold Frogs of 1947 turn hot behind Stout's running and upset the best of the Big Eight.)

TCU 19, SMU 19
Nov. 29, 1947, Fort Worth
Season records at kickoff: TCU 4-4-1, SMU 9-0
Head Coaches: TCU's Dutch Meyer, SMU's Matty Bell
Top Players: TCU backs Lindy Berry, end Morris Bailey, SMU's all-America tailback Doak Walker
(Walker's greatest game can only gain a last-minute tie for nation's No. 2 team against Frogs.)

Ole Miss 13, TCU 9 (Delta Bowl)
Jan. 1, 1948, Memphis, Tenn.
Season records at kickoff: TCU 4-4-2, Ole Miss 8-2
Head Coaches: TCU's Dutch Meyer, Ole Miss' Johnny Vaught
Top Players: TCU backs Lindy Berry, Pete Stout, Ole Miss all-America quarterback Charley Conerly
(Frogs dominate game but Conerly's late drive saves the day for Rebels.)

Oklahoma 21, TCU 18
Oct. 23, 1948, Fort Worth
Season records at kickoff: TCU 4-1, Oklahoma 3-1
Head Coaches: TCU's Dutch Meyer, Oklahoma's Bud Wilkinson
Top Players: TCU tailback Lindy Berry, Oklahoma backs Jack Mitchell, Darrell Royal
(Lindy Berry and Frogs scare daylights out No. 2 team in nation.)

TCU 7, SMU 7
Nov. 27, 1948, Dallas
Season records at kickoff: TCU 4-5, SMU 8-1
Head Coaches: TCU's Dutch Meyer, SMU's Matty Bell
Top Players: TCU tailback Lindy Berry, SMU twins threats Doak Walker and Kyle Rote
(Conference champion Ponies escape with tie on long pass in fourth quarter.)

TCU 33, Ole Miss 27
Oct. 22, 1949, Fort Worth
Season records at kickoff: TCU 3-1-1, Ole Miss 2-2-1
Head Coaches: TCU's Dutch Meyer, Ole Miss' Johnny Vaught
Top Players: TCU tailback Lindy Berry, Ole Miss fullback John (Kayo) Dottley
(In spectacular night game, Berry's passing attack outscores the Rebels' ground game.)

TCU 14, Texas 13
Nov. 12, 1949, Austin
Sesaon records at kickoff: TCU 4-2-1, Texas 5-3
Head Coaches: TCU's Dutch Meyer, Texas' Blair Cherry
Top Players: TCU's Lindy Berry, Texas halfback Byron Townsend
(Dutch Meyer surprises Texas with 9-man defensive line, stifles Longhorns' T-formation.)

TCU 21, SMU 13
Nov. 26, 1949, Fort Worth
Season records at kickoff: TCU 5-3-1, SMU 5-2-1
Head Coaches: TCU's Dutch Meyer, SMU's Matty Bell
Top Players: TCU's Lindy Berry, SMU's Doak Walker and Kyle Rote
(Berry outshines Rote after Walker leaves game with injury.)

TCU 20, Texas A&M 14
Oct. 20, 1951, Fort Worth
Season records at kickoff: TCU 2-2, A&M 4-0
Head Coaches: TCU's Dutch Meyer, A&M's Ray George
Top Players: TCU quarterback Ray McKown, Texas A&M fullback Bob Smith
(McKown ignites three-touchdown burst in last seven minutes in storybook upset.)

Southern California 28, TCU 26
Oct. 27, 1951, Los Angeles, Memorial Coliseum
Season records at kickoff: TCU 3-2, USC 5-0
Head Coaches: TCU's Dutch Meyer, USC's Jess Hill
Top Players: TCU tailback Ray McKown; Southern Cal halfback Frank Gifford
(Triple-threat McKown and TCU's wide-open style thrill West Coast fans, but Trojans prevail.)

TCU 20, Baylor 7
Nov. 3, 1951, Waco
Season records at kickoff: TCU 3-3, Baylor 4-0-1
Head Coaches: TCU's Dutch Meyer, Baylor's George Sauer
Top Players: TCU backs Ray McKown, Bobby Jack Floyd, Baylor quarterback Larry Isbell
(McKown tops Isbell in quarterback duel as Frogs stun another unbeaten favorite.)

Kentucky 20, TCU 7 (Cotton Bowl)
Jan. 1, 1952, Dallas
Season records at kickoff: TCU 6-4, Kentucky 7-4
Head Coaches: TCU's Dutch Meyer, Kentucky's Bear Bryant
Top Players: TCU's Ray McKown, Bobby Jack Floyd; Kentucky quarterback Babe Parilli
(Frogs control ball, outgain Wildcats, but can't find a goal-line punch.)

Kansas 13, TCU 0
Sept. 20, 1952, Lawrence, Kan.
Season records at kickoff: TCU 0-0, Kansas 0-0
Head Coaches: TCU's Dutch Meyer, Kansas' J.V. Sikes
Top Players: TCU backs Ray McKown, Mal Fowler, Kansas backs Charlie Hoag, Gil Reich
(Speedier Jayhawks trip Frogs in first college football game to be televised nationally.)

Michigan State 26, TCU 19
Oct. 10, 1953, East Lansing, Mich.
Season records at kickoff: TCU 1-1, Michigan State 2-0
Head Coaches: TCU's Abe Martin, Michigan State's Biggie Munn
Top Players: TCU backs Ray McKown, Ron Clinkscale, Michigan State backs Leroy Bolden, Billy Wells
(Frogs throw serious scare into nation's No. 1 team and its 23-game winning streak.)

TCU 20, Southern California 7
Oct. 9, 1954, Los Angeles, Memorial Coliseum
Season records at kickoff: TCU 1-2, USC 3-0
Head Coaches: TCU's Abe Martin, USC's Jess Hill
Top Players: TCU's Jim Swink, Chuck Curtis, Trojan halfback "Jaguar Jon" Arnett
(A young TCU team rudely upsets the Pacific Coast's eventual Rose Bowl representative.)

TCU 20, Penn State 7
Oct. 23, 1954, Fort Worth
Season records at kickoff: TCU 3-2, Penn State 3-1
Head Coaches: TCU's Abe Martin, Penn State's Rip Engle
Top Players: TCU halfback Jim Swink, Penn State halfback Lenny Moore
(Swink shows a glimpse of what's to come as he steals spotlight from Lenny Moore.)

TCU 21, Alabama 0
Oct. 8, 1955, Tuscaloosa, Ala.
Season records at kickoff: TCU 3-0, Alabama 0-2
Head Coaches: TCU's Abe Martin, Alabama's Ears Whitworth
Top Players: TCU halfback Jim Swink, Alabama quarterback Bart Starr
(Frogs attract national attention as Swink rushes for three TD's, a total of nine in only four games.)

Texas A&M 19, TCU 16

Oct. 15, 1955, Fort Worth
Season records at kickoff: TCU 4-0, A&M 3-1
Head Coaches: TCU's Abe Martin, A&M's Bear Bryant
Top Players: TCU's Jim Swink, Texas A&M halfback John David Crow
(Frogs bypass field goal chances, allow Aggie sub to bolt for late score, drop heartbreaker.)

TCU 47, Texas 20

Nov. 12, 1955, Austin
Season records at kickoff: TCU 6-1, Texas 4-4
Head Coaches: TCU's Abe Martin, Texas' Ed Price
Top Players: TCU's all-America Jim Swink, Texas quarterback Walter Frondren
(Swink sprints for four touchdowns, gains 235 yards from scrimmage in his greatest game.)

Ole Miss 14, TCU 13 (Cotton Bowl)

Jan. 1, 1956, Dallas
Season records at kickoff: TCU 9-1, Ole Miss 9-1
Head Coaches: TCU's Abe Martin, Ole Miss' Johnny Vaught
Top Players: TCU's Jim Swink, Ole Miss backs Paige Cothren, Eagle Day
(Frogs lose quarterback Chuck Curtis to injury on opening kickoff, then lose 13-0 lead.)

Texas A&M 7, TCU 6

Oct. 20, 1956, College Station
Season records at kickoff: TCU 3-0, A&M 3-0-1
Head Coaches: TCU's Abe Martin, Texas A&M's Bear Bryant
Top Players: TCU's Jim Swink, Chuck Curtis, Texas A&M's John David Crow
(One of TCU's toughest losses as late Aggie drive wins "the hurricane game.")

TCU 46, Texas 0

Nov. 17, 1956, Fort Worth
Season records at kickoff: TCU 4-3, Texas 1-7
Head Coaches: TCU's Abe Martin, Texas' Ed Price
Top Players: TCU backs Jim Swink, Buddy Dike, Texas fullback Jimmy Welch
(Swink scores four times as Frogs romp over Longhorns on national television.)

TCU 28, Syracuse 27 (Cotton Bowl)

Jan. 1, 1957, Dallas
Season records at kickoff: TCU 7-3, Syracuse 7-1
Head Coaches: TCU's Abe Martin, Syracuse's Ben Schwartzwalder
Top Players: TCU's Jim Swink, Chuck Curtis, Syracuse's all-America halfback Jim Brown
(Swink's running and Curtis' passing are too much for Jim Brown's one-man show.)

TCU 18, Ohio State 14

Sept. 30, 1957, Columbus, Ohio
Season records at kickoff: TCU 0-0-1, Ohio State 0-0
Head Coaches: TCU's Abe Martin, Ohio State's Woody Hayes
Top Players: TCU backs Jim Shofner, Buddy Dike, Ohio State fullback Bob White
(Shofner scores on punt return as Frogs score big upset over eventual National champions.)

TCU 22, Texas 8

Nov. 15, 1958, Fort Worth
Season records at kickoff: TCU 6-1, Texas 6-2
Head Coaches: TCU's Abe Martin, Texas' Darrell Royal
Top Players: TCU fullback Jack Spikes, Texas halfback Rene Ramirez
(Spikes and ground game overpower Longhorns as Frogs head for conference championship.)

TCU 21, Rice 10

Nov. 22, 1958, Houston
Season records at kickoff: TCU 7-1, Rice 4-4
Head Coaches: TCU's Abe Martin, Rice's Jess Neely
Top Players: TCU quarterback Hunter Enis, halfback Marv Lasater, Rice's all-America end Buddy Dial
(Enis guides Frogs to win that sews up SWC crown.)

TCU 0, Air Force 0

Jan. 1, 1959, Dallas
Season records at kickoff: TCU 8-2, Air Force 9-0-1
Head Coaches: TCU's Abe Martin, Air Force's Ben Martin
Top Players: TCU backs Jack Spikes, Marv Lasater, Air Force quarterback Rich Mayo
(Frogs miss numerous scoring chances, settle for tie with outplayed Falcons.)

TCU 14, Texas 9

Nov. 14, 1959, Austin
Season records at kickoff: TCU 5-2, Texas 8-0
Head Coaches: TCU's Abe Martin, Texas' Darrell Royal
Top Players: TCU backs Jack Spikes, Harry Moreland, Texas backs Rene Ramirez, Bobby Lackey
(Harry Moreland's 56-yard run in last quarter shatters nation's No. 2 team.)

TCU 19, SMU 0

Nov. 28, 1959, Fort Worth
Season records at kickoff: TCU 7-2, SMU 5-3-1
Head Coaches: TCU's Abe Martin, SMU's Bill Meek
Top Players: TCU's all-America tackles Bob Lilly, Don Floyd, SMU's all-America Don Meredith
(Frogs grab share of title as Lilly and Floyd smother Meredith and SMU's high-powered offense.)

Clemson 23, TCU 7 (Bluebonnet Bowl)

Dec. 19, 1959, Houston
Season records at kickoff: TCU 8-2, Clemson 8-2
Head Coaches: TCU's Abe Martin, Clemson's Frank Howard
Top Players: TCU's Jack Spikes, Harry Moreland, Clemson quarterback Harvey White
(Frogs lead, 7-3, dominate Tigers for three quarters, but Clemson's aeriel game suddenly clicks.)

TCU 7, Southern California 6

Sept. 24, 1960, Los Angeles, Memorial Coliseum
Season records at kickoff: TCU 1-0, USC 1-0
Head Coaches: TCU's Abe Martin, USC's John McKay
Top Players: TCU quarterback Sonny Gibbs, USC linemen Mike and Marlan McKeever
(Gibbs leads rebuilding Frogs to big intersectional victory on West Coast.)

TCU 14, Baylor 6

Oct. 29, 1960, Fort Worth
Season records at kickoff: TCU 2-2-2, Baylor 5-0
Head Coaches: TCU's Abe Martin, Baylor's John Bridgers
Top Players: TCU's Sonny Gibbs, Baylor's all-America halfback Ronnie Bull
(Another major upset as Frogs knock Bears from the undefeated ranks.)

TCU 7, Ohio State 7

Sept. 30, 1961, Columbus, Ohio
Season records at kickoff: TCU 1-0, Ohio State 0-0
Head Coaches: TCU's Abe Martin, Ohio State's Woody Hayes
Top Players: TCU's Sonny Gibbs, Ohio State's all-America fullback Bob Ferguson
(Frogs control the ball and tie a Buckeye team that will wind up No. 1 in nation.)

TCU 6, Texas 0

Nov. 18, 1961, Austin
Season records at kickoff: TCU 2-4-1, Texas 8-0
Head Coaches: TCU's Abe Martin, Texas' Darrell Royal
Top Players: TCU's Sonny Gibbs, end Buddy Iles, Texas' all-America halfback James Saxton
(A long pass, Gibbs to Iles, stuns nation's No. 1 team in Upset of the Decade.)

TCU 6, Kansas 3

Sept. 22, 1962, Lawrence, Kan.
Season records at kickoff: TCU 0-0, Kansas 0-0
Head Coaches: TCU's Abe Martin, Kansas' Jack Mitchell
Top Players: TCU's Sonny Gibbs, linebacker Tommy Crutcher, Kansas running back Gale Sayers
(Gibbs throws TD pass and Crutcher-led defense does the job on Sayers.)

TCU 28, Baylor 26

Nov. 3, 1962, Fort Worth
Season records at kickoff: TCU 3-2, Baylor 1-3
Head Coaches: TCU's Abe Martin, Baylor's John Bridgers
Top Players: TCU's Sonny Gibbs, Baylor quarterback Don Trull
(Gibbs comes out on top in a wild passing duel with Trull.)

TCU 25, Texas 10

Nov. 13, 1965, Austin
Season records at kickoff: TCU 3-4, Texas 5-3
Head Coaches: TCU's Abe Martin, Texas' Darrell Royal
Top Players: TCU quarterback Kent Nix, Texas all-America linebacker Tommy Nobis
(Bruce Alford Jr.'s four field goals help Frogs surprise the vaunted Longhorns.)

Texas Western 13, TCU 12 (Sun Bowl)

Jan. 1, 1966, El Paso

Season records at kickoff: TCU 6-4, Texas Western 7-3

Head Coaches: TCU's Abe Martin, Texas Western's Bobby Dobbs

Top Players: TCU's Kent Nix, end Sonny Campbell, Texas Western quarterback Billy Stevens

(Superior Frogs build 10-0 lead by halftime, go to sleep, wake up with a loss.)

TCU 24, Texas 17

Nov. 18, 1967, Austin

Season records at kickoff: TCU 2-5, Texas 6-2

Head Coaches: TCU's Fred Taylor, Texas' Darrell Royal

Top Players: TCU backs Ross Montgomery, Norm Bulaich, Texas halfback Chris Gilbert

(Bubba Thornton's 78-yard punt return for TD is biggest play in another memorable upset.)

Purdue 42, TCU 35

Sept. 20, 1969, Fort Worth

Season records at kickoff: TCU 0-0, Purdue 0-0

Head Coaches: TCU's Fred Taylor, Purdue's Jack Mollenkopf

Top Players: TCU quarterback Steve Judy, flanker Linzy Cole, Purdue quarterback Mike Phipps

(Judy and Phipps each throw four touchdown passes in game with 1,100 yards of offense.)

TCU 34, Baylor 27

Oct. 30, 1971, Waco

Season records at kickoff: TCU 2-3-1, Baylor 1-4

Head Coaches: TCU's Jim Pittman, Baylor's Bill Beall

Top Players: TCU quarterback Steve Judy, Baylor defensive end Roger Goree

(Frogs win strange game in which Pittman suffers heart attack, collapses on sideline and dies.)

TCU 18, SMU 16

Nov. 27, 1971, Dallas

Season records at kickoff: TCU 5-4-1, SMU 4-6

Head Coaches: TCU's Billy Tohill (replacing Jim Pittman), SMU's Hayden Fry

Top Players: TCU quarterback Steve Judy, SMU running back Alvin Maxson

(Victory gives Frogs first winning season (6-4-1) in six years despite Jim Pittman's tragic death.)

Notre Dame 21, TCU 0

Oct. 28, 1972, South Bend, Ind.

Season records at kickoff: TCU 4-1, Notre Dame 5-0

Head Coaches: TCU's Billy Tohill, Notre Dame's Ara Parseghian

Top Players: TCU running back Mike Luttrell, Notre Dame quarterback Tom Clements

(Frogs venture into football lore but meet team that will be national champs a year later.)

TCU 28, Arkansas 24

Oct. 3, 1981, Fort Worth

Season records at kickoff: TCU 1-2, Arkansas 3-0

Head Coaches: TCU's F.A. Dry, Arkansas' Lou Holtz

Top Players: TCU quarterback Steve Stamp, Arkansas halfback Gary Anderson

(The Miracle. Stamp throws TD passes to Stanley Washington and Phillip Epps in last five minutes.)

TCU 39, Texas Tech 39

Nov. 7, 1981, Lubbock

Season records at kickoff: TCU 2-5-1, Texas Tech 1-7

Head Coaches: TCU's F.A. Dry, Texas Tech's Jerry Moore

Top Players: TCU's all-America end Stanley Washington, Tech quarterback Ron Reeves

(To gain tie, Frogs score three touchdowns, field goal, and safety in game's last minutes.)

TCU 32, Arkansas 31

Oct. 6, 1984, Fayetteville, Ark.

Season records at kickoff: TCU 2-1, Arkansas 2-0-1

Head Coaches: TCU's Jim Wacker, Arkansas' Ken Hatfield

Top Players: TCU halfback Kenneth Davis, Arkansas end James Shibest

(Behind 31-17 with 10 minutes left, Frogs drive 80 yards twice and add two-point conversion.)

Texas 44, TCU 23

Nov. 17, 1984, Fort Worth

Season records at kickoff: TCU 8-1, Texas 6-1-1

Head Coaches: TCU's Jim Wacker, Texas' Fred Akers

Top Players: TCU's all-America Kenneth Davis, Texas all-America defensive back Jerry Gray

(Longhorns' superior depth slowly wears down Frogs in nationally-televised game.)

West Virginia 31, TCU 14 (Bluebonnet Bowl)

Dec. 31, 1984, Houston, Astrodome

Season records at kickoff: TCU 8-3, West Virginia 7-4

Head Coaches: TCU's Jim Wacker, West Virginia 7-4

Top Players: TCU quarterback Anthony Gulley, end James Maness, Mountaineer quarterback Kevin White

(Kenneth Davis goes out early with injury, West Virginia's passing game does the rest.)

TCU 48, Tulane 31

Sept. 13, 1986, New Orleans, Superdome

Season records at kickoff: TCU 0-0, Tulane 0-0

Head Coaches: TCU's Jim Wacker, Tulane's Mack Brown

Top Players: TCU running back Tony Jeffery, Tulane quarterback Terrence Jones

(Jeffery rushes for an amazing 343 yards in only three quarters on a mere 16 carries, a conference record.)

TCU 33, Brigham Young 12

Sept. 19, 1987, Fort Worth

Season records at kickoff: TCU 0-2, BYU 2-0

Head Coaches: TCU's Jim Wacker, BYU's Lavell Edwards

Top Players: TCU running back Tony Jeffery, BYU quarterback Sean Covey

(Jeffery scampers for 207 yards as Frogs upset the heavily-favored visitors.)

TCU 27, Air Force 9

Oct. 21, 1989, Fort Worth

Season records at kickoff: TCU 3-3, Air Force 6-1

Head Coaches: TCU's Jim Wacker, Air Force's Fisher DeBerry

Top Players: TCU quarterback Leon Clay, end Stephen Shipley, back Tommy Palmer, Falcon quarterback Dee Dowis

(Palmer gains 177 yards, Clay hits Shipley twice for scores, favored Falcons tumble.)

TCU 54, Arkansas 26

Oct. 6, 1990, Little Rock, Ark.

Season records at kickoff: TCU 3-1, Arkansas 2-1

Head Coaches: TCU's Jim Wacker, Arkansas' Jack Crowe

Top Players: TCU quarterback Leon Clay, end Kelly Blackwell, Arkansas quarterback Quinn Grovey

(Clay's passing, Curtis Modkins' running, Blackwell's receptions add up to sweet revenge.)

TCU 49, Houston 45

Nov. 23, 1991, Fort Worth

Season records at kickoff: TCU 6-4, Houston 4-5

Head Coaches: TCU's Jim Wacker, Houston's John Jenkins

Top Players: TCU quarterback Matt Vogler, end Kelly Blackwell, Houston quarterback David Klinger

(Last-minute TD pass, Vogler to Shipley, concludes TCU's first winning season in seven years.)

TCU 23, Texas 14

Nov. 7, 1992, Fort Worth

Season records at kickoff: TCU 1-6-1, Texas 5-2

Head Coaches: TCU's Pat Sullivan, Texas' John Mackovic

Top Players: TCU backs Leon Clay, Curtis Modkins, Texas quarterback Peter Gardere

(TCU's entire defensive unit deserves most of the credit for first win over Texas in 24 years.)

TCU 44, New Mexico 29

Sept. 10, Albuquerque, N.M.

Season records at kickoff: TCU 0-1, New Mexico 0-1

Head Coaches: TCU's Pat Sullivan, New Mexico's Dennis Franchione

Top Players: TCU running back Andre Davis, New Mexico quarterback Stoney Case

(Davis dashes for incredible 325 yards, becoming only second Frog to gain over 300 in a game.)

TCU 24, Texas Tech 17

Nov. 25, 1994, Fort Worth

Season records at kickoff: TCU 6-4, Texas Tech 6-4

Head Coaches: TCU's Pat Sullivan, Texas Tech's Spike Dykes

Top Players: TCU backs Andre Davis, Max Knake, Texas Tech linebacker Zach Thomas

(Davis rips off crucial gains in late game-winning drive as Frogs grab share of SWC title.)

Virginia 20, TCU 10 (Independence Bowl)

Dec. 28, 1994, Shreveport, La.

Season records at kickoff: TCU 7-4, Virginia 8-3

Head Coaches: TCU's Pat Sullivan, Virginia's George Welsh

Top Players: TCU backs Andre Davis, Max Knake, Virginia backs Mike Groh, Kevin Brooks

(Cavaliers make fewest mistakes on a cold, rainy, muddy evening.)

TCU 19, SMU 16

Nov. 4, 1995, Fort Worth

Season records at kickoff: TCU 5-2, SMU 1-7

Head Coaches: TCU's Pat Sullivan, SMU's Tom Rossley

Top Players: TCU end John Washington, safety Rick LaFavers, SMU quarterback Derek Canine

(Victory assures Frogs of 6-5 record and first back-to-back winning seasons since 1958-59.)

EARLY ERA ~ 1896-1945

Position	Player	Best years
End	Rags Matthews	1925-26-27
	Pappy Pruitt	1931-32
	Walter Roach	1934-35-36
	Don Looney	1937-38-39
	Bruce Alford	1941-42
Tackle	Ben Boswell	1930-31-32
	I.B. Hale	1936-37-38
	Derrell Palmer	1941-42
	Clyde Flowers	1943-44
Guard	Bear Wolf	1925-26
	Mike Brumbelow	1928-29
	Johnny Vaught	1931-32
	Tracey Kellow	1934-35
	Cotton Harrison	1935-36
Center	Darrell Lester	1933-34-35
	Ki Aldrich	1936-37-38
Quarterback	Sammy Baugh	1934-35-36
	Davey O'Brien	1937-38
Halfback	Cy Leland	1929-30
	Grassy Hinton	1929-30-31
	Blanard Spearman	1931-32
	Jimmy Lawrence	1933-34-35
	Earl Clark	1937-38-39
Fullback	Tillie Manton	1934-35
	Connie Sparks	1938-39

MODERN ERA ~ 1946-1995

Position	Player	Best years
Receiver	Morris Bailey	1947-48-49
	Sonny Campbell	1964-65-66
	Mike Renfro	1975-76-77
	Stanley Washington	1981-82
	Kelly Blackwell	1990-91
Lineman	Herb Zimmerman	1950-51
	Morgan Williams	1952-53
	Norman Hamilton	1955-56
	Don Floyd	1958-59
	Bob Lilly	1958-59-60
	Norman Evans	1963-64
	Tracy Simien	1987-88
	Fred Washington	1987-88-89
	Mike Sullivan	1989-90
	Royal West	1993-94
Center	W.C. Nix III	1985-86
	Barret Robbins	1993-94
Quarterback	Lindy Berry	1947-48-49
	Ray McKown	1951-52
	Chuck Curtis	1955-56
	Sonny Gibbs	1960-61-62
	Max Knake	1994-95
Running back	Jim Swink	1954-55-56
	Buddy Dike	1954-55-56
	Jack Spikes	1958-59
	Ross Montgomery	1967-68
	Mike Luttrell	1972-73
	Kenneth Davis	1983-84
	Tony Jeffery	1985-86-87
	Andre Davis	1993-94-95
Linebacker	Keith Flowers	1950-51
	Hugh Pitts	1954-55
	Dale Walker	1957-58
	Tommy Crutcher	1962-63
Defensive back	Marshall Robinson	1951-52-53
	Ronald Fraley	1952-53
	Jim Shofner	1956-57
	Frank Horak	1965-66
	Lyle Blackwood	1971-72
Placekicker	Michael Reeder	1994-95
Punter	Chris Becker	1985-86-87-88

A

Charlie Abel, 1977-79
Tony Accomando, 1976-77
Ab Acker, 1925-26-27
Will H. Acker, 1918-19-20
Scott Ackroyd, 1985-88
Earl W. Adams, 1968
Homer Adams, 1921-23-24
Larry Adams, 1966-68
Mike Adams, 1966
Robby Adams, 1987-89
Trotter Adams, 1942
Woodrow Adams, 1939-40-41
Harry Akers, 1928
Ki Aldrich, 1936-38
Bill Alexander, 1953-55
Bob Alexander, 1928
Bret Alexander, 1988-89-90
Clarence Alexander, 1938-39-40
C. T. Alexander, 1897-98-1900
Ivan Alexander, 1921-22
Bruce Alford, 1940-42
Bruce Alford, Jr., 1964-66
Rex Alford, 1947-49
Andrew Allan, 1975-77
Anthony Allen, 1981-82
Cedric Allen, 1993-94-95
Egypt Allen, 1982-84
Jimmy Allen, 1977-79
Marcus Allen, 1992-95
Richard G. Allen, 1939
Ricky Allen, 1977-78-80
Tony Allen, 1985
Richard Allison, 1933
Angel Alvarez, 1991
Jim Amburg, 1950
Henry Anders, 1989
Carl Anderson, 1939-40
Duke Anderson, 1926
E. N. Anderson, 1910-11
Grantland Anderson, 1909-10
Greg Anderson, 1972-74
John Anderson, 1914
Marcus Anderson, 1995
Reggie Anderson, 1990-91-93-94
Shirley Anderson, 1943
Scott Ankrom, 1984-85-87-88
John Archer 1948-49
Ramon Armstrong, 1957-59
Greg Arterberry, 1981-83
Mitch Ashley, 1991
Charles Ashmore, 1904-05-09
Noble Atkins, 1928-38
Chad Avery, 1993-94-95
Phillip Ayres, 1922-24

B

Dean Bagley, 1940-42
Erik Bahr, 1987-89
Morris Bailey, 1946-49
Paul Bailey, 1982-83
Don Baker, 1980-82
Bob Balaban, 1942
Marshall Baldwin, 1908-09
Charles Bales, 1967-68
Ken Balfanz, 1971
Joe Ball, 1963-65
Elton Baptiste, 1982-83
Fred Barber, 1966-68
Bobby Barker, 1965
Mike Barmore, 1970
H. C. Barnard, 1906
Clifford Barnes, 1992-95
Steve Barnes, 1976-79
Milford Barr, 1927-29
Lee Barron, 1898
Bernard Bartek, 1960-62
Leon Bartlett, 1972-73
Gilbert Bartosh, 1950-52
Jim Barwegen, 1976-77

Brian Bass, 1975
Dexter Bassinger, 1949-50
Lee Bassinger, 1931-33
Charles Bassler, 1912
Russell Bates, 1978-81
Bobby Batton, 1963-64
Sammy Baugh, 1934-36
Howard Baxter, 1928
Ernest Bayer, 1963-65
Jim Bayuk, 1977-80
Steve Bayuk, 1975-77
Richard A. Beach (Dee), 1965-67
Scott Bednarski, 1984-86-87-88
Trey Becan, 1990-1991
Chris Becker, 1985-88
John Beilue, 1969-70
Thomas Bell, 1979-80
Phillip Bendele, 1992
Ken Bener, 1979-82
James Benson, 1983-84
Mitchell Benson, 1985-88
Lenward Bentley, 1995
Bill Berry, 1916
Lindy Berry, 1946-49
Ray Berry, 1978-79
Tookie Berry, 1970-72
Miles Bevins, 1908
Tony Biasatti, 1974-77
Bobby Biehunko, 1959-61
Gus Bierman, 1940-41-45
Albert Billingsley, 1906-08
Linden Binion, 1938-39
Phil Birdwell, 1969
Bill Bishop, 1974-76
Hugh Bishop, 1923
John Bishop, 1970
Melvin Bishop, 1920-23
Tom Bishop, 1946-48
Jude Bivins, 1913
Miles Bivins, 1907-08
Mike Black, 1989-92
Linnon Blackmon, 1936-37
Billy Blackstone, 1940-42
Jim Blackwelder, 1974-77
Kelly Blackwell, 1988-91
Lyle Blackwood 1971-72
Mike Blackwood, 1975
Bob Blair, 1950-52
Rusty Blair, 1969
Bertram Bloor, 1904-07
David Bloxom, 1946-48
Shankle Bloxom, 1947-49
George Boal, 1946-49
Tunji (Olatunji) Bolden, 1989-92
Duke Bolen, 1943
John Bond, 1941-42
Kendall Bond, 1943
Sidney Bond, 1971-73
Richard Booker, 1987-90
John Booty, 1986-88
Kelly Bostick, 1970-71
Ben Boswell, 1930-32
Brad Bowen, 1977-79
Lane Bowen, 1970-72
Bill Bowers, 1962-64
Mike Bowers, 1977
Chuck Boyd, 1974
Sterling Boyd, 1995
Ted Brack, 1978-81
Steve Braddock, 1971-73
Cecil Bradford, 1916-19
Patrick Bradford, 1984-86
Marion Brally, 1917
Buster Brannon, 1931-32
Chris Brasfield, 1994-95
Kenny Brasher, 1976
Mike Bratcher, 1965-66
G. P. Braus, 1908-09
David Braxton, 1978-79
Brian Brazil, 1983-85-86-87
David Breedlove, 1989-92

Joe Breedlove, 1980-82
Jeff Breithaupt, 1973-74
Kevin Brewer, 1992-95
Ron Zell Brewer, 1981-83
Horace Brewster, 1925-26
Rick Bridges, 1966
Charles Brightwell, 1966-68
Douglas Brightwell, 1945-48
Charles Britton, 1989
Marion Broadley, 1916
Larry Brogdon, 1969
Cliff Bronson, 1988
Daryl Brookins, 1982-83
Brian Brooks, 1991-94
Tony Brooks, 1985-86-88
West Brooks, 1969-70
Allen Brown, 1967-68
Clinton Brown, 1984
Danny Brown, 1973
George Brown, 1946-48
Hal Brown, 1984-86
Larry Brown, 1989-90
Lynn Brown, 1932-33
Leslie Brown, 1966
Marvin Brown, 1975
Tony Brown, 1993-94-95
Wilbur Brown, 1914
Orein Browning, 1947-48-49
Ronnie Brumbaugh, 1939-40-41
Andre Bruce, 1995
Mike Brumbelow, 1927-29
I. B. Bryan, 1945

Charles Bryant, 1973-74
H.H. Bryant, 1904-08
Harold (Butch) Buchanan, 1976
Bill Buck, 1950-51-52
Larry Bulaich, 1962-63-64
Norman Bulaich, 1966-69
Stanley Bull, 1954-55
Mike Bulla, 1986-89
David Buller, 1981-83
Clyde Burnett, 1904
Keith Burnett, 1975-76
Aaron Burton, 1993-94
James Busby, 1944
Bob Bushman, 1944
Guy Bob Buschman, 1971
Edgar Bush, 1909-10
W. M. Busy, 1905
Clarence Bussey, 1911-12
Bill Butler, 1979-80
Leo Butler, 1929-30

C

E. D. Caffey, 1946-47
Jerry Caillier, 1974-75-76
David Caldwell, 1977
David A. Caldwell, 1983-86

James Calhoun, 1983
Pug Calvert, 1916
Hillard Camp, 1921-22
Charles (Sonny) Campbell, 1964-66
Reggie Campbell, 1989
Jerry Cannaday, 1965
Frank Cantelmi, 1923-26
Ralph Cantrell, 1921-24
W. G. Carnahan, 1897-98
T. W. Carpenter, 1931
Barney Carroll, 1942
Harold Carson, 1924-26
Kit Carson, 1922-23
Benny Carter, 1964
Cecil Carter, 1957
Dan Carter, 1967-69
Don Carter, 1970
Douglas Carter, 1943
Adan Casas, 1988-89-90-91
Charles Casper, 1932-33
Jason Cauble, 1987-90
C. E. Chambers, 1898
Terry Champagne, 1973-74
Charles Champine, 1979-80
Blair Cherry, 1920-22
Daren Childs, 1991
Brown Chiles, 1945
Jason Chilton, 1990-92
Marv Chipman, 1961-63
Zygmunt Choroszy, 1982-84
Ivory Christian, 1989

Zeke Chronister, 1943-44
Earl Clark, 1937-38-39
Eddie Clark, 1981-82
Herman Clark, 1923-26
John Clark, 1913
Rex Clark, 1933-35
Leon Clay, 1989-90-91-92
Pat Clifford, 1936-38
Kyle Clifton, 1981-83
Ronald Clinkscale, 1952-54
David Cody, 1975-76
Danny Colbert, 1970
Linzy Cole, 1968-69
Carter Coleman, 1992
Joe Coleman, 1932-34
B. F. Collins, 1907
Brian Collins, 1992-95
Roosevelt Collins, 1988-91
Terry Collins, 1967
Perry Colston, 1975-77
Larry Compton, 1977
Doug Conaway, 1949-50-51
Stephen Conley, 1987-90
Adrian Conlin, 1945
Patrick Connelly, 1990-92
Bud Conway, 1977-80

Charles Conway, 1940-42
Bob Cook, 1937-39
Lee Cook, 1973-75
James Cook, 1981-85
John Cook, 1944-47
Aubrey Cook, 1915
Don Cooper, 1954-56
Gary Cooper, 1963-65
James Cooper, 1944-45
James Cooper, 1954
Jerry Cooper, 1968-69
Steve Cooper, 1976
Kevin Cordesman, 1989-93
Mark Cortez, 1994-95
LaBron Cornell, 1993
Thomas Costello, 1943
Steve Cotaya, 1981-82
Reginald Cottingham, 1980-83
H. C. Couser, 1931
Bobby Cowan, 1973-75
Glenn Cowart, 1938-39-40
John P. Cox, 1911-15
Norman Cox, 1944-45
Jeff Craig, 1978-79
Albert Cragwall, 1944
Barry Crayton, 1977
Bill Crawford, 1939-40-41
Gary Crawford, 1973
Bob Creech, 1968-69-70
Ted Crenwelge, 1959-60
Dub Crocker, 1945
John Cromwell, 1992
Danny Cross, 1965-67
J. G. Crouch, 1974-76
Johnny Crouch, 1952-54
Ronny Crouch, 1961
Brandy Crow, 1994
Ashley Crowley, 1921
Henry Crowsey, 1954-56
Levoil Crump, 1986-8-9-90
Bill Crunk, 1918
Tommy J. Crutcher, 1961-63
Derrick Cullors, 1991-93
Gidden Culver, 1916
Bob Cummings, 1977
Gerald Cumpton, 1958-59
Jazz Cunningham, 1918-19
Bill Curtis, 1953
Charles (Chuck) Curtis, 1954-56

D

H. B. Dabbs, 1906
Jeff Daily, 1986-88
Don Danford, 1988
Hicks Daniel, 1947
Milton Daniel, 1909-10-11
Tony Darthard, 1986-88
Jay Davern, 1993-94
Andre Davis, 1992-95
Bobby Davis, 1969-70-71
Bobby Davis, 1985-88
Charles Davis, 1971-73
Darrell Davis, 1986-89
David Davis, 1981-82-83
Donald Davis 1976-77
Greg Davis, 1995
Kenneth Davis, 1982-84
Lynn Davis, 1975-77
Reggie Davis, 1985-88
Larry Dawson, 1958-60
Kevin Dean, 1983-86
Bill DeFee, 1966
Jay DeFee, 1969-70
Jarrod Delaney, 1985-88
Kim Deloney, 1978-79
Hubero Dennis, 1930-32
Roy Dent, 1960-62
John Denton, 1981-84
Tony DeStefano, 1981
Ad Dietzel, 1930-31
Larry Dibbles, 1970

Average Points Per Game

Year	Points/Games	Per Game
1984	376 points/12 games	31.3
1955	306 points/11 games	27.8
1990	292 points/11 games	26.6
1932	283 points/11 games	25.7
1912	230 points/9 games	25.6
1991	279 points/11 games	25.4
1994	302 points/12 games	25.2

Setrick (Stu) Dickens, 1989-90-91-93
Chuck Dickenson, 1984-87
William Dickerson, 1991
Melvin Diggs, 1933-35
Buddy Dike, 1954, 56-57
Steve Dingler, 1981-82
David Dixon, 1970-71-72
Robert Dobry, 1974-75
John Dodson, 1961
R. E. Dodson, 1958-59-60
Rex Doerre, 1976
William Doherty, 1899
Jon Donahue, 1995
Bill Doty, 1951
Dan Dougherty, 1990
A. Douglas, 1916
Astynax Douglas, 1920
Zane Drake, 1980-82
Lloyd Draper, 1970-72
Terry Drennan, 1972-74
Mike Dry, 1979-80-81
Ronald Dublin, 1952
Carroll Dubose, 1963-64
Woodrow Duckworth, 1938-39
John Dull, 1986-87
Dave Duncan, 1973-74
George Dunlap, 1936-37
Johnny Dunn, 1948-49-50
Ken Durham, 1978-80-82
Andy Durrett, 1968-69
Loraine Dutton, 1917

E

Jim Eddlemen, 1928
Joe Edens, 1915-16
Trent Edwards, 1985
Weldon Edwards, 1946-47
Melville Ehlers, 1928
Delzon Elenburg, 1955-57
Kent Elenburg, 1976
Bill Elliott, 1948-49
Bill Elliott, 1987-90
Criss Elliott, 1916
Drew Ellis, 1934-36
Doug Elms, 1983-86
Jimmy D. Elzner, 1974-77
Bryan Engram, 1953-55
Hunter Enis, 1956-58
Hubert Eoff, 1946-49
Bart Epperson, 1993-94
Phillips Epps, 1978-81
Graham Estes, 1922
Max Eubank, 1947-50
J. R. Eubanks, 1969-70
Roy Eury, 1928-29-30
Greg Evans, 1990-93
H. E. Evans, 1943
John Evans, 1899
Larry Evans, 1970
Lon Evans, 1930-32
Norman Evans, 1962-64
Tom Evans, 1951-52
Beekie Ezell, 1945-46
Don Ezell, 1941-42
Larry Evans, 1970

F

Gerald Falls, 1975
Drake Farmer, 1969-70
Milton Farmer, 1948-49-50
Tim Faulk, 1973
Jim Fauver, 1962-64
Ted Fay, 1967-69
Dick Fencer, 1922-23
Bill Ferguson, 1968-69
Jarrett Ferguson, 1990
John Ferguson, 1976-79
H. E. Field, 1897
Bob Fields, 1981-82
Charles Fields, 1907-10
Craig Fife, 1969-70-71
David Finney, 1952-54
Dick Finney, 1955-57
Todd Fitzgerald, 1995
Heard Floore, 1934

Clyde Flowers, 1942-44
Keith Flowers, 1949-51
Bobby J. Floyd, 1950-51
Donald Floyd, 1957-59
Mike Flynn, 1981-84
Billy Fondren, 1967-69
G. A. Foote, 1897
Corey Ford, 1990-92-93
Gary Ford, 1984-88
Alan Foret, 1987-89
Chuck Forney, 1967-69
Harry Fortson, 1995
Bill Foster, 1982
Bob Foster, 1969-70
Marvin Foster, 1981-83
Chester Fowler, 1919-20-21
Malvin Fowler, 195153
Jim Fox, 1961-62-63
Raymond Fox, 1913-15
C. J. Fraley, 1943-46
Ronald Fraley, 1951-52-53
Don Frazee, 1923-25
Allen Freeman, 1910-13
Bonner Frizzell, 1904-05-06-08
J. B. Frizzell, 1906
T. P. Frizzell, 1915
Bill Frost, 1976
Steve Frost, 1969-70
Kevin Frye, 1989-1991
Pete Fulcher, 1920-21
Al Futrell, 1978-79

G

Foy Gaddy, 1947
Bill Gaffney, 1943
Jerry Gaither, 1974-77
Edward Galaviz, 1988-91
Lee Gallagher, 1944
T. B. Gallaher, 1905
Ben Gantt, 1911-14
Cliff Gantt, 1985-88
Harry Garder, 1943
Bernee Garcia, 1994
James Gargus, 1981-84
Steve Garmon, 1961-63-64
Ervin Garnett, 1970
Rick Garnett, 1971
John Garrard, 1904
Dub Garren, 1943-44
Ronald Garrett, 1914
Craig Garrison, 1989-90-91
George Gartner, 1943
Billy Gault, 1958-59-60
Donald George, 1958-59-60
Mack George, 1975-76
Wilson George, 1949-50-51
Chuck Giammalva, 1975-77
Donnie Gibbs, 1965-67
Sonny Gibbs, 1960-62
Merle Gibson, 1944-46
Marcus Gilbert, 1979-82
Kyle Gillespie, 1939-40-41
Butch Gilliam, 1965-66
Jimmy Gilmore, 1957-59
Lee Glasgow, 1932
David Glass, 1970
S. S. Glasscock, 1897-99
Dale Glasscock, 1959-60-61
James Glenn, 1951-52
O. Glover, 1907
Jeff Godley, 1993
Manuel Godwin, 1933-35
Oscar Golson, 1912
Justo Gonzalez, 1986-87
Rode Gonzales, 1959
Dennis Gooch, 1985-88
Rocky Goodman, 1965
Paul Gorman, 1978
Leon Gough, 1910
J. R. Graham, 1989-90
Jimmy Grant, 1927
Jimmy Green, 1970
Jack Graves, 1931-33
Roy Graves, 1917
T. C. Graves, 1910-11

Allen Greeman, 1911
Guy Green, 1897
Harlos Green, 1929-30-31
A. D. Green, 1920-23
Ansel Greer, 1925
David Gregg, 1973
Abe Greines, 1915-16
E. A. Gresham, 1965-67
Aaron Griffing, 1913
Austin Griffith, 1928-29-30
Eddie Grimes, 1977-80
Frankie Grimmett, 1970-72
Hardy Grissom, 1905
John Groom, 1955-57
Wilson Groseclose, 1933-35
O. Grover, 1907
Howard Grubbs, 1928-29
Anthony Gulley, 1982-84
Steve Gunn, 1967-68

H

Fred Haberstick, 1984-85
John Hadaway, 1944
Joel Haden, 1917-18-19-21
Carl Hagman, 1945
Clint Hailey, 1986-87
Tony Haire, 1917
Billy Hale, 1943-46
I. B. Hale, 1936-38
Jerry Hale, 1970
Randy Hale, 1968-69
Shadie Hale, 1917
Chet Hall, 1943
Colby D. Hall, 1898-99
Jesse Hall, 1961
Johnny Hall, 1936-38
Keith Hall, 1981-82
Mike Hall, 1966-68
Van Hall, 1941-42
Vernon Hallbeck, 1954-56
Danny Hallmark, 1951-53
Milton Ham, 1958-59-60
Norman Hamilton, 1954-56
James Hampton, 1940-41
Phil Handler, 1928-29
Kevin Haney, 1978-81
Mike Hanna, 1973-74
Ken Hanson, 1970
I. C. Harbour, 1904
Bill Harp, 1982-83
Baraka Harper, 1990-92
Bob Harrell, 1935-36-38
Monroe Harrelson, 1944
Don Harris, 1977
James Harris, 1976-78
Larry Harris, 1970-72
Lee Harris, 1970
Marshall E. Harris, 1951-53
Marshall Harris, 1957-59
Marshall K. Harris, 1974-78
R. C. Harris, 1951-53
Scott Harris, 1985-88
Ted Harris, 1967
Wylie Harris, 1920
Greg Harriss, 1992
Wilbert Harrison, 1934-36
Dan Harston, 1933
Brian Hart, 1988
Mike Harter, 1940-42
Frank Hartman, 1977-79
Mike Hartman, 1979-80-81
John T. Hartness, 1958
John Harville, 1950-52
A. M. Harwood, 1907
Froggie Hawes, 1916-17
Frank Hawkins, 1985-88
Wade Hawkins, 1927
Sherrill Headrick, 1957-58
Billy Hearne, 1942
Shellie Hearran, 1960
John A. Heatherly, 1969-70-71
Mike Hebert, 1985-86-87
Richard Hein, 1975-76
Jeff Heinichen, 1973
James Helwig, 1970

Richard Henderson, 1948
Colvern Henry, 1919
Russell Hensch, 1936-38
Ken Henson, 1962-64
Bernie Henyon, 1984
C. W. Herman, 1897
Gene Hernandez, 1972-74
Jack Herring, 1939
John Hetherly, 1969-70-71
Bobby Hickey, 1970
Jimmy Hickey, 1948-49-50
Anthony Hickman, 1989-92
Brandon Hickman, 1993-94
Morelle Hicks, 1946-49
W. B. Higgins, 1914-15
Rodney Higgs, 1985-88
Brooks Hill, 1961
H. Hill, 1918
Paul Hill, 1934
Pete Hill, 1960-61
Ray Hill, 1953-54
William (Loey) Hill, 1949
Joe Hines, 1981-82
Scott Hines, 1990-91
J. W. (Grassy) Hinton, 1929-30-31
James Hodges, 1969-70
Robert Hogg, 1917
Carlos Holcomb, 1926
Richard Holden, 1960
Jerry Holland, 1956
Phillip Holler, 1991-94
Kevin Holmes, 1992-95
Todd Holmes, 1988-89
David Holt, 1968-69
R. Holt, 1897
Solon Holt, 1934-36
Bill Honey, 1921-24
Allen Hooker, 1973-75
Charles Hooper, 1914
Pud Hooser, 1919
Robert Hoot, 1977-78
Doug Hooten, 1967-68
Manvel Hopes, 1992-95
Jeff Hopkins, 1986-88
T. B. Hopkins, 1911
Frank Horak, 1964-66
Durwood Horner, 1938-40
Albin Houdek, 1944
Mike Houston, 1989-1991-92-93
Loren Houtchens, 1920-21
Alex Howard, 1906
Randy Howard, 1963-64
Foster Howell, 1929-32
Stephan Howland, 1985-88
Glen P. Hudgins, 1976
Tom Hudgins, 1945
Cubby Hudler, 1965-67
Jerry Huffman, 1960-61
Royce Huffman, 1970-72
Norman Hughes, 1949-50-51
John Hulse, 1964
Burl Hulsey, 1910
Ray Hummel, 1978
Jimmy Hunt, 1947-49
Kam Hunt, 1995
Hal Hunter, 1912
Gaylon Hyder, 1993-94-95

I

Buddy Iles, 1959-61
Jason Illian, 1995
Guy Inman, 1897
Michael Isaac, 1958-61
Michael Isaac, 1977-79
Rich Isel, 1974-75

J

Lindsey Jacks, 1921-24
Cedric Jackson, 1988-90
Charlie Jackson, 1946-50
Don Jackson, 1960-61
G. P. Jackson, 1920
Michael Jackson, 1989-92
Ralph Jackson, 1982
Ransom Jackson, 1944

Sadd Jackson, 1990-93
Henry Jacot, 1980
Steve Jamail, 1965-66-67
Royal James, 1943
Michael Janak, 1993-94-95
Chris Jeffery, 1995
Tony Jeffery, 1984-87
Ron Jiles, 1986-89
Darryl Johnson, 1995
David Johnson, 1982
Dole Johnson, 1964-66
Fred Johnson, 1993
Joe Johnson, 1985-86
Lawrence Johnson, 1981
Mike Johnson, 1980-81
Dale Johnson, 1966-67
Billy Jones, 1983-86
Bobby Jones, 1991
Calvin Jones, 1990-93
Dan Jones, 1963-65
Dub Jones, 1905
Glen Jones, 1951-52
Gregg Jones, 1985-87
H. Jones, 1918
Jimmy Jones, 1945
Lenoy Jones, 1992-95
Paul Jones, 1982-84
Reuben Jones, 1980-82
Bob Jordan, 1937
Robert Jordan, 1934
Charles Joslin, 1945-48
Chris Judge, 1976-79
Keith Judy, 1974-75
Steve Judy, 1969-70-71

K

Danny Kasper, 1975-77
Tracey Kellow, 1933-35
Jason Kelly, 1992-94
Robert Kemp, 1977
James Kennedy, 1987
Ennis Kerlee, 1938-40
Bill Kerr, 1924
Calvin Kiker, 1917
Carlton Kile, 1977
Kyle Killough, 1976-77
Harold Kilman, 1947-49
Bill Kinder, 1977
Bryan King, 1973-75
David King, 1992-95
Doug King, 1975-76
Shawn King, 1980
Gerald Kirby, 1968-70
Johnny Kitchen, 1932-33
David Kline, 1966
Forrest Kline, 1936-38
George Kline, 1933-35
Max Knake, 1992-95
H. H. Knight, 1904-07
Carl Knox, 1946-47
H. C. Knox, 1952
Walter Knox, 1922
Carl Koch, 1945-47
Alexander Kornegay, 1915-16
Frank Kring, 1939-40-41
Mark Krug, 1974-75-77
Joe Kucera, 1944
La Juan Kyles, 1988-9-90

L

Mark Labhart, 1977-78
Lane Ladewig, 1966-67
Dale Ladner, 1971-72-73
Jim Ladner, 1994
Rick LaFavers, 1992-95
Danny Lamb, 1968-69
Duke Lamb, 1992-93
Blake Lambert, 1978
Hal Lambert, 1951-52-53
Standard Lambert, 1929-30-31
Tom Lamonica, 1908-10
Steve Landon, 1965-67
Jack Langdon, 1932-34
Roy (Brick) Largent, 1921
Albert Lasater, 1957

Average Margin of Victory

Year	Season	Per Game
1932	260 points/11 games	23.6
1929	216 points/10 games	21.6
1930	249 points/12 games	20.8
1912	177 points/9games	19.7
1938	209 points/11 games	19.0
1955	201 points/11 games	18.3
1935	192 points/11 games	14.8

Mike Renfro, 1974-77
Jackie Resch, 1978
Dave Rettig, 1962-64
Fain Reynolds, 1927-28
Felix Reynolds, 1927
Jordy Reynolds, 1988-89
Raymond Rhodes, 1970
Donald R. Richard, 1978-81
John Richards, 1964-66
Bobby Richardson 1977-80
Craig Richardson, 1978-79
Toby Richardson, 1988
Bob Richey, 1971
William Riley, 1967-69
Jason Ritchmond, 1991-93
Aubel Riter, 1909
Claude Roach, 1952-53
Phil Roach, 1939-40-41
Rollin Roach, 1924
Walter Roach, 1934-36
William Roach, 1957-59
Joe Robb, 1956-58
Barret Robbins, 1991-94
Clyde Roberson, 1928-29-30
Allen Roberts, 1977
Glen Roberts, 1934-36
Graham Roberts, 1943
Rex Roberts, 1989
Wesley Roberts, 1976-79
Dana Robinson, 1995
Ed Robinson, 1971-73
Marshall Robinson, 1951-53
Morris Robison, 1908
Charles Rogers, 1950-52
Glynn Rogers, 1935-36-37
Randy Rogers, 1944-48
Wayne Rogers, 1947-49
Curtis Rollins, 1957
Henry Rose, 1944-46
Ricky Rougely, 1985-86
Homer Rowe, 1902
Justin Rowland, 1958-59
Allen Rowson, 1920
Tyrone Roy, 1992-95
Marvin Ruchti, 1976
Bob Ruff, 1944-45
Carl Rush, 1976
Scottie Rutherford, 1918-19
John Ruthstrom, 1968-69-70
Sam Rutledge, 1897
Joe Ryan, 1945
Raleigh Ryan, 1920-21
Hayes Rydel, 1994-95

S

Billy Sadler, 1971-72
Dan Salkeld, 1930-32
Everett Salley, 1954-55
Jerry Salley, 1956-57
Ikey Sanders, 1918
Bobby Sanders, 1962-64
Don Sanford, 1953-55-56
Steve Sanford, 1970
John Saunders, 1978
Luther Scarborough, 1925-26
Tim Schade, 1991
Chris Schirmer, 1982-83
Bubba Schmid, 1945
Bob Schobel, 1969-70-71
Darren Schultz, 1990-91-92
Anthony Sciaraffa, 1982-84
Bennie Scott, 1990-91
Danny Scott, 1973-74
E. U. Scott, 1907-08
Ken Scott, 1950-51
Joe Segulja, 1974-76
Perry Senn, 1972-73
P. D. Shabay, 1965-67
Paul Shabay, 1987-88
Jack Schackelford, 1930-32
Terry Schackelford, 1967-69
Dan Sharp, 1983-84

M. R. Sharp, 1897
Tommy Sharp, 1984-87
Harold Sharpe, 1917
Chris Shaw, 1985-86
Paul Shearer, 1977
Rick Sheddy, 1966-68
Young Sheffield, 1956
Tommy Shehan, 1982-85
Buster Shelton, 1993
Joe Sherrell, 1965-66
Bobby Sherrod, 1938-39-40
Johnny Sherrod, 1944-45
Stephen Shipley, 1989-92
W. M. Shirley, 1921-23
Jim Shofner, 1955-57
Fred Shook, 1938-39
Bernard Short, 1944
Garland Short, 1979-82
Wade Shumate, 1899-1903
Kurt Shunkey, 1979-80
Bill Sikes, 1952-53
Butch Silvey, 1970-72
Tracy Simien, 1985-88
Berl Simmons, 1971-73
Paul Simmons, 1993
Dave Singletary, 1918
Adon Sitra, 1964-66
Jack Sledge, 1957-59
Drummond Slover, 1940-42
Al Smith, 1987
Allanda Smith, 1981-83
Billy Joe Smith, 1945
Bobby Smith, 1963-64
Brad Smith 1985-86
Brad Smith, 1989-90-91-92
Charles Smith, 1899
Coke Smith, 1973-74
David Smith, 1964-66
Derek Smith, 1980
Dick Smith, 1943
Don Smith, 1961-63
Don L. Smith, 1932-33
Don L. Smith, Jr., 1961-63
Herman Smith, 1944-46
James Smith, 1964-66
John Smith, 1942
Martinez Smith, 1977
Paul Smith, 1940
Paul Smith, 1965-67
Paul Smith, 1968-69
Ray Smith, 1919
Robert Smith, 1992-94
Romeo Smith, 1984-86-87-88
Ted Smith, 1899
Billy Snow, 1964
Paul Snow, 1930-31
Paul Snow, 1937-38
Gary Spann, 1981-84
Connie Sparks, 1938-39-40
Earle Sparks, 1897
Jon Sparks, 1970
Nolan Sparks, 1940-41
Larry Speake, 1969-70-71
Blanard Spearman, 1930-32
Jerry Spearman, 1961
Andre Spencer, 1987-88
Houston Spikes, 1917
Jack Spikes, 1957-58-59
Red Spillar, 1918-19-20
David Spradlin, 1983-84-85-87
Steve Stamp, 1978-79-80-81
Ray Standley, 1940
Todd Stanford, 1994-95
Edward Stangl, 1915-16
Frank Stangl, 1922-24
Chris Staten, 1994-95
Oran Steadman, 1926-27
Ken Steel, 1970-72
Fabian Stegall, 1995
Beau Stephens, 1994-95
Geoff Stephens, 1993-94-95
B. J. Stephenson, 1954

Clint Stephenson, 1990-91
Dudley Stephenson, 1979
Ronny Stevenson, 1956-57-58
Bobby Stewart, 1978-79-80
Ed Stewart, 1912
Grover W. Stewart, 1911-12
Lon Stewart, 1913
M. C. Stewart, 1907
Russell Stewart, 1974-75
Cecil Stiles, 1910-11-12
Duncan Still, 1977
Ricky Stone, 1984-85-87-88
Gary Stout, 1969-70
Pete Stout, 1946-47-48
Russell Stout, 1963-64-65
Robert Stow, 1934
Jack Stratton, 1912
Alvin Street, 1912-13-14
Chester Strickland, 1977-78-79
True Strong, 1910
Frank Struska, 1948-49-50
James Stuart, 1926
Mike Sullivan, 1987-90
Richard Sullivan, 1964
W. W. Sumner, 1931-32
Spencer Sunstrum, 1979-81-82
Clinton Swink, 1993
Jim Swink, 1954-55-56
Jeff Sypert, 1897

T

Clifford Taft, 1961-63
Scott Taft, 1994-95
Mike Taliferro, 1982
Stan Talley, 1979-80
Lawrence Tankersley, 1922-24
Roscoe Tatum, 1984-86-87-88
Aaron Taylor, 1932
Alton Taylor, 1949-50-51
Bud Taylor, 1932-33
Bud Taylor, 1938-39
Fred Taylor, 1941-45-46
Gearld Taylor, 1982-84
Harry Taylor, 1923-26
Ray Taylor, 1954-55
Spud Taylor, 1937-39
Wilbur Taylor, 1937
Mickey Teems, 1951-52
Alan Teichelman, 1975-77
Arthur Teixeira, 1943
Jack Temple, 1952
Floyd Terrell, 1983-84-85-87
Jerry J. Terrell, 1960-62-63
Larry Terrell, 1958-59-60
Dedrick Terveen, 1972-73-74
Donnie Terveen, 1967-69
James Teter, 1960-62
Lester Thannisch, 1912
Garry Thomas, 1961-63
John Thomas, 1980-83
Larry Thomas, 1961-63
Manley O. Thomas, 1906-07-09
N. B. Thomas, 1943-44
Rob Thomas, 1984
Sean Thomas, 1982-84
Billy Thompson, 1994-95
Guy Thompson, 1953-55
Ody Thompson, 1926-28
Chris Thomsen, 1988-89-90
Bubba Thornton, 1967-68
Elmer Tidwell, 1946
Jimmy Tidwill, 1968-69
Otha Tiner, 1932
Mark Tipps, 1984-86
Jack Tittle, 1935-37
Marlin Toler, 1926-28
Bill Tommaney, 1983-86
Pete Tomme, 1922
Homer Tompkins, 1949-50
Roy Topham, 1970
Greg Townsend, 1981-82
J. W. Townsend, 1931-32

Vince Townsend, 1987-88
David Towson, 1995
Kent Tramel, 1983-87
Ben Trcalek, 1964
Julius Truelson, 1933-34
Dave Tudor, 1916
Jason Tucker, 1994-95
Ryan Tucker, 1993-94-95
Darron Turner, 1982-84
Elwood Turner, 1945-46
Kevin Turner, 1978-79
Ike Tyre, 1981-82-83
Paul Tyson, 1906-09

U

Vernon Uecker, 1954-56
Busty Underwood, 1968-69-70
Ken Upchurch, 1960-62
Gene Uptegraph, 1964
Chad Utley, 1972-73

V

Carlos Vacek, 1955-58
Al Vaiani, 1947
Joe Vail, 1979-80
James Vanderslice, 1967-68-69
Trey Van Pelt, 1993
Tommy Van Wart, 1972-73-74
Howard Vaughn, 1914-15-16
Johnnie Vaught, 1930-31-32
Ted Vaught, 1950-51-52
Lanny Verner, 1960
Steve Vest, 1974
Matt Vogler, 1990-91

W

Wayne Waddy, 1984-87
John Wade, 1977-78
Wallace Wade, 1905
Robert Waggaman, 1913
Howard Wagner, 1968
Keith Wagner, 1989-90-91
Ray Wakefield, 1908
Kent Waldrep, 1974
Bubba Walker, 1988-89
Dale Walker, 1956-58
Elbert Walker, 1933
Jimmy Walker, 1962
Pat Walker, 1967-69
Ralph Walker, 1928-29
Scott Walker, 1970-72
Brad Wallace, 1989-92
J. H. J. Wallace, 1912-13
J. O. Wallace, 1906-07
Jewell Wallace, 1932-33
Malcolm Wallas, 1952-54
Willie Walls, 1934-36
Charlie Walton, 1912
Kenneth Walton, 1987-90
Merle Wang, 1972-74
Trix Ward, 1923-25
Tom Warden, 1975-76
Bryan F. Ware, 1911-12
Logan Ware, 1938-39-40
Scott Warren, 1979
Fred Washington, 1986-89
George Washington, 1974-75
John Washington, 1993-94-95
L. B. Washington, 1981-84
Stanley Washington, 1979-82
Johnny Washmon, 1924-26
H. H. Watson, 1903
W. T. Watts, 1898
Sam Weatherford, 1942
Greg Webb, 1968-71
Ronnie Webb, 1972-73
Billy Weems, 1991
Vernon Wells, 1975-76
Rico Wesley, 1990-93
Royal West, 1991-94
Richard Westbrook, 1965
Marty Whelan, 1967-69

Allie White, 1936-38
Bob White, 1953
Godfrey White, 1994-95
Gary Whitman, 1971-73
Dan Wilde, 1949-50
Dean Wilkerson, 1968-69-70
Jeff Wilkinson, 1990-92
Ward Wilkinson, 1936-38
Bernard Williams, 1925-27
Charlie Williams, 1937-38-39
Chris Williams, 1982
Derryl Williams, 1994-95
Fred Williams, 1978-79
Jake Williams, 1926-28
Jess Williams, 1985-88
Joe Williams, 1954-56
Lance Williams, 1995
Lee Williams, 1974
Lionel Williams, 1980-81
Lynwood Williams, 1982
Morgan Williams, 1951-53
O'Day Williams, 1954-56
Porter Williams, 1964-66
Raymond Williams, 1977
Ricky Williams, 1962-63
Scott Williams, 1980-82
Steve Williams, 1978-79
Troy Williams, 1995
Willie Williams, 1977-79-80-81
Lee Willie, 1916
Billy Willingham, 1948-49-50
Frank Wills, 1982-83
Chuck Wills, 1993-94
Lorance Wills, 1976
Steve Wilson, 1979-80-81
Travis Wilson, 1995
Vaughn Wilson, 1919
Frank Windegger, 1955-56
Ken Wineburg, 1954-56
Oscar Wise, 1910-11
Richard Wiseman, 1970-72
Raymond (Bear) Wolf, 1925-26
A. F. Wood, 1898
Larry Wood, 1966-67
Mike Wood, 1974
Raymond Woodard, 1975
James Woodfin, 1941-42
Richard Woodley, 1990-93
Ronnie Woodman, 1969
Audie Woods, 1976-77
Koi Woods, 1993-94-95
Vance Woolwine, 1929-32
J. N. Wooten, 1898-99
Richard Wooten, 1993
Charles Wrenn, 1952
Fred Wright, 1966
G. A. Wright, 1904
James Wright, 1975-77
L. C. Wright, 1904-07
Larry Wright, 1968-69
Mike Wright, 1979-80
Ricky Wright, 1975-76
Buddy Wyatt, 1986-89
Randall Wylie, 1960
Mike Wyman, 1973-74-75

Y

Armen Yates, 1908-09
Cameron Young, 1976-79
Charles Young, 1965-66-67
Chester Young, 1973-74
Clarence Young, 1958
Jimmy Don Young, 1974-75-76
Joe Young, 1982-83-84
Bill Yung, 1953-54-55

Z

Herbert Zimmerman, 1949-50-51

DAN JENKINS is one of America's most renowned sports-writers. Jenkins is also the author of more than a dozen books, including the bestsellers *Semi-Tough* (1972), *Dead Solid Perfect* (1974), *Limo* (1976), *Baja Oklahoma* (1981), *Life It's Ownself* (1984), *Fast Copy* (1988) and *You Gotta Play Hurt* (1991). An alumnus of TCU, '53, and a Fort Worth native, Jenkin's most memorable boyhood memories are having watched Sammy Baugh and Davey O'Brien lead TCU in the national championship seasons of 1935 and 1938.

FRANCIS J. FITZGERALD is a noted sports researcher and editor. He has recently edited the book and video box set, *Hail to the Victors: Greatest Moments in Michigan Football History* (1995); *The Nebraska Football Legacy* (1995) and *That Championship Season: The 1995 Northwestern Wildcats' Road to the Rose Bowl.*

AP/World Wide Photo: 16, 159, 160.

Cotton Bowl: 95 (top), 133, 134, 139, 150, 152, 154.

The Detroit News: Front cover.

Dan Jenkins: 8 (top), 32, 34, 35, 36, 43, 48, 50 (right), 54, 56 (bottom), 61, 63, 65, 67, 71 (all), 73, 76, 78 (top), 81, 84, 87, 98, 101, 107, 109, 113, 117, 132, 138, 147, 162, 191, 192.

Orange Bowl: 93, 94.

Southwest Conference: 153, 161, 164 (both), 165 (all).

Street & Smith: 142.

Sugar Bowl: 14, 15 (both), 59 (top).

Sun Bowl: 172.

Texas Christian University Sports Information: Back cover (all), iii, 10, 11, 12, 17, 18, 19, 21, 23, 24, 25, 27, 28, 29, 30, 31, 39, 40, 41, 42, 44-45, 46, 49, 50 (left), 52-53, 57, 60, 64, 66, 70, 72, 78 (bottom), 82, 83 (all), 85, 88, 89, 90, 91, 92, 95 (bottom), 96, 97 (all), 99, 102, 103, 105, 106, 108, 111, 114, 115, 116, 120, 121, 122, 124, 125, 129, 141, 143, 144, 145, 148, 151, 155, 156, 157, 158, 166, 167, 168, 169, 170, 171, 174, 175, 176, 177, 178, 179, 180, 181, 183 (both), 184, 185, 187, 188, 189, 190, 193, 194, 195, 198, 199, 201, 202, 203, 204, 206, 207, 208, 210, 211, 213, 214, 215, 216, 217, 218, 219, 220, 221, 222-223.

Texas Football: 186.

Time, Inc.: 130.

University of Texas at Arlington Archives: 8 (bottom), 9, 13, 20, 22, 26, 33, 43, 58, 74, 75, 77, 79, 80, 110, 112, 118, 119, 123, 126, 128, 136.

Gary E. Martzolf, Sports InfoGraphics: 235, 237.